Washington Burning

Washington Burning

HOW A FRENCHMAN'S VISION FOR OUR NATION'S CAPITAL SURVIVED CONGRESS, THE FOUNDING FATHERS, AND THE INVADING BRITISH ARMY

LES STANDIFORD

THREE RIVERS PRESS
NEW YORK

Library of Congress Cataloging-in-Publication Data

Standiford, Les.
Washington burning : how a Frenchman's vision for our nation's capital
survived Congress, the Founding Fathers, and the invading British Army /
Les Standiford.—1st ed.
p. cm.
Includes bibliographical references and index.
1. L'Enfant, Pierre Charles, 1754–1825.   2. City planning—Washington
(D.C.)—History.   3. Architecture—Washington (D.C.)—History.
4. Washington (D.C.)—Buildings, structures, etc.   5. Washington
(D.C.)—History.   6. Washington (D.C.)—History—Capture by the
British, 1814.   I. Title.
F195.S79 2007
975.3'02—dc22   2007044751

978-0-307-34645-2

Printed in the United States of America

Design by Lauren Dong

10 9 8 7 6 5 4 3 2 1

First Paperback Edition

Contents

Author's Note

THE SEED FOR this book was planted in my mind in the aftermath of September 11, 2001, as I listened to so many around me wonder aloud how such atrocities could take place in this country. That is when I found myself remembering a long-ago tour of the White House, where a solemn tour guide pointed to a soot-stained and scorched cellar archway, and related to a group of surprised and suddenly attentive schoolboys how their capital was once invaded and destroyed by a terror-bent "foreign" army.

That memory led me to begin reading about the British assault on Washington during the War of 1812, not with a book of my own in mind, but with a desire to answer the very questions that friends, pundits, and politicians posed in the wake of September 11: How could such things happen here? What might anyone hope to gain? What endures in the wake of such tragedy? Tugging on those threads of history soon led to quite a heap of yarn.

As I read, I was reminded that before there could be a Washington to burn, there had to be a Washington built, and before it was built, men had to want to build it, particularly when there were any number of cities already in existence that could be used as a capital . . . and on and on . . . and before long I became a prisoner of the story of how a city that today so many take for granted had come to be. It is a story that I have spent considerable time unraveling—a story that I ultimately felt compelled to pass along.

In the end, I came to see the efforts of Washington, L'Enfant,

Jefferson, Madison, and Monroe to build, defend, and rebuild Washington, D.C., in its fledgling years as a microcosm for the building of the nation itself, the first in a never-ending series of internal struggles to preserve our nation and its way of government, prefiguring conflict and political platform-building—hawks versus doves, states-righters versus tax-and-spenders, red-staters versus blue—that plague and inspire us to this day. Furthermore, I found it ironic and instructive that although many of those Britishers who meant to lay waste to Washington had the same surnames and basic religious affiliations as the Presbyterian and Methodist Smiths and Nicholsons and Stuarts with whom they traded musket fire, their intentions had much in common with the men who flew planes into buildings on September 11. For me, it is a reminder that "terrorism" is not the province of any nation or sect. Or, to put it in the words of the immortal Pogo, "We have met the enemy, and he is us."

Nor was my reading without its more delightful elements. It struck me as equally ironic and instructive, given the general Francophobia of our day, that the man who believed most passionately in the city under attack was French. Maddening, self-absorbed, out of touch, and brilliant, P. Charles L'Enfant became for me as intriguing and powerful a presence as the legendary generals and statesmen of his day. Auden says that "poetry makes nothing happen," but in essence, L'Enfant was a poet, and, as I hope this account will bear out, he as much as anyone made Washington, D.C., "happen."

The final irony to touch upon is that it took the burning of Washington by the British to end the controversy as to whether the upstart city should stand as this nation's capital. Until that time, opinion on the matter was so divided that the Union nearly broke apart at its outset. The city that burns so brightly in the modern political and symbolic firmament was in fact born of its own demise.

Given the amount and quality of scholarship devoted to the founding of this country, I have not aimed to unearth a welter of unreported details but rather to offer a fresh appreciation of this dramatic story. And, because I came to the writing life as a maker of novels, the dictum that all stories spring from character guided me as I went about the telling of this factual one. My hope is that readers will be as intrigued by the parallels between past and present, and as taken by these individuals and their relationships, as I have been.

MIAMI, FLORIDA
2007

Be it enacted by the Senate and House of Representatives of the United States of America . . . that a district of territory not exceeding ten miles square, to be located as hereafter directed on the River Potowmack . . . and the same is hereby accepted for the permanent Seat of the Government of the United States.

—RESIDENCE ACT OF 1790

As imagination bodies forth the forms of things unknown, the poet's pen turns them to shapes, and gives airy nothing a local habitation and a name.

—A MIDSUMMER NIGHT'S DREAM

PART ONE
Idea of Order

1

Sentinel

THE VANTAGE POINT FOR THIS SURVEILLANCE IS ATOP a hill 571 feet above sea level, looking east from Virginia across the broad Potomac River toward the capital city of the United States. The view, shaded by a dense overhang of trees, is as striking as it is strategic. In the far distance, the dome of the Capitol Building gleams in the late afternoon sun, commanding all the storied monuments that dot the verdant landscape in between. From this spot, Washington looks anything but the locus of world-politik, not at all the picture of an ever-roiling center of intrigue. It looks almost peaceful.

Just across the river below is the Doric assemblage of the Lincoln Memorial, anchoring one end of the Reflecting Pool. At the other end is the giant stone obelisk—once the world's tallest building—that pays tribute to the founder of the city. On a line thirty degrees or so to the south of the Reflecting Pool is the memorial to the author of the Declaration of Independence, and at an equal angle to the north, just beyond the Federal Reserve Building, is the White House, flanked on the west by the Executive Office Building and on the east by the U.S. Treasury.

One could walk the boundary of this diamond-shaped territory in a little more than an hour: two-thirds of a mile from the Lincoln Memorial northeastward to the White House; a mile or so southeast along Pennsylvania Avenue to the Capitol; a matching leg southwest to the Jefferson Memorial; and a final three-quarters-of-a-mile march back to Lincoln, whose impassive visage has gazed down upon a great range of human activity, from the "I have a dream" oration of Martin Luther King and the massive anti–Vietnam War demonstrations that filled the Mall, to Michael Rennie as a space invader taking a lesson in democracy from a child actor in *The Day the Earth Stood Still*.

Within the bounds of that trek is virtually every structure of significance to the republic for which they stand—in addition to those named are the Smithsonian Castle, the National Archives, the Supreme Court, the Library of Congress, the National Gallery, the Museum of Natural History, the U.S. Holocaust Memorial, the Vietnam Veterans Memorial, the House and Senate office buildings, and on and on.

It is, by any standards, the ultimate destination—for aspirants, admirers, and enemies alike. Over the years, assassins have plied their trade there, as have cause-driven bombers and lunatics of every stripe. By many accounts, the infamous "fourth plane" of September 11, 2001, had set its sights on the Capitol or the White House, before the heroic efforts of the passengers brought it to the ground in rural Pennsylvania.

Such assaults, varied as they have been in nature and motivation, are united in one way: their perpetrators have been drawn to that stretch of territory as inevitably as lightning snaps from roiling storm clouds to the aluminum capstone atop George Washington's 555-foot monument. The various attacks might have had practical intent and woeful consequences for individuals, but they were in essence symbolic actions, meant to strike against an entire nation. In short, they were acts of terrorism.

The history of such attacks extends well beyond the range of memory. The first, in fact, took place long before much of what is now visible from this spot in Virginia was even built. To be sure, there was a White House, a Capitol, a Patent Office, a Navy Yard, and a War Department. But all that had been built over fierce opposition, and controversy still swirled over Washington's status as the nation's capital.

To the invaders, however, the utter obliteration of the Federal City of the United States was a goal of great significance, far more important for its psychological impact than for any tactical value. They understood exactly the sentiments of Peter Charles L'Enfant, the man who designed the city of Washington, when he reasoned that its construction should be accomplished in such a fashion "as to give an idea of the greatness of the empire, as well as to engrave in every mind that sense of respect due to a place which is the seat of a supreme sovereignty."

L'Enfant, born the son of Pierre Lenfant, a painter employed by the courts of Louis XV and XVI at Versailles, was something of an enthusiast. But he did give up a life of relative ease to travel across the Atlantic with Lafayette and join his alliance with the Continental Army in its fight for independence. L'Enfant spent time as a prisoner of the British during the Revolutionary War, and afterward opted to remain in the former colonies, even anglicizing his given name of Pierre as a sign of his affection for his new home.

Making use of talents inherited from his father, he worked as an artist and architect and would eventually design the first seat of Congress at Federal Hall in New York City. In time he was appointed by George Washington to draw the plans for the controversial new Federal City on the Potomac.

To L'Enfant, Paris was a wonder, and Versailles grand, but the blank canvas that existed at the bend of the "Potowmack" in 1789 offered the possibility for even more. "No nation has ever before the opportunity offered them of deliberately deciding on the spot where their Capital City should be fixed," he pointed out. And while he acknowledged that "the means now within the power of the Country are not such as to pursue the design to any great extent," he argued that "the plan should be drawn on such a scale as to leave room for that aggrandizement and embellishment which the increase of the wealth of the Nation will permit it to pursue at any period however remote."

L'Enfant's acknowledgment of the difficulties that lay in the path of the development of Washington turned out to be a model of understatement. It was, after all, nearly a hundred years before so much as the placement of a monument to the city's founder could be resolved. In the interim, critics complained mightily of the city's isolated nature, of its torrid summer weather, of a lack of everything from firewood to theater to sidewalks.

When Abigail Smith Adams and her husband, John, became the first residents of the President's Home in November 1800, she described her approach in dramatic terms: "You find nothing but a forest and woods on the way for 16 or 18 miles. Not a village. Here and there a thatched cottage without a single pane of glass."

To her sister Mary Cranch she spoke of Washington itself as "a quagmire after every rain . . . and always the chill and the dampness." They were sentiments shared by many—Northerners dismayed by its geographic setting and Southern opponents of anything that smacked of expansiveness in government—but even Adams's successor Jefferson, who opposed the choice of Washington as capital, realized that the die was cast. This rawboned Federal City would become the indisputable seat of the United States government, and in 1812 it was the spot from which James Madison, the nation's fourth president, proclaimed a second war against the British, aiming to settle, once and for all, issues that had dragged on from the end of the Revolution nearly thirty years before.

The War of 1812 was a ragged conflict, crippled in the States by a lack of resolve among the decidedly less-than-united former colonies, and in Britain by a parliament and populace weary from fending off the relentless advances of Napoleon Bonaparte. It was full of indecisive battles, bloody Indian raids on frontier outposts, and desultory interference, on the part of the British, with American shipping interests. During the summer of 1814, there were reports of a significant massing of British naval forces off the Maryland shores, but there had been regular depredations up and down that part of the American coastline, and most conjectured that the target would be the port of Baltimore.

Certainly, little thought was given to Washington. The unfortified city had next to no commercial trading, and its tactical value was nil. Not much was changed from the days when Abigail Adams described the area as "romantic . . . but a wilderness." When Congress was out of session, the place became a ghost town, and there was still the occasional proposal being floated around Congress to move the seat of government back to Philadelphia.

But on the morning of August 24, 1814, pandemonium erupted when an elite force of British infantrymen was discovered to be marching on Washington City with the intent of teaching the upstart Americans a lesson in "hard war" and reducing their capital to ashes.

History is silent as to the exact whereabouts that day of L'Enfant, whose influence and circumstances had considerably diminished. "In Washington, though not living on the streets, I hope," offers the noted historian and L'Enfant biographer Kenneth R. Bowling. L'Enfant had refused to leave the city that shunned him, frequenting its streets in eccentric garb, trailed by a faithful hound. Whatever his feelings as British troops poured across the ill-defended bridge at Bladensburg, astonishment could not have been among them, however. If he had overheard Secretary of War John Armstrong dismiss the designs of the British for "this sheep walk," L'Enfant would have very heatedly begged to differ. Had he still held the ear of the commander-in-chief and his advisers, the magnitude of the disaster might not have been so great.

L'ENFANT STILL KEEPS watch over his city, though the vigil is a symbolic one. His resting place—moved from a Maryland pasture nearly a century after his death—sits here, atop the highest point in Arlington National Cemetery, a hundred yards or so uphill from the grave of John F. Kennedy and in the shadow of the formidable Arlington House, once the residence of Robert E. Lee and taken by the Union during the Civil War.

Crowds are guided by park rangers through Arlington House every hour on the hour, and—no news—there is a steady flow of visitors to the Kennedy graves. Few are drawn to disturb L'Enfant's quiet contemplation, however.

His monument is a simple, table-shaped sculpture that reverts his name to "Major Pierre Charles L'Enfant," and bears a carved likeness of his 1791 blueprint for the city, which has finally come to exist in the shimmering distance beyond.

We do not know what L'Enfant thought of the irony that it took the devastation of the city by an invading army to bring his countrymen around to an appreciation of what Washington could become. Still, gazing out across the Potomac at the "idea of the greatness of empire" that has taken shape, it is tempting to speculate. He would feel pride, unquestionably. As for the events of days such as September 11, 2001, and August 24, 1814, grim resignation, too.

2

If You Build It, They Will Come

EVEN BY THE CRUEL STANDARDS OF WASHINGTON SUMmers, the late-August day was shaping up as a scorcher. By noon the temperature was nearing 100 degrees and the humidity nearly matched it. It was weather that sapped energy, frayed tempers, and threatened to tip the already desperate mood of the populace—which had never expected that war would come so close to the American capital—into full-fledged panic.

The president had already fled Washington, and the commanders of three separate military defense teams struggled to bring their forces into a tenable position at the northeastern fringes of a rapidly emptying city. As they scrambled about, an invading army headed by two of the world's most feared military leaders—one a cool tactician, the other a brutal master of force—advanced steadily from their beachhead on Chesapeake Bay.

It was no dream, no drill, no fanciful scenario from the pages of a doomsday novel. An ill-prepared and fractured army, crippled by partisan wrangling over whether a need for military preparedness truly existed, was the only obstacle to the obliteration of the seat of the world's premier experiment in democratic rule.

LAST-MINUTE EFFORTS to mount a defense proved futile. Communication between the president—driven to ground somewhere in the tangled forests of Virginia or Maryland—and U.S. commanding general William Winder had broken down, and the only forces with significant combat experience (fewer than two thousand) were routed when the invaders loosed a barrage of experimental rockets upon their positions. By midnight, all U.S. forces were in full retreat, and their commanders—save for one able captain of privateers—were discredited and disgraced.

The Capitol Building was destroyed, and with it the Library of Congress and the Supreme Court. The U.S. Treasury lay in ashes. Also in ruins were the War Department and the State Department and the Navy Yard. The nation's capital lay lit by the flames of its own demise.

As for the ultimate symbol of the city, the president's home: "We found a supper there all ready," one of the invading officers reported, "which many of us speedily consumed . . . and drank some very good wine also." After they had eaten the president's dinner and upended the table where they had sat, they set a torch to that building and, as it burned, stumbled out into the Washington night, drunk not only with wine but also with the ease with which they had routed the American defenders.

They were a small but seasoned group of operatives, well skilled in this sort of mission. It was no classic military undertaking, this assault on Washington, but a carefully calculated guerrilla strike, meant to bring "hard war" to America, to instill fear in the hearts of the populace and deliver an unequivocal message: Submit or die.

And by all appearances, this first terrorist attack launched on American soil had succeeded beyond all expectations. The operation had been carried out with the loss of only sixty-four men, and in the space of one afternoon and evening. Every hallowed institution of the American capital had been obliterated, and the remnants of the citizenry cowered as the boot heels of foreign invaders cracked on the District pavement.

3

The Winds of a War

THE DEVASTATION OF THE NEW CAPITAL CITY WAS AS much a shock to the young nation as it was an outrage. Few had seen it coming, but then that is the very aim of terrorist operations. As for the roots of the assault, however, the perspective of history suggests that the thirty years that had passed since the end of the Revolutionary War constituted a temporary pause in battle between the two sides rather than a cessation and a new beginning.

Military historians have only recently begun to reconsider the importance of what was once dismissed as "Mr. Madison's War." In his 1989 book, *The War of 1812: A Forgotten Conflict*, Donald R. Hickey began a process of reevaluation that continues to this day, arguing that the true end of the American Revolution came with the resolution of the War of 1812, formalized by the Treaty of Ghent in 1815. Only then, Hickey and others now contend, were the issues settled that had opened the rift between the American colonies and Great Britain. With the conclusion of the War of 1812 the United States became truly independent of its former colonial ties and took its place as a player on the world stage with the great powers of Europe.

Prior to America's declaration of war in 1812, the country's reputation remained that of the upstart prodigal, and England continued to harbor substantial concerns about its former and current North American colonies. The Crown was determined that Canada should remain its possession, in spite of the covetous glances cast toward their northern neighbor by certain expansionist-minded American politicians. There was also some fear that one day the colonists might make their way across the vast U.S. continent to the Pacific Coast and threaten British holdings in Oregon.

But of far greater concern to Great Britain and her various allies—including the Germans, Russians, and Austrians—was Napoleon Bonaparte, who had been successfully pursuing his stated goal of world conquest since the turn of the century. Napoleon had trounced the Prussians at Jena-Auerstedt in 1806 and the Austrians at Wagram in 1809, and had gained command of the continent of Europe. As Admiral Horatio Nelson's decisive victory over the French fleet at Trafalgar in 1805 had proven, though, the power of the French navy remained second to that of Britain. If he could not defeat the British on the seas, Napoleon reasoned, he could try to subvert that British navy's power though diplomatic and economic maneuvering. In 1806 he issued the Berlin Decree, forbidding any European nation to trade with Great Britain.

King George III countered with the Orders in Council, which declared that no nation's ships could dock at any continental port (and thus trade directly or indirectly with France) unless those ships docked first in England to be inspected and to pay appropriate duties for the privilege of carrying on trade with the continent. Napoleon responded with the Milan Decree of 1807, arguing that any ships submitting to these British conditions were, in effect, agents of Great Britain and thus could be seized by the French.

Traders and manufacturers in the United States—their ships and property now subject to seizure at the whim of two foreign powers—were outraged at being caught in the middle of this European tit-for-tat. Thomas Jefferson, president since 1801 and suspicious of "entanglements" in European politics, attempted to withdraw the United States from the economic battlefield by issuing the Embargo Act of 1807, which banned American trade with *any* foreign nation. It was a miscalculation on Jefferson's part, however, for during the two years the act was in place the U.S. economy nearly collapsed. Foreign trade plummeted—from more than $100 million in 1807 to slightly more than $20 million the following year. The only trade that continued was illegal, much of it conducted by American trading ships that moved to home ports in the Caribbean, from which they plied only foreign cities, thus risking capture by both British and French naval forces.

Adding to the anger in the United States was the regular practice of impressment of Americans by the commanders of British naval vessels. A captain of a British warship might at any time force an American merchant ship to heel to at cannon-point, board her, and remove any American sailors deemed to be deserters, remanding these unfortunate men for duty in the British navy. Chronically short of hands in their fight with the French, British naval officers were not at all troubled that most of the so-called "deserters" were U.S. citizens; good help was increasingly difficult to come by.

British support of the indigenous Indian populations on the northern and western frontiers of the new nation further aggravated Anglo-American discord. The British supplied arms and other assistance to tribes opposed to American encroachment on their lands as a pragmatic form of foreign aid. Armed and able bands of Native American tribes formed a convenient barrier between the United States and Canada and also slowed the inexorable movement of settlers toward the West. But the practice infuriated such westerners as Kentucky congressman Henry Clay and governor of the Indiana Territory William Henry Harrison, who in 1811 joined the vociferous "War Hawks" hounding President James Madison (a Democratic-Republican like his predecessor Jefferson) to declare a formal state of war with Great Britain.

Though the issues of trade barriers, kidnapped sailors, and marauding Indians had contributed to significant discontent among Americans, the fervor of the War Hawks was matched by the staunch opposition to war of the much-diminished but still combative Federalist Party. The remaining influence of the Federalists lay with New Englanders, who were particularly opposed to funding a war that they believed would be fought primarily at the behest of Western expansionist interests, especially when the country was in such dire financial straits.

The stalemate between the hawks and the doves might have continued longer were it not for President Madison's announcement in March of 1812 that a British spy had been apprehended in Washington, D.C. John Henry, an Irishman alleged to be in the employ of the Crown, was reportedly found in possession of papers documenting a supposed plot hatched between Massachusetts governor Elbridge Gerry and the British government for the secession of the New England states and a return of their allegiance to the British Empire.

Subsequent inquiry proved the far-fetched "plot" to be a politically motivated fiction given unwarranted credence by both Madison and his secretary of state, James Monroe (think "Remember the Maine" or "weapons of mass destruction"). But the scare nonetheless gave Representative Henry Clay of Kentucky the leverage he needed to persuade his colleagues in Congress to authorize a significant expansion of the regular army, at the time just 4,000 men, and of a navy that could not claim a single major gunship. Congress's approval of a standing army of 30,000 and the building of a dozen men-of-war was largely a symbolic action for a country with only $100,000 in its national treasury, but the decision nonetheless constituted the first significant and deliberate step toward war.

In Great Britain, meanwhile, many members of Parliament were calling for a reconsideration of their strained relationship with the former colonies. Napoleon's mighty march toward Russia was under way, and if that campaign proved successful, France would have control of nearly half the world's landmass. In the face of such a prospect, the last thing Britain needed was an armed conflict with the United States to drain away its resources.

Others in Parliament worried that secret negotiations were under way for an alliance between France and the United States, though those fears were actually as groundless as the preposterous claims that the New England colonies were plotting to rejoin the Crown. The truth was that Napoleon still harbored a desire to reclaim the

Louisiana territories, if not the whole of the North American continent. He intended to turn to America once he had dispensed with the
Russians and added the larger part of Asia to his fold.

Certainly the former colonies harbored no fondness for the French,
for the economic sanctions and predations imposed on American sea
trade by Napoleon's government were every bit as oppressive as the
Orders in Council shipping restrictions levied by Great Britain. Furthermore, in an 1812 report to Congress, Madison calculated that
while the British navy had seized 389 American ships since 1807, the
French had taken 558.

Ironically enough, debate on the necessity for war reached its
height in the U.S. houses of Congress at the same time that the British
government was moving steadily toward a repeal of the onerous Orders in Council. On June 1, Madison—up for reelection that fall—
sent a message to Congress declaring that war with Great Britain had
become a necessity. The House, swayed by the bombast of Representative Clay and his fellow War Hawks, endorsed the president's call,
voting for war on June 4 by a margin of 79–49.

Matters were not so simple in the Senate. One alternative measure introduced there called for armed engagements between the two
countries to be limited to those between British naval vessels and
American commercial ships defending their rights to free passage.
Another would have allowed for similar limited naval engagements
against both Great Britain and France.

But the end was inevitable. Even among Federalists, a party that
for the most part opposed the war, members were influenced by their
own political self-interest, and politicians worried, then as now, that
opposing the war might be seen as unpatriotic. Chief among the
image-makers was one of the staunchest opponents of the call for war,
Senator Stephen Bradley of Vermont, who somehow found it impossible to reach Washington in time for a crucial vote on June 17. On
that day the Senate voted 19–13 in favor of Madison's call, and the following day the president signed a formal declaration of war against
Great Britain.

As fortune would have it, precisely two days before that final vote the British Parliament announced that it would rescind the much-loathed Orders in Council. In the contemporary world, such news would have flashed across the Atlantic in less than an eye-blink. The good Senator Bradley from Vermont would have found himself a helicopter or private jet to rush him down to Washington for an impassioned excoriation of those who would have the country go to war with a nation willing to compromise. As it was, however, more than two weeks passed before the packet ship carrying the momentous news from London docked in New York City. By that time the United States had already geared up the engines of battle.

Secretary of State James Monroe, a decorated veteran of the Revolutionary War and a man considered by many to be Madison's intellectual equal, declared on June 13 that in spite of America's shaky finances, her military deficiencies, and the divided opinion of the populace as to the wisdom of the undertaking, "we shall succeed in obtaining what it is important to obtain, and that we shall experience little annoyance or embarrassment in the effort."

It was widely predicted that, at the very least, U.S. ships would soon be able to ply the high seas in safety again and the supply of British aid to marauding frontier Indians would be brought to a halt. And perhaps, as some of the nation's politicians hoped, the United States might just take possession of Canada as well.

History contains examples of times when the mission of war is accomplished as easily as predicted, and without great cost. But, to put it mildly, they have been few and far between. Had anyone whispered to Madison or Monroe what the cost of *this* conflict would prove to be, had able soothsayers warned of deadly conflicts with Native Americans stretching onward for the better part of the century, had they portrayed a future Canada resolutely independent of the Union, or had they painted a picture of the capital of the United States as a scorched ruin, would that call for war have come so easily?

There is some recompense for the fact that conciliatory word from Britain came too late and that no convincing soothsayers stepped forward. As Donald Hickey and other historians have argued, despite its high cost and the uncertainties that lingered after its close, "Mr. Madison's War" brought America of age as an independent nation, rallying the union as never before, and ushering in an unprecedented and virtually unduplicated "Era of Good Feeling" in American politics. And it created in Washington, D.C., a city of power and a locus of national pride where none had existed before.

It can be argued that the nation as a whole was forged in this conflict's fire, and in particular by the fires that consumed its capital in 1814. But to fully appreciate the events that finally turned the tide in this "second war of independence," we have to turn to a few matters surrounding the conclusion of the first.

4

First Orders of Business

SOME MODERN PUNDITS MIGHT QUIBBLE WITH THE notion of Washington as the "preeminent" American city, mentioning others that are older, richer, or more culturally influential, but few would argue against its position as the dominant political symbol of the country. As a friend once noted in passing, "Washington is like Paris. It's just there. It's always been there." Which is, of course, an exaggeration.

When George Washington defeated Lord Cornwallis at Yorktown, Virginia, in October of 1781, the city of Washington was not "there," nor had it yet been conceived of. Two and a quarter centuries later the two communities have swapped positions in the world order. Yorktown still exists, now a tiny hamlet of 203 souls on the outskirts of Newport News; about 125 miles north on the Potomac is Washington, now with 582,000 residents.

Yet at the time that George Washington was laying siege to it, Yorktown was the most important community in all America. Cornwallis had established a position there at the mouth of the York River on Chesapeake Bay, from which he could maintain contact with the forces of General Clinton, his counterpart operating in New York. Washington, who had been readying a major campaign against Clinton, realized that Cornwallis's position was the more vulnerable, and with the aid of the French fleet and the ground forces of Count de

Rochambeau, he decided to head south instead. The combined French and American forces surrounded Cornwallis, forced his surrender on October 19, 1781, and effectively put an end to the War of the Revolution.

Shortly thereafter, Parliament voted against further hostilities against the colonies and authorized King George to begin negotiations for peace. Though there were some minor skirmishes—including several retaliatory raids by troops on Native American settlements—Yorktown marked the close of serious fighting, and the Treaty of Paris, signed on September 3, 1783, confirmed the settlement of the war.

On November 2 of that year, George Washington delivered his farewell address to his army, and on December 23 he appeared before the U.S. Congress to resign his commission. While a number of Washington's troops were mustered out in November, most of the Continental Army was officially discharged on the first day of the new year of 1784. Among them was Pierre Charles L'Enfant, who had come to the colonies in 1777, having accepted a commission as a lieutenant in the Continental Army offered by Silas Deane, the Connecticut member of the Continental Congress who had been secretly dispatched to Paris in search of support for the war effort.

L'Enfant had studied architecture and drawing under his father, Pierre Lenfant, at the Royal Academy of Painting and Sculpture, and like many of his young French counterparts he had been inspired by the American cause for liberty. He was not yet twenty-three when he volunteered, sailing from France on February 14 with Major General Jean-Baptiste Tronson de Courday and a corps of fellow French engineers. They arrived in Portsmouth, New Hampshire, in April, about a month before the nineteen-year-old Lafayette and his swashbuckling troops.

If as eager as Lafayette, L'Enfant (who may have added the apostrophe to his family name in order to add luster to his image) lacked any training whatsoever as a soldier, and beyond his architecture studies he had no schooling or practical experience in the field of engineering. Courday's own evaluation of L'Enfant to the U.S. Congress noted that while the young man may have been a talented illustrator, he exhibited little potential as an engineer, save perhaps for the decorative embellishment of plans.

In December of 1777 the Congress ordered L'Enfant to Boston to serve as an assistant to another newly arrived European sympathizer with the American cause, the German army hero Frederich von Steuben, former aide-de-camp to Frederick the Great and future author of the standard U.S. military regulations manual. L'Enfant accompanied von Steuben from Boston to York, Pennsylvania, where the Continental Congress had been forced to relocate after the British occupied Philadelphia. In York, von Steuben undertook preparations for his most valuable contribution to the American war effort, the training of George Washington's troops during the miserable winter of 1777–78 that they spent bivouacked at Valley Forge.

The ability of von Steuben to marshal his rigorous Prussian style to create a sense of esprit de corps among the bedraggled, ill-provisioned Continental Army may have turned the tide of the war. When Washington and his lightly regarded troops managed a draw with the British forces of General Clinton at Monmouth in the following summer, it forced a withdrawal of the British from Philadelphia and cemented von Steuben's influence with his new allies.

Meanwhile, von Steuben introduced his ambitious young French assistant L'Enfant to various aides to Washington, including Alexander Hamilton, Henry Knox, John Laurens, and James Monroe, as well as to the great General Washington himself. L'Enfant executed a portrait of Washington there at Valley Forge, and though the simple penciled sketch has long since been lost, the drawing and its maker apparently pleased the subject greatly. Washington made regular use of L'Enfant as a courier from that point on, and he found himself defending the talents of the exuberant young Frenchman on many occasions to come.

Von Steuben too seemed pleased with his young assistant, who was described by his contemporary William W. Corcoran as "a tall, erect man, fully six feet in height, finely proportioned, nose prominent, of military bearing, courtly air and polite manners . . . a man who would attract attention in any assembly." (L'Enfant's appearance remains a matter of some conjecture, given that Corcoran's remarks—the most detailed that survive—were reported secondhand nearly one hundred years after the Frenchman's death. The only verified contemporary likeness that exists is a silhouette executed by Sarah DeHart in 1785, featuring that prominent nose and still hanging in the U.S. Department of State.) In April of 1779, von Steuben was successful in persuading Congress to promote L'Enfant to the rank of captain of engineers, retroactive to the time of his arrival in Valley Forge the previous February. In addition, von Steuben commissioned L'Enfant to provide eight illustrations for his *Regulations, Orders, and Discipline for the Army of the United States* (it would endure until 1812 as the basic manual for the service), an endeavor that brought the young new captain a congressional bonus of $500.

Though his association with von Steuben provided political and financial benefits, the irrepressible L'Enfant seemed to chafe in his assistant's role. When John Laurens offered him the command of a corps of slaves he hoped to raise near Charleston, South Carolina, L'Enfant quickly accepted, leaving von Steuben for the American South, intent on an active role in countering the British offensive there.

Laurens, a staunch abolitionist who had grown up in South Carolina, nonetheless seems to have underestimated the political realities he was up against in the region, and was unable to raise the troops he hoped for. L'Enfant found himself without the promised command and reattached to the engineering corps. Worse yet, he was isolated in the American South and subject to the whims of superiors who lacked the same appreciation von Steuben had held of his talents.

L'Enfant had not come this far to sit on his hands, however. In October of 1779 he joined an attempt to set fire to the British fortifications at Savannah, a city that had fallen to the British late the year before. While leading the advance guard of an American column, L'Enfant suffered a serious leg wound that left him unconscious and presumed dead on the field. When a fellow soldier realized he was still breathing, L'Enfant was dragged to safety, then taken to a Charleston hospital where he stayed until the following January. Still leaning on a crutch and dependent upon alcohol and opiates to dull the lingering pain in his leg, L'Enfant helped to defend Charleston against the British siege of May 1780. Ultimately, however, the Southern defenders were forced to surrender and he was taken prisoner.

In accordance with practices of the time, L'Enfant was soon paroled by the British to the adjacent Christ Church Parish, on the condition that he provide no further military service to the American forces. In July of 1781 he was released from his confinement to the parish. He traveled to Philadelphia, where, in January of 1782, he became part of a formal prisoner exchange, which permitted him to resume his duties as an officer.

At that point his old friend Laurens wrote to revive the prospect of a command of freed slaves, but experience seems to have hardened L'Enfant to such schemes. He turned Laurens down and instead wrote to Washington himself, requesting a promotion to major in the corps of engineers. The leader of America's forces responded by praising the young man, but he did not offer a promotion.

Still, the engineer would not be stymied long. In April of 1782 the French ambassador, Anne-Cesar La Luzerne, approached Washington with a request that a pavilion be built in Philadelphia to honor the birth of the French Dauphin, the child who would become Louis XVII. Luzerne furthermore proposed that one Pierre Charles L'Enfant, French-trained architect and noted hero of the American war effort, be commissioned for the building's design. Washington, who had favored L'Enfant from their days together at Valley Forge, and who depended mightily on the maintenance of cordial relations with the French, was quick to give his assent.

The commission was L'Enfant's first, and unlike projects that would follow, this one was completed quickly and without incident. The celebration of the Dauphin's birthday took place in L'Enfant's newly constructed pavilion just three months later, on July 15, 1782. With eleven hundred influential individuals in attendance, it was said to have been the most extravagant party ever to take place in the fledgling republic. Guests, who included Washington, Thomas Paine, Robert Morris, John Dickinson, and Count Rochambeau, gathered in a sixty-by-forty-foot hall that L'Enfant had decorated in the exuberant fashion that would become characteristic of his work: one end of the room was dominated by a rendering of a rising sun and thirteen stars, evocative of the emerging colonies; the other end was anchored by a fulsome sun beaming down from its zenith, standing for France. It was a triumph for the novice architect, and one that would change the course of his life.

WASHINGTON'S DEFEAT OF Cornwallis at Yorktown had proven to be a watershed event, and the remainder of 1782 was marked by a steady winding down of efforts on both sides. The British had withdrawn from Savannah on June 11, and a minor engagement between U.S. and Crown forces on the Combahee River in South Carolina on August 27 marked the last fighting between the two sides. On November 30, 1782, the British signed a preliminary peace agreement in Paris recognizing American independence and pledging to withdraw forces from the former colonies. On December 14, the British left Charleston, giving up their last significant foothold in the United States. Though the formal Treaty of Paris would not be signed for nearly a year and the Continental Army would remain standing meanwhile, the war was over.

L'Enfant's fortunes continued on the rise as well. On May 2, 1783, he received his long-sought promotion to major by a special resolution of Congress, recommended by a committee that included another supporter from the Valley Forge days, Alexander Hamilton. Says biographer Kenneth Bowling, "The rank was so meaningful to L'Enfant, and he clung so tightly to it for the rest of his life, that many of his contemporaries . . . could have believed that his first name was 'Major.'"

Shortly thereafter, a group of Continental Army veterans, including L'Enfant and presided over by von Steuben, met in Fishkill, New

York, to form the Society of the Cincinnati, an organization open to both French and American army and navy officers who had served during the war. The aim of the group, named after the fifth-century BC Roman military leader, was partly honorific and partly social, but there were also common interests to pursue with Congress, including issues of back pay, pensions, and payments to widows and children of those who had died in action.

Von Steuben thought it a good idea that a medal be struck for members of this society and appointed L'Enfant to design it, along with other appropriate iconography. In short order, L'Enfant returned with the concept of the eagle as the central symbol for the society, no doubt inspired by the actions of Congress, which had adopted the same creature for the country's official seal during the previous year.

In her discussion of the symbology chosen to represent the newly formed nation, the architectural historian Pamela Scott notes that the Great Seal eagle—initially proposed by the Philadelphia lawyer William Barton—was destined to become the most popular emblem of them all, a veritable shorthand notation for the United States itself. Some assume that the bald eagle was chosen because its range is limited to North America. They also point to such occasions as Creek chief Tomo Chachi Mico's presentation in 1734 of a clutch of eagle feathers to King George II with the words "These are the feathers of the Eagle, which is the Swiftest of Birds and who flieth all round our Nation." But as Scott points out, the eagle has been a symbol of supreme authority since the days of the Romans.

L'Enfant's renderings for the society, though decidedly less bellicose than those featuring the arrow-clutching bird of the federal seal, found great favor in the group. Washington, who was elected the first permanent president of the Cincinnati, was so taken with the design and motto ("He abandons everything to serve his country") that he asked L'Enfant to travel to Paris, where he was to share news of the society with their French counterparts and have his drawings engraved and the society's medals struck. Society members raised $300 for the costs associated with the enterprise, though, as Washington made clear, those monies were to be used solely for the expenses of producing the society's artifacts.

The return to Paris might well have been one more in a series of small but significant triumphs for L'Enfant, who still had yet to reach his thirtieth birthday. Around this same time, in June of 1783, little more than a month after he had received his long-coveted promotion to major in the Continental Army, he was appointed by Louis XVI to the rank of captain in the French Provisional Army and was awarded an annual pension of 300 livres (equivalent to perhaps $1,500 in today's dollars).

In addition, Steuben appointed L'Enfant as chief engineer on what would turn out to be an ill-conceived mission to Canada, where he was to inspect the British forts erected on the Great Lakes and help prepare for their transfer to United States control. L'Enfant agreed willingly, but the transfers never took place, and when the young inspector applied to Superintendent of Finance Robert Morris for reimbursement of the expenses he had incurred, Morris denied the petition. Only pressure from von Steuben and others sympathetic to L'Enfant resulted in the payment of the claim. It might have seemed a needless complication at the time, but history would come to prove that where money and L'Enfant were connected, nothing was ever simple.

L'Enfant had returned to his duty station with the Corps of Engineers at West Point by the time Washington authorized leave for the trip to Paris. L'Enfant assured the general that he would undertake this travel at his own expense, and with copies of the society's constitution and letters of introduction to every French officer of influence in hand, he reached Paris in December of 1783.

Although he succeeded in finding artists he considered qualified to render the society's artifacts and soon persuaded the king to permit French officers to join the society and wear its insignia, L'Enfant was having problems on another score. "The reception which the Cincinnati met with," he wrote his friend Hamilton, ". . . induced me to appear in that country in a manner consistent with the dignity of the society of which I was regarded as the representative. . . . My abode at court produced expenses far beyond the sums I first thought of."

From a young man who had come of age amid the excess at Versailles, such a statement sounds disingenuous, but there is no doubt that L'Enfant far outstripped his budget and that of the society within a very short time. The bill from Duval and Francastel, where he had ordered the medals struck, came to 22,303 livres (the equivalent of more than $100,000, and a rather shocking sum, given the sixty or so livres [$300] that his fellow society members had sent him off with for such purposes).

By April, L'Enfant was back in the United States, leaving behind that enormous unpaid bill and several others, as a matter for the new American ambassador to France, Thomas Jefferson, to deal with. Though Jefferson may not have been happy with the mess he had inherited, Hamilton and other society members were delighted with the quality of the medals and other materials that L'Enfant brought back, and Hamilton promised to see what he could do about the bills.

Although the society did eventually pay most of the debts incurred on its behalf, L'Enfant was still suffering from the results of his profligacy nearly three years later. In 1786 he wrote an impassioned letter of some forty pages to the Cincinnati, complaining that he was still being hounded for debts undertaken on their behalf in Europe, and that his honor was at stake. Years later, L'Enfant would complain to Washington that the matter of his French debt had cost him the support of Lafayette, and that his dashing young fellow countryman was now standing in the way of any further favors he might receive from the French court.

Meanwhile, money matters came more and more to occupy L'Enfant's attention. In 1784, shortly after his discharge from the Continental Army, the government issued a statement estimating that he was owed $29,323 in back pay, a sum that would earn him an annual interest payout of $1,759. L'Enfant quarreled with the government's figures, however, insisting in a letter to Continental Army commander and society president Henry Knox that he was due in addition several months' pay for his time spent in Paris on the Cincinnati's behalf, and that he was in line for promotion to the rank of brigadier general. With that promotion he hoped to lead a newly created permanent Army Corps of Engineers, the establishment of which he saw as crucial to "the securing to the United States of a peaceful and tranquil enjoyment of liberty."

On December 13, 1784, L'Enfant sent Congress a lengthy "memorial," or petition, proposing the formation and detailing his concept of the new agency, which he felt should be charged with the responsibility of building and maintaining the new nation's harbor fortifications and frontier outposts. Though the war with England was at an end, L'Enfant argued, the protection of the country's harbors and the settlers willing to push the western boundaries outward were matters "necessary" to the continued development of the nation. His warnings were prescient, considering the dire struggles that would ensue in extending the frontier over the following decades, but L'Enfant was hard-pressed to convince the war-weary, cash-strapped, and still divided Congress that such a costly program should be undertaken.

In addition to the ambitious expansion of the nation's defenses, L'Enfant proposed that the corps would also be responsible for maintaining all forts already in existence, for the upkeep of all federal buildings—civil and military alike—and for the repair of all the country's roads and bridges. As something of an afterthought, L'Enfant also suggested that the corps be given the added duty of building the still hazily conceived "Federal City."

Nor was L'Enfant above attempts to elicit the sympathies of his audience. If Congress did not find its way clear to an adoption of his plan, he declared, "I should now be doubly disappointed . . . for by remaining here I have lost the opportunity of getting employment in my own country." He went on to add that no less distinguished a patron than Brigadier General Thaddeus Kosciusko, the Polish engineer who had designed the fortress called "America's Gibraltar" at West Point, among other notable fortifications, "gave me the flattering expectation at being at the head of a Department. . . . The attachment I bear and the anxiety I feel for the present and future happiness of a country for which I have fought and bled" was the motivating force behind the submission of his proposal, L'Enfant asserted.

In advocating for the establishment of the corps, he enumerated the various qualifications of the capable engineer: "the good performance of their duty being to depend upon their real knowledge of several sciences." He included in these arithmetic, geometry, mechanism (physics), architecture, hydraulics, drawing, and natural philosophy, and expounded upon the latter as "being necessary to judge of the nature of [building materials] . . . the quality of the elements, that of the water and of the air being necessary . . . with a view to avoid making establishment in any place which might be injurious." For an individual who had received no formal education in engineering, civil or otherwise, L'Enfant's detailed memorial suggests that he managed to pick up a fair amount of useful knowledge in his few years of on-the-job training. And whatever the depth of his scientific expertise, his stated concerns for the impact of a project on its environment placed him well ahead of his time.

To undertake all of this work, L'Enfant proposed the authorization of three companies of one hundred men apiece, headed by a command structure of ten officers: an adjutant, three lieutenants, three captains, a major, a lieutenant colonel, and a brigadier general, who would decide exactly what these troops would do, and who would be, of course, L'Enfant.

As biographer Bowling points out, the document is a remarkable work, notwithstanding its self-serving aspects, for it had no precedent in America. The United States barely had a government, much less a bureaucracy, when L'Enfant laid out his vision for a department of public works. But that same nascent and fragile quality of the government was what doomed any realistic hopes for such an ambitious undertaking.

The Congress, while a body that represented the whole of the new United States, was composed of individuals who, then as now, represented a wide range of competing local interests. Though enough of a consensus had been reached among the colonies' representatives to fight and win the war against the British, it is telling that more than 100,000 of the 2.5 million residents of the colonies, or four percent, declared themselves loyal to the king and decamped for Canada, England, and points beyond over the course of the conflict. That figure does not reflect the vastly greater number of individuals who essentially "rode the fence" throughout the war, far more concerned with their personal well-being than with questions of allegiance to a government.

When the conflict finally came to an end, representatives to the Continental Congress were most concerned with the practical question of who was going to foot the bill for what had been spent and with ensuring that their states were adequately compensated. They had little interest in costly new federal programs, no matter how compelling in outline or nature. The committee to which L'Enfant's proposal was diverted reported back promptly that no such program seemed necessary, and though L'Enfant was to renew his plea when Henry Knox was appointed secretary of war a few months later, that appeal fared no differently.

Now a civilian and with no apparent prospects for a renewed commission in the peacetime army, L'Enfant followed Congress to its temporary seat in New York City. The relocation of the government also attracted a number of L'Enfant's influential friends and associates to the city, including Alexander Hamilton and the French ambassador, Comte de Moustier.

Despite Congress's rejection of his plans for a permanent and powerful corps of engineers, it must have been a hopeful period for the thirty-year-old L'Enfant. He had journeyed from his native France, arriving even before such luminaries as Lafayette, to fight and nearly die for the ideals of liberty. Not only had he lived to tell the story, but he had found friendship and patronage among the most prominent men in this new world. He had been entrusted with missions of military and diplomatic significance, and with a romantic temperament forged in the extravagant milieu of prerevolutionary Versailles, he could easily put behind him the matters of a few outstanding debts and a politically motivated rebuff.

In New York City, as the new democracy took shape, he would surely find the important role that he was meant to play.

5

Coming of Age

I F THE MOVE TO NEW YORK DID NOT CATAPULT L'ENFANT to immediate success, it nonetheless allowed for his steady advancement. He enjoyed the friendship of Hamilton, who had risen to prominence as an attorney and banker in the city, as well as the patronage of Moustier, who made regular petitions to the French government in support of L'Enfant's requests for relief of his debts. In one letter to his mother, L'Enfant suggested that he had at long last come to feel as if he had a place in his adopted land, and even hinted at the possibility of romance. "If I were easy enough in my mind to enjoy the pleasures of society," he wrote, then Moustier's "charming" sister-in-law, the Marquise de Brehan, "would make any man happy," but nothing ever came of that attraction.

L'Enfant landed the first of his choice assignments when, in 1787, Congress finally decided upon the placement of a monument to honor General Richard Montgomery, killed during the Battle of Quebec on New Year's Eve of 1775 (thereby becoming the first of the American generals to die in battle). The statue had been authorized in 1776, and was executed—at the behest of then minister to Paris Benjamin Franklin—by Jean-Jaques Caffieri, youngest in a long line of sculptors to serve the king of France. The sculpture arrived in North Carolina in 1778, packed in several boxes, but as there were more immediate concerns facing the colonies at the time, it languished in a warehouse until the end of the war.

Congress originally intended for the work to be installed in Philadelphia's Independence Hall, but the move to New York apparently prompted that body to rethink the matter. More than eleven years after the first national monument was authorized, the statue was finally ordered assembled and placed under the portico at St. Paul's Chapel on Broadway at Wall Street (across the street from where the towers of the World Trade Center would one day stand).

Though the statue would lend an impressive presence to the great avenue before it, officials realized that something would have to be done about an embarrassing problem. Caffieri had left the back of the piece unfinished, and its rough backside was clearly visible through the window behind the altar. L'Enfant was hired to oversee the placement of the monument itself and to design an elaborate altar screen to block the view out the chapel's east window. The still-extant reredos features a Louis XIV–inspired cloud-and-sunburst motif; an altar rail that L'Enfant added to complement his composition is said to be unique in American architecture.

Though a writer for the *New York Daily Advertiser* opined that the ornamentations that the designer had added to the pediment of Montgomery's statue were so tasteless as to "even discredit the mind d'un enfant," the vestry of the church issued a proclamation expressing their great satisfaction with L'Enfant's work, saying that his efforts reflected nothing but "honor on his taste."

Soon afterward, the French sculptor Jean-Antoine Houdon asked L'Enfant to accompany him on a trip to Mount Vernon; Houdon, who had come to the United States in hopes of landing the commission for the equestrian statue of Washington authorized by Congress in 1785, had meanwhile been commissioned by the Virginia General Assembly to execute a statue of Washington for its own, and Houdon employed L'Enfant to serve as his assistant on the latter project. Houdon took measurements of their subject, executed a life mask, and fashioned a preliminary terra-cotta bust that served as model for the finished marble product. The rendering, now standing at the state house in Virginia, was greatly admired by Washington's contemporaries and is generally held to be the authoritative likeness of the first commander-in-chief.

Houdon was not the only one to admire his countryman's talents. If some judged L'Enfant's artistic expression too exuberant, others found in him the perfect spirit. In July of 1788, the demonstrative and unquestioned champion of liberty was commissioned to oversee the design and iconography of the lavish parade held in New York City to celebrate the ratification of the new Constitution of the United States, and it was by all accounts a wise choice. "The taste and genius of Major L'Enfant, so often displayed on public occasions, were never more conspicuous," gushed one observer.

L'Enfant advised on the design of a number of floats in the parade—including one upon which Hamilton was carried—as well as the attendant banners and decorations, but his most significant contribution was his plan for a 6,000-seat temporary banquet pavilion erected at the terminus of the grand march, near the present-day intersection of Grand Street and the Bowery. As a contemporary drawing by David Grim shows, the pavilion took the shape of a great triple-domed half-wheel with spokes formed by 440-foot-long tables radiating out from a central axis where sat Washington, members of Congress, foreign diplomats, and other dignitaries. The festivities took place under the watchful eye of a grand figure of Fame executed on the main ceiling by L'Enfant, and proclaiming the glory of the new era to come.

The affair was deemed a triumph in the press, cementing L'Enfant's reputation in the city as a successful and esteemed architect and planner. In September of 1788 the acting Congress decided that the temporary seat of the federal government would in fact remain in New York, rather than return to Philadelphia. The city's commissioners donated their own government building at the top of Wall Street for the use of Congress and selected L'Enfant to oversee its redesign from City Hall to Federal Hall.

While it might have seemed a magnanimous patriotic gesture for the city fathers to vacate their own building and authorize more than $50,000 for renovations needed by Congress, the largesse was in large part motivated by politics. Ever since the shift of the government from Philadelphia, there had been steady lobbying from Pennsylvanians and others distrustful of "northern" interests who wanted Congress to return to quarters in the Pennsylvania state house; New York's offer of a newly renovated building to a cash-strapped Congress was seen as an effective foil to the back-to-Philadelphia bloc's efforts. Clearly, politicians and influence-peddlers in 1788 were no less savvy than their twenty-first-century counterparts when it came to appreciating the importance of where the nation's political business was conducted, and they understood perfectly well what advantage was to be gained by ready access to the legislative chambers.

THE ISSUE OF a location for the seat of the federal government had been contentious for years before the 1788 controversy. In fact, the question had been raised as early as 1754, when Benjamin Franklin penned his Albany Plan of Union, suggesting a confederation of the seven British North American colonies at the time (Connecticut, Maryland, Massachusetts, New Hampshire, New York, Pennsylvania, and Rhode Island) for the purposes of seeking better relations with Indian tribes and the establishment of a common defense against the marauding French. In a codicil that presaged the difficulties to come, Franklin proposed that the capital rotate from one colony capital to another on a yearly basis, beginning with Annapolis. That plan never came to fruition, and by the time the question of the location of an American capital became a practical issue, Franklin (who died in 1790 at eighty-four) was aging and in ill health and took no active role in the debate.

In June of 1783 the Congress of the Confederation was meeting in rooms provided by the Pennsylvania Council when a group of several hundred unhappy Pennsylvanian soldiers marched upon the state capitol to demand back pay from their legislature. Congress immediately decamped from Philadelphia for Princeton, New Jersey, though the reasons are still debated by historians. Some say the move was made out of fear; others contend that the appearance of a coerced displacement was simply a way for Congress, sympathetic to the soldiers' cause, to pressure the state to meet its obligations.

Complicating the matter of where the nation's capital should reside—and many other matters as well—was the fact that, in the years immediately following its founding, Congress had no source of income beyond voluntary contributions from the individual states. Representatives might pass resolutions and acts all they wished, but paying for anything was a matter of wheedling, coaxing, and otherwise persuading the leaders of state delegations to pony up.

Shortly after the move to Princeton, the leaders of Congress made what the historian Rubil Morales-Vazquez describes as an unequivocally political move by inviting General Washington for a several-months'-long consultation. Ostensibly Washington would be available to advise on various military and political issues, but Morales-Vazquez argues that Congress's true intention was to associate itself publicly with the unassailable national hero and to raise its own stock in the bargain. It was at this time, not coincidentally, that the resolution was passed authorizing that a bronze equestrian statue honoring Washington was to be installed at "the place where Congress shall be established."

In light of the recent reestablishment of that "place" in Princeton, debate ensued in late 1783 as to just how permanent the move from Philadelphia was to be. The result was a compromise engineered by Massachusetts representative Elbridge Gerry and Virginia's Arthur Lee: there would be *two* seats of government, they proposed, one to be located somewhere along the north bank of the Potomac River near Georgetown, and the second on the Delaware. While those final locations were being prepared, Trenton, New Jersey, and Annapolis, Maryland, would stand in as temporary bases.

To the modern eye the complex plan seems to be the result of the same sort of committee work that had produced a camel when the aim had been a horse, and even at the time there were plenty of detractors of the Lee/Gerry plan. Francis Hopkinson, delegate from New Jersey and the designer of the original "stars and stripes" flag, quipped that since Congress had already resolved that the statue of Washington was to be placed "where Congress shall be established," perhaps a set of wheels would have to be added to it.

Still, the compromise temporarily defused a fundamental tension that had haunted the earliest attempts to form a coalition among the American colonies. The division among the states was geographical, of course, but it was motivated principally by economics. Federalists from a densely populated and industrialized New England favored a powerful central government with the intricate organization necessary to manage the affairs of a large and growing nation. Such thinking was anathema to men such as Thomas Jefferson and James Madison, who represented the interests of an agrarian south and who feared the consolidation of power in any locale distant from the interests of those governed. For Jefferson, the best federal government was the simplest and most minimal version possible. To place the permanent seat of the federal government in any established city of the Northeast was simply unthinkable. If there had to be a national capital, Southerners believed, then, at the very least, situating it along the Potomac on the northern border of Virginia guaranteed some distance, both politically and geographically, from the big money in the Northeast and the sophisticated political machines allied with it.

A movable capital might have seemed workable in the abstract, but the expense involved caused lawmakers to rethink the issue, and by December of 1784 Congress agreed that a dual capital was impractical. The body would situate itself temporarily in New York City while a single site near Trenton was prepared for the permanent home of government.

Though Southern interests were dismayed, Washington worked behind the scenes to reassure them. The lack of support in the South meant that no appropriations would be forthcoming for the building of so much as a national privy in Trenton. It was Washington's personal belief that a site along the Potomac, on the dividing line between the industrialized North and the agrarian South, represented not only a philosophical but a practical compromise on the matter.

When the Constitutional Convention was assembled at the Philadelphia state house in 1787, Washington successfully persuaded the fifty-five delegates to authorize the establishment of an independent federal district "ten miles square," and with exclusive dominion over all affairs undertaken within its boundaries, including the construction of "forts, magazines, arsenals, dockyards, and other needful buildings." As to where exactly that ten miles square should rest, the convention was silent, leaving the matter to be determined by the new Federal Congress.

The action alarmed a wide range of opponents of a central government who feared that any such enclave, no matter what its location, would become an insular and self-interested fiefdom, unresponsive to the needs of the country at large. Writing in *The Federalist*, James Madison—enough of a realist along with Jefferson to understand that there would have to be a capital city *somewhere*—reasoned that such fears were groundless and that by joining together in the enterprise of building such a district, the various states and interests would create a physical and lasting manifestation of the philosophical ties that brought the nation into being in the first place.

Nor was such thinking confined to the realm of fine rhetoric. The *Pennsylvania Packet* reported that at the L'Enfant-designed parade in 1788 celebrating the work of the Constitutional Convention, the flag carried by the bricklayers' union featured a representation of workmen carving a new Federal City from the midst of a forest. Its motto was "Both Buildings and Rulers are the works of our Hands."

Of course, the wrangling over the placement of the government continued. Jefferson was instrumental in keeping the government from moving back to Philadelphia for the first federal session. His reasoning was somewhat Machiavellian: given his grudging support for a site on the Potomac, he feared that it would be far more difficult to dislodge the government from Philadelphia than to build a coalition to force a move from New York City.

Debate in Congress was acrimonious, stretching on into the summer of 1788, and leading some to fear that the shaky national alliance might actually collapse. North Carolina still had not ratified the Constitution, and the New York delegation had called for a new constitutional convention to reconsider matters. Former finance minister Robert Morris remarked to a colleague that if Congress were to allow the matter of a permanent governmental seat "to sleep much longer, they will probably meet the reproaches of the major part of the people of America."

Proposals were floated for other sites in New Jersey, as well as at Wilmington in Delaware, Lancaster in Pennsylvania, and Annapolis in Maryland, as alternatives to the major contenders, though none proved popular. When a last effort for Princeton by the Philadelphia coalition failed, even Pennsylvania's editorial writers had seen enough. "Let the place of meeting . . . be anywhere; but for Heaven's sake . . . let the government be put in motion," one writer opined.

Finally, on September 12, Virginia's Lee introduced the seventh proposal to be debated, suggesting that the "present seat of Congress" in New York should become the temporary site of its new federal incarnation, and on the following day, an exhausted body voted unanimously to do just that, setting the date for the first meeting of the constitutionally authorized Congress for the fourth of March, 1789.

Of course, there would be a need for a building to house the new Congress, and that necessarily brings us back to Pierre Charles L'Enfant.

6

A New American Order

WHILE THE DECISION ON WHERE TO SETTLE ITSELF had occupied Congress for the better part of two months, the choice of the man to make its new home ready was apparently an uncontested matter, owing perhaps to the memories of the successful and popular ratification celebration the Frenchman had orchestrated—or perhaps to the personal influence of Hamilton, Washington, and his other powerful backers. In any case, before the end of September, L'Enfant had submitted a design for "additions, alterations, and repairs" necessary to convert the City Hall of New York for use by the First Federal Congress.

The hall, originally constructed in 1704, had a long and storied history of its own. In 1735 it was the site of the trial of John Peter Zenger, a newspaper publisher accused of libeling the New York governor in print. Zenger's acquittal established the concept of the legally protected freedom of the press, an issue that the new Congress would soon address as it crafted the first ten amendments to the Constitution, also known as the Bill of Rights.

City Hall had also played a significant role in the events leading up to the Revolution. In 1765 the building served as the meeting place of the so-called Stamp Act Congress, at which representatives of nine colonies met in opposition to the Crown for the first time. At issue was the short-lived decree of George III that all official documents, newspapers, pamphlets, and even playing cards were to carry his imprimatur, and that publishers and manufacturers would have to pay a tax for each stamp.

Because the tax was instituted to underwrite the cost of maintaining the British army's presence in the colonies and provided only minimal benefit to the citizens, protests were vehement and the law was widely flouted. John Dickinson, delegate to the Stamp Act Congress from Philadelphia, drew up the formal petition, arguing that colonists were owed the same respect and rights as other subjects of Great Britain and were therefore were exempt from "taxation without representation." While pressure from merchants in Great Britain was probably more effective in causing Parliament's eventual repeal of the measure than were the petition and protests of the colonists, it is generally agreed that the Stamp Act Congress and its "Declaration of Rights and Grievances" constituted a dress rehearsal for the Continental Congress and its Declaration of Independence.

Given the building's historic association with the cause of liberty and its grand new national purpose, there is little wonder that L'Enfant threw himself fully into the project. By October 6, once the city's prisoners had been moved from the basement cells to a hastily constructed jail, more than two hundred men were hard at work on the renovations. As von Steuben wrote a friend, his former assistant was already causing himself "a great deal of pain," primarily in anticipation of the glory involved.

If the old City Hall had enjoyed an illustrious past, its physical manifestation—one newspaper described it as a "gothic heap"—did not measure up. L'Enfant, mindful of the symbolic significance of structure and design, set out to create a building that outwardly expressed the importance of the work being done within, embodying the unprecedented aspirations of the country in its architecture.

Beginning with a modest two-story, seven-bay, three-arched Jacobean structure about ninety feet wide and fifty feet deep, L'Enfant expanded the building's footprint to nearly three times that size. He also created a grand new façade for the building, with a soaring tower and an imposing four-columned loggia. The new frieze atop the Doric loggia featured thirteen stars representing the colonies, and the pediment featured an imposing rendition of the now-ubiquitous warlike eagle, thirteen arrows clutched in one claw. The magnificence of the design clearly marked the building, a reporter noted, as one "set apart for national purposes."

While several engravings and watercolors of the building's exterior survive, its architectural plans long ago disappeared, so historians are left with a few newspaper accounts and fragmentary descriptions from which to reimagine the interior. The *New-York Journal and Weekly Register* of March 26, 1789, describes an entry hall paved with marble leading to a spacious central vestibule illuminated by the dome's glass cupola high above. On the second floor was an impressive lobby of some twenty by fifty feet that was sometimes called the "picture room," a reference to the portraits by John Trumbull of Washington, Hamilton, and George Clinton that hung there. An iron-railed balcony bordered the open vestibule below, allowing, as one reporter noted, a convenient track of more than two hundred feet for any senator needing to pace and ponder a troublesome issue.

The Senate Chamber was located off that second-story lobby in a room of about forty feet by thirty, with its arched, twenty-foot ceiling plain except for a rendering of a sun and thirteen stars in its center. Though it had a pair of fireplaces and was said to be "neatly wainscotted," with "handsome" carpet and drapes of crimson damask, it was not the most memorable of the newly created rooms.

More impressive—"the master piece of the whole, and most entitled to the name of Federal Hall"—was the ground-floor House chamber. At roughly sixty feet square, it was more than three-quarters the size of the original building all by itself. With a soaring thirty-six-foot, two-story-high ceiling, four marble fireplaces, and opposing banks of windows that began sixteen feet above the level of the floor, the room was a grand space for the new government. At the south end a two-tiered, cantilevered spectators' gallery faced the Speaker's table on the opposite end of the hall, and desks for each of the fifty-nine members of the House sat in a semicircle between.

A writer for *The Massachusetts Magazine* took particular note of the building's decorative touches: "the capitals are of a fanciful kind, the invention of Major L'Enfant, the architect . . . amidst their foliage appears a star and rays, and a piece of drapery below suspends a small medallion with U.S. in a cipher. The idea is new and the effect pleasing; and although they cannot be said to be of any ancient order, we must allow that they have an appearance of magnificence."

That magazine concluded on a note of high praise for the architect, "who has surmounted many difficulties, and has so accommodated the additions to the old parts, and so judiciously altered what he saw wrong, that he has produced a building uniform and consistent throughout, and has added to great elegance every convenience that could be desired."

Although L'Enfant found himself criticized by at least one editorial writer for using too many "foreigners" on the job (concern over the number of French immigrants fleeing the fallout from the revolution there would lead to the first restrictive legislation in 1790), his liberal use of American symbols suggests he was far more concerned about what was left behind once the workers had departed. He had even made sure that American marble—"for beauty of shades of polish . . . equal to any of its kind in Europe"—was used for the fireplaces in the building. With the exception of some quibbles over the decorative grillwork and panels, other architects found the end result pleasing and unified, agreeing that L'Enfant had been successful in expressing strength and pride without sacrificing function and in striking an effective balance between patriotic zeal and classical restraint.

There were some politically motivated grumblings, of course: Pennsylvania Senator William Maclay sneered at the thought that the government should reside in New York for the sake of the "Jimcrackery and Gingerbread of an old building new vamped up," and quipped that he would not employ any "infants" if the job of commissioning a capitol were left up to him. His colleague in the House, Frederick Muhlenberg, chimed in that the building was "really elegant and well designed—for a trap."

But the response of most was highly enthusiastic. The *Gazette of the United States* said that the building was "on the whole, superior to any building in America . . . the great design for which it is constructed does honor to the architect." And James Duane, the mayor of New York, wrote L'Enfant "with great esteem" to praise his "distinguished merit and services," adding that "while the Hall exists it will exhibit a most respectable monument of your eminent talents." Taking particular note of the fact that the work had been completed within five months, one New York paper called the building "superb," exceeding the "most sanguine expectations."

Adressing L'Enfant's loftier aspirations, French ambassador Moustier wrote home to say that the architect had transformed the old building to such an extent that it now retained little more than its name. "In the end he created a monument that can serve as an allegory to the new constitution," Moustier enthused. "Both have been entirely changed by their architects, who brought their clients a great deal further than they had thought to go."

In a retrospective assessment published in 1970, architectural historian Louis Torres called L'Enfant's work on both the interior and exterior of the building "so extensive and unique as to place it in the vanguard of a new style of architecture in America." And in her 1995 book, *Temple of Liberty*, Pamela Scott calls this first Federal building "a harbinger of more flexible and cosmopolitan" public structures for the new republic. She goes on to agree with Torres, crediting L'Enfant's combination of classical style and American architectural entablature as constituting the invention of a "new American order," initiating "a national emblematic language in both its architectural forms and its decorative details."

Such praise would surely have been music to the ears of L'Enfant, who was watching a different kind of American order taking shape before him, and—even more satisfying, one assumes—within the walls of a place he had constructed. On March 4, 1789, the new Congress of the Constitution convened in the still-unfinished Federal Hall, and on April 6, electors chose George Washington, running unopposed, as the nation's first president. On April 30, Washington, then fifty-seven, stood on the portico of the new Federal Hall, designed by L'Enfant for just such an occasion, to take the oath of office of the President of the United States before New York State Chief Justice Robert Livingston.

In his address Washington stressed the need for unity as the country now began the long process of building what the Revolution had only begun. "The preservation of the sacred fire of liberty and the republican model are . . . finally, staked on the experiment entrusted to the hands of the American people," Washington intoned, gazing out over Wall Street from the porch where red and white bunting designed for the occasion by none other than L'Enfant had been placed. The architect, however, was nowhere to be found.

L'ENFANT'S ABSENCE FROM the occasion, honoring the man who had championed him for years and taking place in a building that was being hailed as a triumph of the imagination, might seem peculiar. Congress had, after all, chosen him as one of seven "special assistants" in charge of arrangements and security for the inaugural.

But, while the record of history is silent as to why he did not attend, it is possible to make some suppositions. First of all, the inauguration of the first president was not the pageant that the ceremony has become today. It was assumed by everyone that Washington would become the nation's first executive, and with no formal political parties yet formed, there was no great sense of drama or triumph surrounding the installation of the former leader of U.S. forces in his new position.

In fact, Martha Washington herself did not bother to attend the ceremony. It was more than a month later that she made her way to

New York from Mount Vernon, and when she did seek a tour of Federal Hall, it was not in the company of her husband. In a letter of June 11, her secretary requested that Major L'Enfant himself accompany the First Lady: "Miss Washington having postponed an engagement she had for Saturday next; is desirous of seeing the Federal Building on that day.—I have; therefore; taken the liberty of informing you; and of inquiring the hour which will be most convenient; in all respects; for making the visit."

Kenneth Bowling theorizes that it was wounded pride that kept L'Enfant from watching as Washington became the first to swear to "preserve, protect and defend" the nation's new Constitution. Given his longtime association with the new president, his status as a war hero, and his work on the new seat of government, it is possible that being appointed a "special assistant" in charge of ceremonial design and security might have struck L'Enfant as an honor far smaller than he believed he was due. It would not be the last time that L'Enfant would consider himself slighted.

Still, the hall he designed quickly became an inextricable part of American popular culture. Philip Freneau, poet and publisher of the *New York Daily Advertiser*, ran a paean to the building's irresistible appeal:

> Four hours a day each rank alike,
> (They that can walk or crawl)
> Leave children, business, shop and wife,
> And steer for Federal Hall.

Crowds not only thronged the galleries during congressional debates, but the building also traveled to the crowds themselves: as part of a play produced in the city that summer, a painted rendering of the façade descended as if from the clouds, to be praised by an actor as "that Temple, sacred to patriotism, liberty and virtue." In October of 1789, the New York City Council passed a resolution praising L'Enfant and making him an honorary citizen of their town.

And yet, when it came to recompense for his achievement, it must have seemed to L'Enfant that von Steuben had been prophetic when he noted that all this hard work was done "pour la Gloire" alone. In March of 1790, nearly a year after construction on the building ended, the council offered L'Enfant only a parcel of land in payment for his services. Though the modern mind might falter in an attempt to calculate the value of ten acres of midtown Manhattan property, comprising most of the area between 66th and 70th streets, just east of Third Avenue, L'Enfant found the offer of the then far-flung pastureland an affront. When the council inquired if it was true that he was not willing to accept their proposed settlement, L'Enfant wrote back in his characteristically oblique way that it was "perfectly agreeable with my sentiments and disposition to refuse the gift."

It is impossible to know whether L'Enfant spurned the offer purely out of pique, or because he hoped that the shamefaced city government would return with a more generous counteroffer. Or perhaps he had already set his disappointment aside to hope for better things ahead. For the truth was—whether he suspected it or not—he was about to be entrusted with the project of his dreams.

7

Quid Pro Quo

DESPITE THE DECISION TO SEAT THE FIRST FEDERAL Congress in New York City, debate continued as to just how long the body would continue to meet there. Even New Yorkers seemed resigned that their city would never serve as the permanent seat of government for a country that was firmly set on westward expansion. From the moment that Henry Lee's resolution was adopted by a debate-weary Congress, a fresh wave of lobbying by spurned Philadelphians began.

In the spring of 1789, shortly before the election that proclaimed Washington the nation's first president, Benjamin Rush, a prominent Pennsylvania surgeon and delegate to the Constitutional Convention, approached his old friend John Adams to let him know that he could count on Pennsylvania's support in the race for vice president—on the condition that Adams lend his support to a site on the western banks of the Delaware River as the permanent site for the capital. As Pennsylvania senator William Maclay explained in his diary, he and Rush undertook a campaign to boost Adams in the newspapers: "We knew his vanity, and hoped by laying hold of it to render him useful among the New England men in our scheme of bringing Congress to Pennsylvania."

The moment Adams was elected as Washington's vice president, Rush wrote to remind him of the help that Pennsylvania had rendered and hoping that his influence would be "exerted immediately in favor of a motion to bring Congress to Philadelphia." In a letter back to Rush, Adams protested that he had little influence to exert in the matter, though he did profess his personal regret that Philadelphia had not been the choice of Congress to begin with.

Meanwhile, Philadelphia newspapers were relentless in their own campaign to smear New York and tout the advantages of their city as the preferred site. Most of the arguments were familiar: Philadelphia was more centrally located and better suited as a gateway to the West (privately, Washington and James Madison thought this was in fact the most compelling argument for an even more southerly site); the influence of wealthy New England merchants and established politicians did not extend to Pennsylvania (an issue of great importance to Southern interests); and, as would be claimed on both sides, the cultural amenities were greater and the women better looking in their respective cities.

For their part, New Yorkers pointed out that Philadelphia and its well-entrenched interests were every bit as devious and power-hungry as any group of New Englanders, and that any proposal for a temporary move back to Philadelphia was unnecessary, wasteful, and a transparent ploy to locate the government there permanently. If nothing else, New York's proponents argued, New York had a much better climate, especially in the summertime. In March, the New York legislature went so far as to authorize the expenditure of $20,000 to build a lavish new residence near Federal Hall for the use of the president—with L'Enfant's name floated as the likely architect.

Back and forth the promises and the charges flew. Congressmen were lobbied brazenly, treated to dinners and entertainments during their travels, and pressured to place the matter on the agenda the moment a quorum was reached in New York. Only when a group from the Virginia delegation, headed by James Madison, approached the Pennsylvania leadership to ask that they comport themselves with decency did they agree to back off their lobbying for the time being.

The lull allowed Congress to focus on other pressing matters. On

July 4 the first import tariff on foreign goods was approved, and on July 20 the Tonnage Act followed, creating an assured source of revenue for the federal government for the first time. On September 13, Hamilton was appointed the first secretary of the treasury to mind these monies and guide future fiscal policy.

Also in September, Congress passed the Judiciary Act, creating a six-member Supreme Court authorized to rule independently on the constitutionality of any law in the land, and thereby addressing one of the chief complaints about life under the capricious rule of King George. Before the month was out, Congress had also proposed a dozen amendments to the new Constitution, ten of which would eventually be ratified and become known as the Bill of Rights. By any standards, it is a significant record of achievement for one term.

With such fundamental matters under its belt, Congress returned to the issue that simply would not die. Because they understood that their own city had little chance of becoming the permanent site, New York interests were willing to back the establishment of various other locations for the Federal City, so long as the temporary home of government could remain in Manhattan, and so long as its rival city of Philadelphia was not the final choice. In order to distract Congress from Philadelphia's lobbying, New York's backers proposed a mind-boggling cascade of sites in Pennsylvania—including Germantown, Old Philadelphia, Reading, Peach Bottom, York, and Carlisle—most motivated by the specter of Philadelphia as a hotbed of entrenched interests and big-city vices. (Those backers presumably were not reassured by Pelatiah Webster, a Philadelphia businessman and influential political economist, who opined that if the enticements of big-city living proved distracting to its members, Congress could simply enact legislation forbidding members' immoral and licentious behavior.)

Not to be left out of the fray, civic leaders in Baltimore readied their own proposal and secured pledges of $20,000 for the construction of a new Federal Hall and other necessary buildings. On the opposite side of the Maryland peninsula, the remote outpost of Georgetown lobbied for consideration, its hopes bolstered by the support of nearby landowner President Washington, who had long championed the Potomac River as the future gateway to the West.

On August 27, 1789, representative Thomas Scott of Pennsylvania introduced a resolution to determine a permanent seat of government. Scott, who had earlier told his colleagues, "Westward the path of Empire takes its way," proposed no specific choice of his own but did stipulate that the site chosen should have "convenience to the navigation of the Atlantic Ocean, and . . . due regard to the particular situation of the western country."

As to the gravity of the matter, he argued that the very future of the Union depended upon its swift resolution. The issue may have been a political football, but Scott was not exaggerating the stakes regarding where this one bounced. For a fragile republic still feeling its way toward reconciling its varied interests, the choice of a symbolic and physical home was crucial.

Debate in the House soon crystallized into a fight between those championing a site on the east bank of the Susquehanna River in Pennsylvania, a hundred miles or so west of Philadelphia, and those in favor of the north bank of the Potomac in Maryland. Northern interests, including the Philadelphians, backed the Pennsylvania site and held a slight majority in the initial voting, while Southerners fought for Maryland. The deadlock continued until a crafty amendment was attached to the Susquehanna proposal. The "proviso," as it became known, simply required that no construction on the capital could begin until all obstructions to navigation on the river between the site and its mouth on the Chesapeake Bay were removed.

The amendment was introduced by Southerners who supported the Potomac site. They expected that the Philadelphia-based members of the Pennsylvania delegation would never support a proposal that would allow commercial traffic from the center of their state to be diverted down a newly navigable waterway to the Chesapeake and away from Philadelphia's port. It was a rather cynical maneuver, but ultimately it would prove an effective one.

On September 22, after nearly a month of intense debate, the

House passed along a bill to the Senate approving a federal district of ten square miles to be situated on the banks of the Susquehanna River in Pennsylvania. The bill set aside $100,000 for acquisition of land and building improvements and gave the president authority to appoint three commissioners to choose the specific site. All of it was contingent upon that proviso: the opening of the river for navigation to the Chesapeake, where Baltimore was poised to take the place of Philadelphia as broker for central Pennsylvania trade interests.

When the bill reached the Senate, things began to unravel. Pennsylvania senator Robert Morris, former superintendent of finance under the Articles of Confederation and said to be the richest man in America, opposed the Susquehanna location not only because he was troubled by the proviso, but also because he owned considerable lands in and around a previously considered site on the Pennsylvania bank of the Delaware River opposite Trenton. After considerable maneuvering, Morris amended the House bill to move the site from the middle of his state back to Germantown, a suburb of Philadelphia, and into his own backyard.

The amended bill was returned to the House, where a weary membership approved it, along with a minor amendment inserted by Madison, who had noted an inconsistency in the language concerning interim governmental jurisdiction over the new district. It might have seemed that the matter was settled once and for all, the capital slated for Philadelphia . . . but the Senate would have to debate Madison's amendment, and its adjournment had already been scheduled for the following day, so the matter was postponed until the next session of Congress.

The postponement was seen as a great triumph for Madison and fellow proponents of the Potomac site, but it also pleased a number of moderate interests, who feared that the debate had come close to splitting the union of the states before it was effectively under way. As proof, they pointed to the fact that despite any number of modifications and compromises, neither the New England interests nor the Southerners had been able to assemble a clear majority—and as for the rascally Pennsylvanians, they were nothing more than self-centered opportunists. Perhaps, they thought, the matter should be postponed until the new Western states sure to come had a chance to form and add their own input.

As the most powerful spokesperson for Southern interests, James Madison found himself in a difficult position. He believed any site north of the Potomac was unacceptable, but he was deeply concerned that the controversy over the capital had stirred talk among New Englanders that secession from the young Union, based on economic interests, was the only practical course of action. Nor was Madison unmindful of the concern that the Western states, which just months earlier had seemed sure to join the Union, might instead choose to ally themselves apart for similar reasons.

Unwilling to risk the nation over the issue of the capital, Madison tentatively favored a continuing series of delaying tactics. The longer the decision was put off, the greater the chance that fresh voices would join the chorus and an unassailable majority would form, placing the site outside the controversial spheres of established interest. On the other hand, he worried that regional tensions bred by the uncertainty might be the fuel that fed secessionist fires to a blaze. In the end he agreed with Vice President Adams that a decision would have to be made sooner rather than later, and set about lending his support to that aim.

In the meantime, civic boosters of the Potomac site were taking direct steps to advance their cause. An Irishman named John O'Connor, who had immigrated to Georgetown, published a popular pamphlet that described the area in florid terms: "From every ascent, and in every dale, Georgetown will affect the imagination in presenting new beauties," he wrote. Of the neighboring Potomac River he added, "The branch is wide, and deep enough to receive all the ships in the river Thames . . . under the protection of elevated hills . . . as if, formed by nature, for the express purpose of sheltering ships and commerce from the North-west wind."

O'Connor's writings inspired a group of local merchants and

landowners to draw up a similar broadside for distribution among their counterparts in New England, in an attempt to appeal to their business interests. The broadside was crafted by David Stuart, an investor in the Potomac Company and the man who had married George Washington's widowed daughter-in-law. Stuart emphasized the potential of the Potomac as a conduit to the Ohio and Mississippi rivers, and lauded the climate, the rich soil, and the ready availability of timber and quarry rock for building. He also attempted to turn the often-heard criticism that the area was woefully underdeveloped into a positive, pointing out that while New Englanders could not be expected to reap many benefits from development and trade with a well-established site near Philadelphia, they could become early investors in a freshly minted port city on the Maryland-Virginia border.

George Walker, another prominent Georgetown landowner, published an article that appeared in a January issue of the *Maryland Journal*, echoing Stuart's sentiments on the importance of the Potomac as a trade conduit. New England businesses already controlled what commerce existed on the river, he pointed out, and when the magnificent treasures of the West began to pour eastward between its banks, those who owned the ships that carried the cargo would become extravagantly wealthy. Not only would their Northern brethren enjoy untold profits from those raw materials flowing eastward, the Southerners argued, but the waters of the Potomac would "groan under the pressure of New England manufactures" headed in the opposite direction.

With this nationwide discussion as background, the Federal Congress met for its second session in January, and the postponed bill for the Germantown site was immediately called. Given that this was the first such instance of a bill carried over from one session to the next, Congress had not yet adopted rules to govern the situation. The Pennsylvania delegation argued that the Senate should proceed to consider the Madison-amended bill as if no time had passed. The friends of the Potomac interests countered that any matter taken up in a new session was in fact "new" business, and any previously unresolved matters should be wiped off the slate and introduced afresh. But Alexander Hamilton had just introduced a matter of some pressing importance, and final consideration of the bill was postponed.

Hamilton's business was more than a diversion. He delivered a report to Congress that called for it to assume responsibility for the debts incurred by the former colonies during the fighting of the Revolutionary War a decade before. He suggested that Treasury notes should be issued in exchange for any paper money printed by states to pay soldiers and suppliers during the conflict, and he argued further that the federal government should repay all the loans made by foreign governments as well.

Hamilton's proposal opened a new firestorm of debate. The states that had incurred the most debt during the fighting—Massachusetts and South Carolina—were behind the plan, of course. Virginia, with the smallest debt and the largest population (750,000 of the nation's 4 million—nearly twice as many as second-place Pennsylvania), was firmly opposed.

And there was another issue as well: since the value of the states' notes had long been in decline, much of that tender had fallen into the hands of speculators, who now stood to reap a fortune simply by strolling into the Treasury offices and demanding redemption of their holdings at face value. Lawmakers found themselves facing what would become a familiar quandary, where legislation that seemed necessary for the common good would inevitably reward the perfidious as well.

Hamilton's own reasoning went beyond such proximate concerns. Not only would federal assumption of the debt affirm the nation's credibility, he asserted, but freeing the states from their burden would also boost the economy, putting money, goods, and services immediately into circulation. The arguments over such thinking—whether debt can be a good thing—began immediately, and while the battle over Hamilton's particular proposal would eventually be resolved, the political war over economics that he began has never ceased.

When a motion in support of the debt assumption failed in April, some Northern congressmen began to talk openly of secession. And if that were not enough, the House had begun debate on petitions to strike the provisions of the Constitution reserving matters of emancipation to the states alone. That led Thomas Tudor Tucker, representative from Georgia, to declare that the South would wage "civil war" rather than submit to federal dominion over the slave trade.

The outlook for the Union, not yet fourteen years old, was bleak. Virginia senator Henry Lee confided to Madison, "I had rather myself submit to all the hazards of war . . . than to live under the rule of a fixed insolent northern majority," and urged that Madison do all he could to settle the matter of moving the seat of government to the Potomac. A resolution might be enough to stave off secession, Lee reasoned. Madison did not share Lee's gloomy prospect for the Union, but, as he wrote back, that did not mean he was as hopeful about their chances of moving the capital to the Potomac.

Before the failure of Hamilton's proposal for debt assumption, most of the secessionist public oratory had come from Southerners feeling dispossessed; now New Englanders were ready to pull out of the Union for their own reasons. The dissolution of the republic might have seemed inevitable.

But seen from a pragmatic view, the possibility of a quid pro quo had finally emerged. Northerners wanted debt assumption; Southerners wanted a capital on the Potomac. Thus began a process of regional-interest horse trading that has never stopped.

Hamilton, the maestro of the new economy and thus the point man for a strong federal order, met with Madison, who was finding himself more and more a states'-rights man. Mediating was the newly appointed secretary of state, Thomas Jefferson, just back from Paris, where he had served as ambassador. With typical aplomb, Jefferson described the dinner meeting that he had arranged:

"It was observed, I forget by which one of them, that as the pill [of assumption] would be a bitter one to Southern States, something should be done to soothe them, that the removal of the seat of Government to the Patowmac was a just measure . . . and would be a proper one to follow assumption." Jefferson's tradeoff—the bane of idealists, an inspiration for pragmatists—endures to this day as an object lesson in the American political process.

Before the dinner's last course was cleared away, Madison promised to deliver the Southern votes necessary for assumption if Hamilton would intervene with the New Englanders on behalf of the Potomac site—and both went immediately to work. Key to Madison's end of the bargain was securing the vote of Maryland senator Charles Carroll. Given that he owned a 10,000-acre estate just off the banks of the Potomac a few miles north of Georgetown, it is not surprising that Carroll quickly saw the benefits of dropping his opposition to assumption. With Carroll in his fold, Madison next approached Representative Richard Lee of Virginia, who agreed to support assumption in return for Madison's implied promise that Alexandria, across the Potomac from Georgetown, would be included in the new federal district.

For Hamilton it was crucial to persuade the Massachusetts delegation to keep its distance from the endlessly opportunistic Pennsylvania delegation. Hamilton had already managed to persuade Pennsylvania to accept the deal he had worked out. In return for Pennsylvania's support of the bargain Hamilton had struck with Madison, Philadelphia would become the temporary capital of the nation for ten years, while the new capital was being built. Furthermore, as Hamilton explained to Elbridge Gerry and others, if Massachusetts wanted its debts assumed, there was to be no more collusion with the bloc holding out hope for a permanent home of government anywhere in Pennsylvania.

In the end, Hamilton managed to cobble together the necessary votes in support of the Potomac as the capital's permanent site, and on July 1, 1790, the Senate approved by a vote of 14–12 a bill authorizing the formation of the new capital "in a district of territory not exceeding ten miles square" at a site to be determined on the Potomac somewhere between the Anacostia River (on the eastern edge of present-day Washington, D.C.) and the Conococheague Creek (which empties into the Potomac more than one hundred miles upstream, near the Maryland-Pennsylvania border).

Madison's amendment to the original Scott bill of 1789 was included—Maryland state law would prevail within the new district until Congress took possession of the district. And, as originally proposed, the president was to appoint a three-person commission to choose the final site, purchase public lands, and oversee the construction of necessary buildings. The capital would be transferred to this new site no later than December of 1800, and in the meantime Congress would conduct its affairs in Philadelphia.

The House took up the Senate's bill on July 6, and, as expected, opponents took advantage of every opportunity to ridicule and block the establishment of a government in what they declared to be a loathsome place. Aedanus Burke of South Carolina demanded to know why any intelligent congress would send itself off to "the woods," while Elbridge Gerry of Massachusetts wondered "where in the name of common sense is Connogochuque . . . I do not believe that one person in a thousand . . . knows there is such a place on earth."

Gerry had also gotten wind of Alexandria's hopes to be included in the district and demanded if that were to be so, then it was a matter that ought to be honestly spelled out in the legislation. He went on to say that the whole affair reeked of a conspiracy by the Pennsylvania coalition, claiming that once Philadelphia got its hands on the government, it would never let go. That assertion got considerable play in the newspapers, with some likening Robert Morris's skills as a negotiator for Philadelphia's interests to those of the rabbit who had begged to be thrown anywhere but into the briar patch.

Such histrionic rhetoric and similarly futile amendments, including the dusting off of well-worn proposals for sites in Germantown, Baltimore, and Trenton on Delaware, were bandied about for three days, until, finally, on July 9, after one last attempt by opponents to postpone the matter, the House adopted the Senate bill known as the Residence Act without change by a vote of 32–29.

Three weeks later the debt assumption bill was passed by the Senate, and after some face-saving bluster by Madison, the matter was put to a vote in the House. Alexander White, one of the Virginia representatives who understood from Madison that Alexandria would be included within the boundaries of the district, claimed that he had still not made up his mind. But when it came time for the vote, it appeared that he had. He fell in line with Richard Lee, and by a vote of 32–29 the matter of assumption was also approved.

In this manner, some contend, the fledgling Union had been saved. And yet, for the new president, such a momentous accomplishment would not come without its personal cost.

8

Court of Public Opinion

THOUGH WASHINGTON'S OWN ENTHUSIASM FOR THE placement of the capital on the Potomac was well known, there was still hope among the die-hard opponents that the president might understand how deep the divide was over the matter and refuse to sign or even veto the Residence Act. Representative William Smith of South Carolina argued that only Congress had authority—granted by the Constitution—over issues of adjournment (where and when it would meet). Thus a bill bearing on such matters that required the president's signature was patently unconstitutional.

Whether or not Washington privately found it a sophist's point, he nonetheless turned for advice on the matter to Secretary of State Jefferson, who assured the president that the bill was safe to sign. On July 16, Washington followed Jefferson's counsel and, as a result, felt the sting of press and public criticism for the first time. A story in the *New York Daily Advertiser* suggested, furthermore, that Washington's personal support of the Potomac site had improperly influenced the decision, and others also complained that in signing the bill he had exposed himself as a powermonger.

To be sure, Washington was by no means the first or the only one to fall under the sway of what was termed "Potomac Fever." The Algonquin tribes had populated the Maryland peninsula and the adjacent territories of Virginia from the ninth century AD, drawn southward from the Great Lakes region by a mild climate, fertile soil, and ample bounty from the broad river on the west and Chesapeake Bay to the east. In an early form of advertising, the tribes chose *Petomeack*, or "trading place," as the designation for their new home, and the name stuck.

Although early Spanish explorers ventured a short way up the river in 1571, no other Europeans are known to have taken an interest there until Captain John Smith sailed up what was known briefly as the Elizabeth in 1608. In 1622 a party of settlers from Jamestown visited long enough to raid an Indian village in the Anacostia area, and in 1629 the first Lord Baltimore arrived in northern Virginia to make his home in the wilderness abutting the Potomac. He eventually acquired title to a significant portion of the lands bordered by the river and the Chesapeake Bay, renamed the area "Maryland," and decreed it a haven for fellow Catholics seeking refuge from persecution in England. Henry Fleet, a fur trader, described the region as abounding "with all manner of fish. . . . And as for deer, buffaloes, bears, turkeys, the woods do swarm with them; and the soil is exceedingly fertile."

By the mid 1630s, a number of Lord Baltimore's heirs and coreligionists had responded to the allure of spiritual asylum and literal haven. They established a permanent settlement at the mouth of what was now being called the St. Gregory, and soon the Algonquin were on the way to oblivion. The typical grant from the British government to a settler was a "manor" of 1,000 acres, and by 1700 most of the land along the 150 miles of navigable waterway between the bay and the two sets of picturesque falls between present-day Rockville and Washington, D.C., had been claimed by families whose names would become a part of history.

Warburton Manor, just across the river from Mount Vernon, was given to the Digges family in 1641. Nearby, on the banks of Piscataway Creek, named for one of the doomed tribes of the Algonquin, was Mount Airy, a swath of land owned by Lord Baltimore's descendant Benedict Calvert, and a place that Washington visited often. In fact, Calvert's daughter married John Parke Custis, Martha Washington's son by her first husband, Daniel Custis. Adjacent to the Anacostia River (or "East Branch" of the Potomac) was an estate of 1,800 acres known as Duddington, controlled in Washington's time by the Carroll and Young families, and regarded as the most valuable tract of land in the area.

The falls posed a barrier to further traffic up the Potomac, but the merchants keenly felt the need to create a shipping route to carry goods to and from the western territories. It was not long before those who controlled lands both above and below the "drop" began to conceive of a system of canals and portages that would ultimately connect their river, through the Monongahela, to the Ohio at Pittsburgh. The importance of such a linkage might be difficult to appreciate for a modern mind accustomed to systems of transport where two-day ground delivery seems tortoiselike, but to families such as the Lees and the Fairfaxes and the Masons, the Johnsons and the Custises and the Washingtons, their place on the Potomac—in a world without air travel, rail lines, or even roads—might well give them a stranglehold on the future of American trade, and a capital city built there at the cultural and economic crossroads might well constitute the Constantinople of the Americas.

There were alternative river routes in contention to be the entryway to the West. The most northerly of these stipulated use of the Great Lakes, then the Mohawk and Hudson rivers down to the port of New York. Another, through Pennsylvania, was to be stitched along the Ohio, Allegheny, and Susquehanna rivers. Whether the terminus of the latter route was to be Philadelphia or Baltimore was a matter still being fought out.

But Washington, whose great-grandfather had been granted the family's original 2,000 acres at Mount Vernon in 1670, believed that the most practical route—requiring dry-land portages of no more than thirty miles and most benefiting the nation and anyone in it who would listen—ran along the Potomac. As a young man he had canoed the upper reaches of the river from Great Falls all the way to

Cumberland in the northwest corner of the state, and, with his surveyor's training and dogged entrepreneur's spirit, had spent many years refining his vision of a trade route cutting through what others regarded as impenetrable wilderness: ". . . steep hills and what is called briery Mountains to cross is intolerable," he wrote in a 1784 diary entry, "but these might be eased and a much better way found if a little pains was taken. . . ."

By that same year, Washington had increased his holdings along the Potomac to nearly 20,000 acres, and after resigning his commission in the Continental Army he became president of the Potomac Company, an enterprise that would construct a series of locks around the two sets of falls at the tide line of the Potomac. Opening traffic between Georgetown and Cumberland would easily double the value of his land, Washington calculated, and he corresponded frankly with Thomas Jefferson on the subject.

After Jefferson had sent him a letter expressing support of the Potomac locks project, Washington wrote back, "I am made very happy to find a man of discernment and liberality (who has no particular interest in the plan) thinks as I do, who have lands in that country the value of which would be enhanced by the adoption of such a scheme."

It may be difficult for a contemporary observer not to assume that Washington's zeal for locating the new Federal City on the Potomac was due more to a desire to line his pockets than to any sincere belief that he was acting in the public interest. But elsewhere in his correspondence with Jefferson, Washington reiterates the argument that Northern interests held too much power to permit situating the capital in an established city: "From trade our citizens will not be restrained," he proclaimed, "and therefore it behooves us to place it in the most convenient channels, under proper regulation, freed, as much as possible from those vices which luxury, the consequence of wealth and power, naturally introduce." Was he sincere, or was it simply a justification? Certainly, Washington would not be the first able businessman to argue that the success of a personal agenda would also bring benefits to a community of the like-minded.

Still, most of the complaints of his opponents on the matter of residence centered on Washington's political insensitivities more than the financial benefits he might accrue. And in any case, Washington did not find it necessary to lead a personal crusade on the matter, for there were plenty of fellow landholders and businessmen from the Potomac area eager to undertake the task for him.

Georgetown merchant George Walker's *Maryland Journal* article of January 1789 claimed that if the capital were placed on lands just east of his city, across Rock Creek, lots that had been purchased for thirty-five or forty dollars an acre could be sold for as much as $1,000. Walker stressed that his figures were supplied as an inducement for the Congress, which needed simply to become involved in land speculation. Once the Congress had quietly purchased sufficient acreage on the Potomac and then designated it as the site of the new federal district, Walker reasoned, it could then turn around and sell off the excess properties, using the heady profits to underwrite the necessary public works on the land it kept. Walker, who had come to Georgetown to work as a tobacco broker for a Scottish exporting firm and was fond of signing himself "A Citizen of the World," was ostensibly offering sober counsel on behalf of the nation. But it is possible to see why a few pundits, even those with no viable city of their own to lobby for, might use such figures to arouse suspicion of a president with neighbors like this Georgetown merchant and 20,000 acres of his own in the area.

For his part, Washington was greatly pleased that the issues of assumption and residence had been resolved and the union preserved. As commentator John Ball Osborne said before a meeting of the Columbia Historical Society on the centenary celebration of the district's founding, "Probably nothing in [his] administration afforded him keener satisfaction," than when he appended his signature to the act establishing "the temporary and Permanent Seat of the Government of the United States."

From Washington's own perspective, the intertwined issues were "more in danger of having convulsed the government . . . than any other points. . . . I hope they are now settled in as satisfactory a manner as could have been expected; and that we have a prospect of enjoying peace abroad, with tranquillity at home." Jefferson, too, saw the so-called Compromise of 1790 as having averted disaster. "Assumption and residence . . . really threatened at one time, a separation of the legislature. . . . It is not foreseen that any thing so generative of dissension can rise again."

With the question of where decided in general, if not in detail, the question of how became paramount for Washington, and it was no small matter. As his contemporary John Carroll put it, had the development of the new Federal City been the president's only task, "he scarcely could have found the future seat of government more time-consuming."

Who to turn to for help, then, but the man who had been waiting in the wings for years: his old friend Peter Charles L'Enfant.

9

Greatness of Empire

IN HIS 1784 MEMORIAL CALLING UPON CONGRESS TO FORM a permanent Corps of Engineers, L'Enfant had added the construction of the then vaguely conceived Federal City as one of the corps' premier duties, adding that the undertaking would take many years and a significant amount of money to complete. The document was the first chance for L'Enfant to express his belief that a noble nation should manifest itself in noble buildings, thereby conveying the greatness of its purpose and principles to the world at large.

Furthermore, as L'Enfant argued at the time, close management of such a project should not be undertaken by Congress itself. The proposed corps was the perfect administrative instrument for efficiently assessing plans, assembling materials, overseeing the various workforces, ensuring adherence to standards, and related matters. In the end, L'Enfant reasoned, the corps would save the country money and ensure a continuity of development through all future political weather.

Though Congress had declined to create the corps, L'Enfant's proposal successfully gained him a nomination a short time later to one of the many interim commissions for the creation of a federal town, this one on the Delaware River. Though he was never formally appointed to that post, L'Enfant would later write that he had traveled to the site and completed significant planning at his own not-inconsiderable expense. Furthermore, he claimed that he had been engaged on several occasions between 1784 and 1791, by Washington and others, to make confidential reports on the feasibility of various sites proposed for the capital.

Whether or not it is true that L'Enfant was acting as a behind-the-scenes consultant for Washington as debate on the placement of the Federal City swirled through the 1780s, L'Enfant did send Washington an updated version of his 1784 memorial during the debates that began in the Congress in 1789. In what took the form of a long letter (perhaps vetted for spelling and syntax by Alexander Hamilton), L'Enfant waxed his most eloquent:

"To lay the foundation of a Federal City which is to become the Capital of this vast Empire, offers so great an occasion for acquiring reputation," he wrote candidly, ". . . Your Excellency will not be surprised that my ambition and the desire I have of becoming a useful citizen should lead me to wish to share in the undertaking." He observed that no country had ever before had the chance to debate the place where its capital would be situated, and he contended that even if the country lacked the present means, it should nonetheless conceive of the prospect on the grandest possible scale. L'Enfant sought Washington's appointment to oversee this grand design, and he closed with a reiteration that he do so in the position he had long ago suggested: Engineer to the United States, and the leader of the Corps of Engineers.

Washington made no such appointment, but ensuing developments suggest that there was nothing to offend him in L'Enfant's dream of a magnificent Federal City. Shortly after the Residence Act became law in July of 1790, Treasury Secretary Hamilton wrote to Washington recommending L'Enfant as the natural choice to oversee the design and construction of the new city. On the other hand, Jefferson, the secretary of state, was not so sure.

He may or may not have remembered L'Enfant's profligate ways in Paris on behalf of the Cincinnati Society, when he left numerous embarrassing debts behind him, and he probably was not enthusiastic that a former protégé of the royal court at Versailles should be in charge of designing the "first city" of the newly democratic United

States. But one thing Jefferson certainly was opposed to was the scale on which L'Enfant thought to work.

There was nothing personal in it, really—Jefferson's view was simply that government should be small in all ways. Whereas L'Enfant envisioned a city of some 6,000 acres fairly palpitating with architectural bombast, Jefferson thought that something closer to fifty acres would be plenty. The whole of the working capital, Jefferson would come to argue, could be contained within an area on the Potomac that he saw as ideal, only a few blocks square, just west of the present-day White House and bounded by D Street and Constitution Avenue, Seventeenth Street on the east, and Twenty-third on the west.

All that said, Jefferson was no fan of urban density, and he and L'Enfant were not opposed on every account. Jefferson had been pleased at certain features he observed in Paris and urged Washington to envision a city with broad avenues no less than a hundred feet wide, a sizable central park, and a square set aside for a central market. Though the concept of a Versailles on American shores would have made him shudder, he did suggest a president's house and a garden, each with a square of its own. He went on to say, "In Paris, it is forbidden to build a house beyond a given height, and it is admitted to be a good restriction. It keeps down the price of ground, keeps the houses low, and convenient, and the streets light and airy."

Washington was also getting advice from Madison, though the congressman was less concerned with architectural features than with more practical matters. While he understood that the president was likely to situate the "ten miles square" in the general vicinity of Georgetown, he felt that the president should propose several possible locations and then give the various groups of landowners the opportunity to offer their land to the government at the most attractive terms—in the end, the group of landowners who agreed to sell the necessary lands for the capital at the lowest price would see their surrounding holdings appreciate greatly in value. Thus both sides would gain.

Washington, of course, saw the wisdom of such advice. Even if L'Enfant's mind was already ablaze with architectural renderings of his vision of empire, the first order of business was to tie up the necessary land, in the best location, at the lowest possible price. If Congress hadn't become land speculators, the president of the United States had, for all intents, become a real estate developer.

In September, Washington, Jefferson, and Madison agreed to put off a move by Virginians to include Alexandria within the bounds of the district and confine the district to the eastern banks of the Potomac. Washington authorized Jefferson and Madison to stop, on their way back to Virginia, for a tour of the lands between the lower falls and the Anacostia River on the Maryland side of the river. Accordingly they met for dinner with a delegation of Georgetown's elite and the following day crossed over Rock Creek to have a look at the lands that lay between that eastern boundary of Georgetown and what was then known as the Tiber, a narrow creek that coursed where present-day Constitution Avenue is laid out.

Chief among the local delegation was Daniel Carroll of Duddington, the nephew of Maryland senator Charles Carroll, who had been persuaded to change his vote on assumption under the compromise engineered by Madison. The younger Carroll owned most of the land along the Anacostia and was considered a key figure in the dealings that Jefferson and Madison proposed.

Though the governments of Maryland and Virginia had pledged monies ($72,000 and $120,000 respectively) from the state treasuries to help secure the lands and construct the buildings of the new capital, the bulk of the support would come from a version of the speculation scheme outlined by George Walker in the *Maryland Journal*. Jefferson proposed to Carroll and the two Georgetown merchants who accompanied him that the Congress might be willing to purchase a 1,500-acre tract in the area for twice its current value; an announcement of the sale would be made, driving up prices, to the great benefit of those in control of adjoining properties. As a further inducement to Carroll as well as to George Mason, who owned 2,000 acres on the Virginia side of the river opposite Georgetown, Jefferson let it be known that Alexandria would somehow be included in the new district, as would additional lands on the eastern banks of the Anacostia.

The meetings seemed to go well. Jefferson wrote to Washington that Carroll and his associates showed "great zeal" for the proposal, and he promised to go to work assembling the necessary 1,500-acre parcel.

On October 13, nine other Georgetown landowners—perhaps dismayed that Jefferson was favoring Carroll and the landowners farther downriver—approached Washington with an offer of appropriate lands in their vicinity on whatever terms the president determined to be fair. A few days later Washington himself arrived to inspect this alternate area bounded by Rock Creek and Tiber Creek and seemed interested enough to ask the group to prepare a map with ownership of parcels and other features outlined.

While the Georgetown group went to work, Washington played a proper bargain-hunter's role, leaving Georgetown for a trip to the Upper Potomac region, where he met with various groups of landowners from towns along the river, including Hagerstown, Sharpsburg, and Monocacy, about ten miles above the Great Falls. To each he gave encouragement and suggested that they prepare maps and arguments for consideration.

The strategy had its effect. Washington had hardly returned from his trip upriver when the "proprietors" of Georgetown presented him with an offer to sell the lands between Tiber Creek and Rock Creek for forty dollars an acre, on the condition that every third lot would be deeded back to the sellers, and that they would retain timber rights to all the property.

Washington's response was to sit tight. When Congress reconvened for its third session at its temporary home in Philadelphia, members expected an announcement from the president on the matter, but still no word came.

It might have been that he was hoping to squeeze a better offer out of the Georgetown group—according to the historian Bob Arnebeck, he had discovered that at least 130 acres of the land on offer was owned by German settlers who might sell for a third of what the consortium was suggesting. More likely, he was preoccupied with the ticklish matter of how to shoehorn Alexandria and the eastern banks of the Anacostia into the confines of the district. He was also facing the prospect of a difficult fight in Congress over the establishment of a national bank, a measure proposed by Hamilton and vehemently opposed by Southern members, who viewed the bank and its proposed permanent placement in Philadelphia as a tool of the moneyed interests in the North.

He knew that it would take a supplemental act of Congress to extend the federal district along the lines he envisioned; but he also knew that he faced an uphill battle to have the banking bill approved. Politics being what they are, he faced the very real possibility of a trade-off that would cost him one goal or the other.

Finally, on January 24, he issued a formal proclamation of his chosen site east of the Potomac, including the city of Alexandria and lands on the southeast banks of the Anacostia River. To his opponents it was bad enough that the president had chosen to locate his city at the southernmost limit of that "Eastern Branch to Connogochegue" area they had limned; but to nudge the line even farther southwestward into Virginia seemed beyond the pale.

When Massachusetts representative Theodore Sedgwick grumbled that the president had shifted the boundaries so that Mount Vernon would now border the new Federal City, he was exaggerating. But had he known that Washington actually did own 1,200 acres of property in Alexandria, or that his wife's grandson George Washington Parke Custis owned the 950-acre plantation that would one day become Arlington Cemetery, his witticisms might have turned to outrage. In a letter written the day of Washington's announcement, Maryland representative William Smith penned an astute assessment of Washington's actions.

Smith did not believe for a moment that Washington had acted with any conscious self-interest, but "almost all men form their opinions by their interest without always knowing the governing principle of their motives or actions." Such insight might have helped Smith understand Washington's actions, but it did not save the president from suffering a surge of public indignation in the wake of the announcement. Long after his own political career had ended, John Adams was still grousing that the decision had raised the value of the Washington and Custis property by 1,000 percent.

For ten days in February the bill establishing the national bank lay on Washington's desk for signature. To buy time, he put out a request to Hamilton for a response as to the constitutionality of the measure, but the stakes had already become painfully clear to the president. If he vetoed the bank legislation so loathed by the South, their Federalist opponents would crush any hopes for approval of a supplement to the Residence Act in retaliation.

On the twenty-third of February, Hamilton's famous defense of the doctrine of implied powers authorizing the constitutionality of the bank act arrived on Washington's desk. The moment that Washington dreaded could no longer be avoided. Even in Philadelphia, the smart money held that Washington would veto the bill, but on that same day, Washington signed the bank act into law.

Debate began immediately on the supplemental seat-of-government bill. True to his word to go along if Philadelphia was named the interim capital, Senator Morris of Pennsylvania gave his blessing. The bill sailed through the Senate and the next day passed the House by a margin of more than two to one. The Federalists had their bank, and Washington had his city. All he had to do now was find a way to buy the land and build it.

10

Habitation and a Name

DURING THE TIME THAT IT TOOK FOR THE BANK BILL/ residence supplement compromise to be worked out, Washington had not been sitting idle. On January 24, he named three commissioners who would oversee the purchase of the land and at some time "prior to the first Monday in December, in the year one thousand eight hundred, provide suitable buildings for the accommodation of Congress, and of the President, and for the public offices of the government of the United States."

Despite Madison's suggestion that it might be politic to include someone from Massachusetts on the panel, Washington had had enough of wrangling. He selected three men who were as resolute as he was in support of the Potomac site: Thomas Johnson of Frederick, Maryland; David Stuart of Alexandria; and Daniel Carroll of Montgomery County, Maryland, formerly that district's representative to Congress.

Johnson was a former governor of Maryland and a partner of Washington's in the Potomac Company, assuming its presidency when Washington stepped down in 1789 to accept a greater presidency. Carroll was a fairly wealthy landowner and speculator in his own right, and a member of an extended family that controlled thousands of acres up and down the Potomac. He was also a confidant of Madison and held a vested interest in the affairs of the Potomac Company. Because

Carroll lived near Georgetown but was related to the Young and Carroll families who controlled vast properties on the Anacostia, Washington counted on him to maintain harmony between what might be called the Eastern Branch, or Anacostia, group and the Western interests, or Georgetown group.

Stuart, the third member of the commission, enjoyed the closest relationship to the president. He was a doctor and the owner of a plantation not far from Mount Vernon, and had married the widowed daughter-in-law of Martha Washington. Stuart was the man with whom Washington would correspond most frankly, and whom he trusted to see that his wishes were carried out.

With the commission in place, Washington sent Andrew Ellicott, geographer general of the United States, to Alexandria, where the starting point for the bounds of the "ten miles square" would be set. Proceeding from that point on the south bank of the Potomac, Ellicott was then to lay the four boundary lines of the district, though a detailed survey could wait for later, after Washington had settled on exactly which lands he wanted to purchase for the capital city itself.

Meanwhile, the president was anxious to get some version of the city's design realized, thereby making the project more tangible in the imaginations of those whose support he needed. Local booster George Walker's 1789 article had suggested that this new city on the Potomac should be based on such esteemed (if somewhat disparate) predecessors as Babylon and Philadelphia, and if a practical conflation of those two models seemed a bit unlikely, other aspects of his proposal were more reasoned. To encourage development and temper harmful speculation, for instance, Walker suggested that deeds should require the improvement of property within a certain number of years. Whatever tangible form the city took was sure to usher in a new architectural era: "The genius of America will rise superior to the Gothic taste that has so long pervaded," he said, "and will . . . revive the elegance . . . and grandeur of the ancients."

While at least one other person—the Maryland architect Joseph Clark, who had designed a few public buildings for Annapolis—offered his services as the hoped-for "purveyor of genius," there was never any doubt in Washington's mind who would have the job. If he had qualms about the significant cost overruns during L'Enfant's redesign of the Federal Hall in New York, they were swept aside by the acclaim for the finished product and the speed with which the architect did his work. Such considerations were not insignificant, given all the years that Washington's hopes for the Potomac site had simmered. He might have been the most powerful man in all the new nation and the wrangling over a site for the federal city might finally have come to an end, but in this regard he was an anxious man, ready to see his dream take shape at last.

L'Enfant also enjoyed the support of Hamilton and others in the government, if not Jefferson's unalloyed enthusiasm. Pennsylvania representative Thomas Fitzsimons had in fact earlier recommended that L'Enfant be hired to renovate Philadelphia's county courthouse to house Congress temporarily. In doing so, Fitzsimons not only pointed to the quality of L'Enfant's work at New York's Federal Hall, but also noted that the architect was of an unassuming nature, willing to roll up his sleeves and work alongside all those "foreigners" hurrying to bring the job in on time. Ambassador Moustier chimed in on the latter point, lauding L'Enfant's skills in dealing with laborers and coworkers.

Washington would have been heartened by the assurances that L'Enfant worked well with others, though that would hardly have been his chief concern at the time. He had been observing L'Enfant's various efforts firsthand for years—from the sketch of himself rendered so long ago at Valley Forge through the work for the Society of the Cincinnati to the triumph of Federal Hall. He was demonstrably talented and he was *known*, and to a president with an imposing and unforeseeably complex task before him, nothing could be more important or more comforting.

Without waiting for his newly appointed commissioners to meet (Johnson was having some difficulty stepping away from his duties at the Potomac Corporation), Washington had Jefferson write to

L'Enfant on March 7, asking the architect to travel to Georgetown and begin making drawings of "the particular grounds most likely to be approved for the site of the Federal town." As for "grounds most likely," since first authorizing the purchase of lands, Washington had discovered that some landowners balked at his price of forty dollars an acre. Even when he increased the offer by two-thirds, an obstreperous landowner along the Tiber named David Burnes suggested that he might sell a portion of his property, but insisted on keeping one hundred of his 350 acres intact.

Faced with the prospect of Burnes's dilapidated tobacco plantation staying in place in the area westward from the foot of what would become Capitol Hill, Washington and Jefferson decided that L'Enfant should begin his work with renderings of the land along the Anacostia, at the eastern boundary of the new district, in hopes that the prospect of a city on the eastern fringes of the district would convince the less tractable owners of western parcels to give in.

Accordingly, Jefferson wrote out instructions to L'Enfant on March 2, 1791: "You are desired to proceed to George town, where you will find Mr. Ellicot employed in making a survey and map of the federal territory. The special object of asking your aid is to have drawings of the particular grounds most likely to be approved for the site of the federal town and buildings," he wrote, asking that L'Enfant "begin on the eastern branch, and proceed from thence upwards, laying down the hills, valleys, morasses, and waters between that [the Anacostia], the Potomac, the Tyber, and the road leading from George town to the eastern branch."

Jefferson asked that L'Enfant make some estimate of the heights of the hills, and directed that "for necessary assistance and expenses," L'Enfant should "be pleased to apply to the Mayor of Georgetown, who is written to on this subject." Finally, Jefferson wrote, "I will beg the favor of you to mark to me your progress about twice a week, by letter, say every Wednesday and Saturday evening."

One week later, following an arduous journey from New York, the architect arrived in Georgetown, ready to go to work. As he wrote

Jefferson on Friday, March 11, "Sir, I have the honor of informing you of my arrival at this place where I could not possibly reach before Wednesday last and very late in the evening after having traveled part of the way on foot and part on horse back, leaving the broken stage behind."

A writer for the local paper duly noted the arrival, describing him as "Major Longfort, a French gentleman employed by the President," come to survey the land for the new Federal City, and adding that "his skill in matters of this kind is justly extolled by all."

While L'Enfant dutifully followed Jefferson's instructions to seek out Georgetown's mayor, Robert Peter (he became the city's first, following its incorporation in 1789), it seems that Peter had no clue that L'Enfant was on his way. As L'Enfant wrote back to Jefferson, "He appeared to be much surprised and he assured me he had received no previous notice of my coming, nor any instruction relating to the business at hand."

If the mayor was surprised, he was nonetheless willing, quickly rounding up four able-bodied men to assist L'Enfant, who reported back, "this being the only thing I was in need of every matter has been soon arranged." L'Enfant also met with George Walker, the inveterate booster of the Georgetown area, and was advised of Walker's many proposals for developing the nearby lands into a grand capital. Thus bolstered, the architect was up and off on his appointed inspection of the lands about the Eastern Branch the morning after his arrival, even if the weather was not in keeping with the spirit of the undertaking.

"I am only at present to regret that an heavy rain and thick mist . . . has been incessant ever since my arrival here," L'Enfant wrote Jefferson. Still, he managed, on horseback and through the rain, "to obtain a knowledge of the whole. I put from the eastern branch towards Georgetown up the heights and down along side of the bank of the main river and along side of Goose [the Tiber] and Rock Creeks as far up as their springs."

"As far as I was able to judge through a thick fog," he continued, "I passed on many spots which appeared to me realy [sic] beautiful and which seem to dispute with each other who command." Though he stopped short of an outright endorsement for the city's location, he did note that the most promising section for development seemed to be the extensive section of level ground that stretched from the eastern branch westward to Tiber Creek. "The remainder of the ground toward Georgetown is more broken," he added.

Foremost on L'Enfant's mind was the fear that unless the weather broke, he would never have a plan of the ground ready by the time the president arrived for his own inspection of the area. Still, though the bad weather continued unabated, L'Enfant soldiered on.

When Washington arrived in Georgetown on March 26, the architect was ready with a report titled "Note Relative to the Ground Lying on the Eastern Branch of the River Potowmack." Given his earlier misgivings and uncertainties, L'Enfant seems to have managed admirably; what he sketched out for Washington in those brief few days would have a remarkable influence upon much that followed:

"After coming upon the hill from the Eastern Branch ferry the country is level and on a space of about two miles each way present a most eligible position for the first settlement of a grand City, and one which if not the only within the limits of the Federal territory is at least the more advantageous" (than the territory to the west, toward Rock Creek). Though it might seem as if he were following the orders that had been handed him by Jefferson to favor the Eastern Branch lands, L'Enfant's commentary certainly sounds convincing: "The soil is dry and not withstanding well watered abounding springs it has an wholesome air and being of an easy ascent," he wrote, adding that the mouth of the Anacostia provided a natural harbor "in every respect to be preferred to that of the Potowmack toward Georgetown."

"All the total of this ground is such as will favour every improvement as may render the City agreeable, commodious and capable," L'Enfant added, noting that "on that part terminating in a ridge to Jenkins Hill . . . many of the most desirable position offer for to Erect the Publique Edifices thereon . . . every grand building would rear with a majestied aspect over the Country all around."

The remark, while characteristically fractured in its grammar, was also prophetic of L'Enfant, given that Jenkins Hill—or Jenkins Heights, as it was also called—would one day be known as Capitol Hill. But that was not the only forward-looking aspect of his initial report.

L'Enfant also proposed a bridge over the Potomac linking Alexandria with Georgetown, with a broad avenue to be constructed thence to Jenkins Hill, with "a middle way paved for heavy carriage and walk on each side planted with double Rows of trees." Perhaps with a vision of a busy Pennsylvania Avenue thronged with traffic already dancing in his head, the architect proclaimed the proportions of such a passage as necessary to project "the greatness which a city the Capitale of a powerfull Empire ought to manifest."

He closed by arguing for a layout that would take into consideration the nature of the land itself: "a grand plan of the whole city combined with the various ground it will cover and with the particular circumstance of the country all around." To that end, there could be no imposition of a grid, "not the regular assemblage of houses laid out in square and forming streets all parallel and uniform . . . for such plan could only do on a well level plain."

Presaging what would become one of the most controversial aspects of the city's design, L'Enfant insisted that "regular assemblage" would "absolutely annilate [sic] every of the advantage enumerated . . . and injure the success of the undertaking." While he admitted that however seductive the application of a grid might be to some, such an approach was but a "mean continance of some cool imagination wanting a sense of the real grand and truly beautiful."

L'Enfant's English is characteristically labored, and it is also apparent that he was mindful of Jefferson's charge to dress up the image of the area around the Eastern Branch. Still, the report is remarkable for its poetry and power of vision. It is in essence the sketch—both physical and philosophical—of what the city would become.

Given L'Enfant's enthusiasm (he had included such flourishes as the building of a grand "Perysomid," or pyramid, in Alexandria, "which would produce the happyest effect and Completely finish the landscape"), one might imagine him hovering at Washington's shoulder as the president read the report. But, its more fanciful aspects aside, the document he submitted was all the more remarkable in what it called for, given the nature of the lands that L'Enfant had been sent to examine.

This was no case of simply extending the borders of an already established urban center, or of redesigning an existing city district or set of buildings for new purposes. The only significant settlements in the area were Georgetown, with a total of 289 households, and Alexandria, across the Potomac in Virginia, with 2,748 residents, nearly a quarter of whom were slaves. As the nineteenth-century commentator Tallmadge A. Lambert put it: "West of Rock Creek the patented Rock of Dumbarton [Georgetown] exhibited a social foundation . . . and Alexandria was a chief emporium of the South. Looking, however, eastward of the Creek, the Federal City, about which speculation was naturally rife, existed, practically, in the imaginations of men . . . stimulated . . . by the plan of the prescient L'Enfant."

L'Enfant had been riding around an untouched wilderness on horseback, peering out from forested hilltops over mist-shrouded vistas, without the benefit of aerial photography or topographical maps, and putting together a vision of how to lay out a mighty city upon one hundred square miles of territory that was about as unformed and rawboned as it gets.

Tobacco was at the heart of the local economy, and with the size of the plantations, planters were accustomed to a ride of many miles to pay a call on a neighbor. There were few hotels, and travelers venturing far from the settlements of Georgetown and Alexandria were forced to seek lodging at private homes, where, as one contemporary put it, "any decent stranger was sure of welcome."

The local gentry lived privileged lives, and their celebrations featured plenty of liquor as well as card games, horseracing, shooting contests, fencing, boating parties, hunting, and riding. But it was also a relatively isolated existence, with a trip to Baltimore or points north easily the work of two days and presenting the same sorts of challenges that L'Enfant had faced coming in the other direction.

There were also small groups of working-class settlers in the area: some were tenant farmers working the less desirable stretches of the great estates and bartering their crops for little more than subsistence goods at stores operated by the prosperous owners. Others were tradesmen who had come from England to work as indentured servants— terms were generally three to five years of service to the planters and merchants who had paid for their passage.

And of course there were the slaves, who lived in shanties tucked out of sight on the manor house grounds. While the former two groups had at least the prospect of one day carving out a place in the new land of opportunity, it takes significant imagination to guess what kept the latter group going.

And while David Stuart, George Walker, and others described the glories of the area in overheated terms, not everyone saw it in the same way. David Burnes, the farmer who seemed to be holding out for a better offer from Washington, described his lands stretching out beneath Jenkins Hill as a few acres of "timothy meadow very much grown up with sedge," and the rest "chiefly cut down, and worn out, very much grubbed and washed."

Furthermore, even Washington seemed to be having second thoughts about his strategy. L'Enfant's stated enthusiasm for the area around the Eastern Branch had not budged David Burnes and had only served to alarm that group of western property owners who were quite ready to go along with the president's original offer. When a representative of that group wrote to ask what was going on, the president sought advice from Jefferson. In turn, the secretary of state quickly drafted a letter to L'Enfant, proclaiming that the central city would in fact be placed on lands between the Tiber and Rock Creek, and instructing him to put an end to his diversionary tactics concerning the Eastern Branch. "The President will go within two or three days, and would wish to have under his eye when at Georgetown, a drawing also of the particular lineaments of the ground between Rock

Creek and the Tyber; you are desired immediately on the receipt of this, to commence the survey of that part."

Jefferson conceded that there were advantages to a site on the Anacostia, but that "there are very strong reasons also in favor of the position between Rock Creek and Tyber, independent of the face of the ground." He closed by telling L'Enfant that the main objective was to maintain harmony between the two competing groups while the president made decisions designed to appease them both, and that meanwhile "we shall be obliged to you . . . to poise their expectations."

These were of course the words of the consummate politician. Unfortunately, the man for whom they were intended was a lifelong enthusiast. Even if he was willing to do Jefferson's bidding, it was doubtful he would be able.

11

Grand Design

THOUGH THE HISTORICAL RECORD ON PETER CHARLES L'Enfant is not voluminous, what is to be found suggests that *compromise* was not a word included in his lexicon. Perhaps it was a holdover of having grown up at Versailles, or perhaps it was simply his artistic nature. In any case, once he had determined what he considered a proper course of action, thinking could stop, and the work itself must begin.

Still, when he received Jefferson's letter ordering him away from the Eastern Branch and to do what he could to keep the competing factions in the area "poised," L'Enfant did not quarrel, though he did write back on March 19, to complain that the weather was keeping him from doing much of anything: "I have only been able this day, to lay down that part which lay between the Eastern branch and the Tiber so much as included Jenkins' Hill . . . leaving for a better time swampy parts which were rendered absolutely impassable."

As for the area to which Jefferson demanded he turn his attention, he offered that he would have "before this day attempted to lay down some part of those laying between the Tiber and Rock Creek had not a fall of snow and stormy wind which succeeded for these three days past prevented me." He made no mention of the charge to deal cleverly with the proprietors, but simply closed his note to Jefferson with the hope that the morrow would bring more favorable circumstances

for surveying, and by promising to consult with the geographer Ellicott to bring the fruits of their separate labors into some kind of harmony before the president arrived.

It is likely that L'Enfant felt no obligation to assume the duties of
a politician, though if it had been Washington himself who had asked
him to moderate his enthusiasm for the good of the project, the response might have been different. The Frenchman had come of age in
an arena where only one person's opinion or orders were of major consequence. In his mind, having been engaged by the American
"monarch" to accomplish a certain task, his sense of duty and chain of
command was a simple one.

As Elizabeth Kite, one of L'Enfant's early biographers, notes,
L'Enfant's familiarity with the monarchical system was surely what
prevented him from ever seeking a contract in advance for his services—Cincinnati medal striking, Federal Hall remodeling, or Federal
City designing alike. When the king requested a "favor," it was simply understood that one would be properly rewarded at the conclusion
of those services. One appeared at the palace to announce the job was
completed, one knelt before the throne for an appropriate blessing,
and one found a bag of florins pressed into one's hand on the way out
of the chambers.

Thus, any orders that Jefferson sent along that L'Enfant had good
reason to believe originated with Washington, and which clearly lay
in the realm of his appointed duties, posed no problem. When it came
to playing politics, however, L'Enfant would have wanted to get those
orders directly from the chief executive himself.

And yet for all that, it was L'Enfant who found a way for Washington to skirt one of the first significant obstacles in the path of his
new city. Imagine for a moment the former general arrived in blustery
Georgetown on a late-March afternoon, with Ellicott's forty miles of
boundaries drawn, L'Enfant's enthusiastic building plans laid out before him, and still no land ready for groundbreaking. Washington's
plan to pit two competing groups of landowners against each other so
that he might get a price that would not break the national bank had

backfired. Now it seemed as though he might not be able to cobble together enough property from either faction to make his plans work.

L'Enfant, however, had a simple suggestion. It may have been born of his natural urge toward excess—and certainly it had self-serving implications—but in this case it was a stroke of genius.

Just make the central city larger, he suggested to Washington. Buy land from both groups. On one end of this spacious district, place a house for the president. On the other, build a house for Congress. Let everyone win.

It is tempting to imagine a scene in which the commander-in-chief sits at a table at Suter's Fountain Inn with plans spread and head in hands. Outside the rain pelts and inside the flamboyant L'Enfant paces a smoky, overheated room, his hands flying as he tosses out ideas in accented, sometimes fractured English—grand public buildings here, pyramids there, who-knows-what in between—and all the while Washington's mind wanders . . . that he could win a war with England and assume a presidency unopposed and unite a Congress as divided as oil from water on the matter of where to build a capital, yet find himself stymied by down-at-the-heels tobacco planters and small-town self-promoters . . .

. . . when suddenly he glances up at the architect, with something like recognition dawning on his face and a hand raised to stanch the flood of words with his own interjection . . .

Hold on, L'Enfant. Hold on. Perhaps you've got something there.

THOUGH IT WAS not in Washington's nature to call together groups of citizens and petition them personally for their assistance (try to imagine a contemporary president appearing before a meeting of the Georgetown Chamber of Commerce to ask for their help on a few matters), this was, after all, the Federal City hanging in the balance. He called for a meeting of the eighteen men and one woman who constituted the leadership of the competing interests in the district, for 6:00 p.m. at Suter's Tavern.

And in his diary he explains what he told those present. He began by letting the proprietors know that their squabbles "did not in my opinion comport either with the public interest or that of their own," that in their dogged self-interest they might "defeat the measure altogether; not only by procrastination but for want of the means necessary to effect the work . . . and that, instead of contending which of the two should have it they had better, by combining more offers make a common cause of it."

Describing what was essentially L'Enfant's plan for a large central city, he pointed out that each side would gain by having one of the major houses in "its" section, that he would have a plan of the city engraved shortly (so that lots could be more easily sold), and that construction on the two principal buildings—the president's home and the chambers of Congress—would begin by the following summer.

When one of the proprietors asked if a plan for a city sprawling over 5,000 or 6,000 acres mightn't dilute the value of individual lots, Washington responded dryly that Philadelphia sat upon an area of about two miles by three (about 4,000 acres), and if the area of the capital of a single state was as large as that, then just how much land would be appropriate for the capital of an entire nation? As a final blandishment to the group, he promised that the commissioners would announce an initial public sale of lots for the coming October, and with that the meeting ended.

Later that night Washington met with a smaller delegation from the group to hammer out details, and on the following day agreement was reached: the proprietors would turn over all their land that lay within the ten-mile-square borders drawn up by Ellicott to a pair of trustees, with the understanding that they would receive about sixty-seven dollars an acre for any lands selected by the president for use for public buildings and parks, up from his original offer of about forty dollars. More land would be allocated for streets, and half of the remaining acreage would be returned to the proprietors.

The half retained by the commissioners would be sold to raise the money to pay for the public building sites and for the costs of construction and other improvements. Proprietors who had already built homes on their property could purchase the lot on which the improvement stood for about fifty dollars an acre, provided that the land was not in the public right-of-way or otherwise needed by the government.

In this way the government would acquire more than 10,000 lots (nearly 1,000 acres), all the necessary lands for streets (about 3,000 acres), and the five hundred or so acres thought necessary for the principal public buildings for a total outlay of about $35,000, a sum that itself would be recouped by the sale of lots to the public. (George Walker had optimistically suggested in his 1789 proposal that such land sales could eventually bring in as much as $10.5 million.)

Thus, thanks to the sagacious advice of L'Enfant and the speculative-financing suggestions of Walker, the project could finally go forward. As Washington wrote, "The business being thus happily finished and some directions given to the Commissioners, the Surveyor [Ellicott] and Engineer [L'Enfant] with respect to the mode of laying out the district—Surveying the grounds for the City and forming them into lots—I left Georgetown—dined at Alexandria and reached Mount Vernon in the evening."

THE AGREEMENT WAS promptly announced by the *Maryland Journal*, reminding the rest of the world that the site was "surpassed by no spot on earth . . . for commercial advantage and elegance of situation." And L'Enfant, who had assured Washington that the city "would soon grow of itself and spread as the branches of a tree does toward where they meet with most nourishment," dashed off a letter to Hamilton in which he expressed some embarrassment at his early enthusiasm. Still, he assured Hamilton, "no position in all America can be more susceptible of grand improvement . . . nor better situated to secure an infinity of advantages to government."

Hamilton wrote back to caution L'Enfant. "I thank you much for the full communication you have made me concerning the intended seat of Government," he allowed. But the treasury secretary seemed far more concerned that L'Enfant not neglect a promise that Hamilton had extracted from the architect before he left New York for Georgetown: to finish designs for the first American coins. "As soon as your imagination shall have fixed upon anything," Hamilton pressed on the matter of the coins, "I shall be glad to know it."

On April 4, Washington wrote to L'Enfant urging him not to stint when setting aside the necessary land for streets and parks and buildings. "Although it may not be immediately wanting," Washington counseled, the extra land would "nevertheless increase the Revenue" and ensure that future design decisions would not be constrained due to a lack of available property.

On the same day, L'Enfant dashed off a note to Jefferson, apologizing for not having written as regularly as he had asked, but explaining that he had simply given "the whole of my time to forwards as much as possibly could be the business I had to perform." He could not restrain his joy at the fact that, even though he was unable to prepare more than rough pencil drawings in advance of Washington's visit, "I had the satisfaction to see the little I had done agreeable to his wish."

Furthermore, L'Enfant told Jefferson, the president had seen enough to approve the completion of the survey "and the delineation of a grand plan for the local distribution of the city." In other words, L'Enfant had landed the commission of a lifetime. At the age of thirty-seven, scarcely fifteen years since his arrival in a foreign country, with no personal fortune, no letters of introduction from influential patrons, no formal training—with little more than abounding self-confidence and a passion for the former colonies' experiment in liberty—he had come to be entrusted with the creation of the American capital from scratch.

"It shall be from this moment my endeavor to answer the president's expectations in preparing those plans," L'Enfant told Jefferson, then went on to solicit any suggestions he might have on the matter. "I would be very much obliged," L'Enfant added, "if you could procure for me whatever map may fall within your reach—of any of the different grand cities now existing."

This did not mean that he intended to copy the plans of such cities as London, Madrid, Paris, Naples, or Venice, L'Enfant was careful to explain. Certainly he meant to study "what exists of well improved situations," for such would "serve to suggest a variety of new Ideas and is necessary to refine and strengthen the Judgement." Ultimately, however, it was his wish "and shall be my endeavor to delinate [*sic*] on a new and original way the plan the contrivance of which the President has left to me without any restriction soever."

If Jefferson had any suspicions that L'Enfant had overstated his situation, they were put to rest when he opened a letter from Mount Vernon the very next day. The president wanted to let Jefferson know that there would indeed be a city of some 3,000 to 5,000 acres and that a survey of lots was under way, "which Major L'Enfant is now directed to do."

Whatever reservations the secretary of state may have had about the scale of the project, he kept them to himself. On April 11, Jefferson wrote back to L'Enfant to concur with the president: "Considering that the grounds to be reserved for the public are to be paid for by the acre, I think very liberal reservations should be made for them." He seemed in agreement with the president's concept of placing the public grounds in the center of the district, with the expectation that the commercial interests would locate on either end, where the deeper waters of the Anacostia and the Potomac near Georgetown would allow the building of ports.

In response to the architect's request, Jefferson agreed to send along copies of the plans of several of the European cities he had found agreeable during his term as ambassador to France, including Frankfurt, Amsterdam, Strasbourg, Paris, Bordeaux, Lyon, Montpelier, Marseilles, Turin, and Milan. He told L'Enfant that he would have the documents rolled up and posted quickly and added, "I am happy that the President has left the planning of the town in such good hands and have no doubt it will be done to general satisfaction."

He closed by refusing any specific advice to L'Enfant on general design matters, "for fear of repeating what [Washington] did not approve." He could not restrain himself from a few suggestions concerning the nature of the Capitol and the President's House, however. As for the former, Jefferson preferred "the adoption of some one of the models of antiquity, which have had the approbation of thousands of years." And as for the President's House, he ventured, "I should prefer the celebrated fronts of modern buildings, which have already received the approbation of all good judges." In Jefferson's mind, these included the Hôtel de Salm, a high-ceilinged home that overlooked the Tuileries and that influenced his later remodeling of Monticello, and the grand display of the Grande Galerie du Louvre, overlooking the Seine.

Speculation fueled by the announcement of the deal was immediate: banking on the fact that Jenkins Hill was likely to be the site of the Capitol, George Walker bought up a 358-acre tract between the hill and the Eastern Branch (where Jefferson envisioned a seaport and other commercial development) for about seventy dollars an acre. L'Enfant himself was shopping for a lot and suggested to Washington's assistant Tobias Lear that he ought to encourage his fellow New Englanders to join in buying lots in the new Federal City instead of speculating in land out west. This would not only speed the development of the Federal City, the architect reasoned, but it might also help to lessen the lingering division between North and South.

Commissioner Daniel Carroll wrote to James Madison to bring him up to date on what had been going on, mentioning that the president was scheduled to return to Georgetown toward the end of June. "By that time he expects Major L'Enfant will be ready . . . with a description of the grounds within the city—it is probably that some plan of the city and the public buildings may be then exhibited."

Carroll explained to Madison that the president wanted a publishable plan in hand in time for a public sale to be held in advance of the next session of Congress, "so that the southern members who may chuse [sic] to purchase may take it in their way and time be allowed for any of the Northern member who may chuse to come down."

Carroll went on to express his opinion that the sale would raise "at least 300,000 pounds [close to $1.5 million at contemporary rates of exchange] for public use."

While Washington had to endure the complaints of a minority group of proprietors that L'Enfant seemed to be gobbling up far too much land for the city, the more influential—George Walker among them—reassured the district supervisors that the deal would stand and that the president should simply ignore the grousing. On April 15 the three commissioners—David Stuart, Thomas Johnson, and Daniel Carroll—presided over a public ceremony of the type that would come to be a part of life in the new district. Standing before a large crowd, they formally installed the southern boundary marker at Jones Point in Alexandria, laying the cornerstone of the president's city at last.

12

Glory Days

T O L'ENFANT, THE WORLD MUST HAVE SEEMED A bright place indeed. As newly appointed architect of the Federal City, he had the full confidence of the president and the stated approval of the secretary of state. He could requisition as much land as he needed to build a city that would outdo the greatest of all Europe, and he had the implicit commission for the design of the nation's principal edifices, including the Capitol and the home of the president. Accordingly, he might have believed himself to be well positioned to overcome almost any obstacle and persuade any critic of the power of his civic vision.

As it happened, he would soon have the opportunity to test his mettle. On April 22, South Carolina representative William L. Smith came through Georgetown on his way home from Philadelphia during a congressional break. A widely traveled man with sophisticated tastes, Smith had been one of the most vocal and vehement opponents of the drive to locate the capital on the Potomac. He wanted a firsthand look at the place where this new district was to sit, and many of its supporters girded themselves for the public excoriation sure to follow. In the end it was L'Enfant who was deputed to take the fire-breathing Smith out for a look, a choice that proved fortuitous:

"The Major pointed out to me all the eminences, plains, commanding spots, projects of canals," Smith reported to his colleagues,

". . . [including] the place intended for the Presidents palace, States House for Congress, public buildings, mercantile part of the City . . . quays, bridges . . . magnificent public walks, and various other projects." Though Smith's report suggested that his tour was comprehensive, more important was his final assessment: "The ground pleased me much . . ." Smith continued, likely stunning many of his colleagues on each side of the debate. "Nature has done much for the place, and with the aid of art it will become the wonder of the World. I propose calling this new Seat of Empire Washingtonople."

The collective sigh of relief might have been heard as far away as Smith's hometown of Charleston, where the president had gone to rally support for the bank act and other matters unpopular with the South. Washington was surely gratified to learn that L'Enfant had served so effectively as an advocate and ambassador for the new Federal City, and Georgetown's supporters were overjoyed. Commissioner Carroll crowed in a letter to Madison that the sales of lots combined with the grants from the Maryland and Virginia legislatures would soon put close to $1 million in the public coffers, and placed the credit for it all succinctly: "Major L'Enfant proceeds."

L'ENFANT WAS INDEED proceeding. By the time Washington returned from his travels through the South, the architect had completed a much more detailed plan. On June 22 he traveled to Mount Vernon to hand over to the president a document explaining that after much mental anguish, "prompted by a fear of being prejudiced in favour of a first option," he had settled on the west side of Jenkins Hill as the site for the Capitol. The spot was "a pedestal waiting for a monument," he told the president, adding that "no situation could stand in competition with this."

Washington and L'Enfant had discussed the placement of the other major building (now unabashedly referred to by L'Enfant as the "presidential palace") when they toured the land. In his letter,

L'Enfant assured the president that the "ridge which attracted your attention at the first inspection of the ground on the west side of the Tiber" was indeed the perfect place: "It will see 10 or 12 miles down the Potowmack" to "the town and harbor of Alexandria and stand to the view of the whole city."

This location would create a subtle psychological benefit as well, L'Enfant pointed out. "The distance from the Congressional House will not be too great," he said—but it would be just far enough away to remind any committee waiting on him just who was in command: "no message to nor from the president is to be made without a sort of decorum." It was advice from a man who knew well, from his time at the French court, the respect due to heads of state.

On the other hand, L'Enfant was aware of the president's need to have his cabinet ministers close by: "To make however the distance less to other officers I placed the three grand Departments of State contiguous to the principle [*sic*] Palace." He then turned to a feature as important to his plan as any building—a sweeping area of open space connecting the two buildings and open to the public: "on the way leading to the Congressional House the gardens of the one together with the park . . . are connected with the publique walk and avenue to the Congress house in a manner . . . as grand as it will be agreeable and convenient to the whole city."

By this time L'Enfant had also settled on another aspect of the plan that he considered vital: the conversion of Tiber Creek—which Jefferson considered a shallow, useless nuisance—into a commerce-bearing canal. As it naturally lay, the Tiber ran south toward the foot of Jenkins Hill, then turned westward to empty into the Potomac near the present-day site of the Tidal Basin. L'Enfant proposed cutting a channel straight on eastward from the hill to join with the Anacostia, or Eastern Branch, providing a convenient means of intracity transport and linking the two branches of the Potomac. In addition to serving a proposed central market, the canal would also encourage trade and shelter "any number of boats." As an added feature, L'Enfant proposed that where the waters of the Tiber had been artificially truncated at the hill, a picturesque, forty-foot waterfall would now cascade into the channel, delighting onlookers and filling the canal. And—bringing L'Enfant to the high point of his proposal—the waterfall would provide a dramatic backdrop to the spot where a "grand Equestrian statue" would be placed, in honor of the president and leader of the Revolutionary forces.

In laying out the streets, L'Enfant had indeed produced a basic underlying right-angle grid, aligned north-south and east-west, but he had laid atop this a number of avenues on "various directions . . . to and from every principal place, wishing by this not mearly to contrast with the general regularity . . . but principally to connect each part of the city with more efficacy." The avenues would connect with existing roads in the area and ensure direct routes of commerce for both the Eastern and Georgetown interests, he was careful to point out.

As to the controversial question of whether the "main Establishment" of the city would be placed upon its eastern or western verge, L'Enfant returned to the argument that had earned him Washington's initial endorsement (and likely his gratitude as well): "I believe the question may be easily reply [sic] if not viewing by part, [but] embracing under one sight the whole extant from the Eastern branch to Georgetown and from the branch on the Potomac across toward the mountains." In the end, he contended, seeing the city as an organic entity, in terms of its ultimate grand and unified destiny, would only hasten "the rapid aggrandizement and settlement of the whole." In other words, L'Enfant saw the placement of the central core of the new city as an issue that transcended politics and special interests—his concern was with the design of a city (his "Plan") that would not only work, but would work in harmony with the geographical realities of its setting. Such an approach, he believed, would encourage investment from a broad spectrum of businessmen and home builders alike, thereby hastening the natural development of a "whole" city—as a national capital, as a center of commerce, and as a place to live.

Washington accepted the report for study, but did not comment immediately, even in his diary. On the morning of Monday, June 27, he left Mount Vernon for Georgetown before six o'clock for a meeting with the District Commissioners at nine. After outlining his intentions for them, Washington called the proprietors together and "readily" answered their lingering objections to an overly grandiose vision for the city. Face to face with the president, all their opposition wilted. As Washington put it, the group "agreed to convey [to the landowners] the utmost extent of what was required."

On the following day, while the commissioners drew up the final deeds for the landowners' signatures, the president went out with Ellicott and L'Enfant "to take a more perfect view of the ground in order to decide finally of the spots on which to place the public buildings," and—apparently in response to vigorous lobbying by one of the proprietors—to "direct how a line which was to leave out a Spring belonging to Major Stoddard should be run."

On June 29, Washington was finally ready: he called a public meeting, and before a sizable crowd at the Fountain Inn he outlined, with a few minor changes, L'Enfant's plan for the city as it had been presented to him. It must have been both a relief and a triumph for the young Frenchman to stand beside the president and hear his master plan endorsed. The "building for the Presidential department," as Washington took care to call it, would be moved slightly to the west so as to rest upon higher ground, and a number of the diagonal avenues would be dispensed with, but the basic plan, including the canal, had not only the support of the president but, by all accounts, that of his audience as well. As Washington put it, "A general approbation of the measure seemed to pervade the whole."

While the murmurs of approval still filled the room, L'Enfant fielded a few particular queries: to proprietor Notley Young, who wondered whether the house he had built was in the way of any road or public building, L'Enfant was reassuring. With Daniel Carroll of Duddington, nephew of Commissioner Carroll, who wondered if he could now resume work on a home he had begun partway up Jenkins Hill, L'Enfant could not be so certain, but the matter was passed over without great issue.

Before Washington left for Philadelphia the following day ("The business which brot me to Georgetown being finished"), he authorized the commissioners to prepare for an auction of lots as early as October 17; he also told them to start work on the canal as soon as possible. L'Enfant's grand "Plan" was finally under way.

13

Headway

THERE IS NO RECORD OF CORRESPONDENCE BETWEEN L'Enfant and the president following that late-June announcement, nor has any proof survived that L'Enfant honored Jefferson's request that he write each Wednesday and Friday to keep the secretary of state apprised of how things stood. And while Washington surely continued his habit of careful diary-keeping through the summer and the rest of his years in the presidency, history laments the loss of virtually all of Washington's diaries and correspondence from mid-1791 until he left office, likely due to the carelessness of the president's nephew Bushrod, who was entrusted with them after Washington's death.

Even without the personal record, it is safe to assume that the summer of 1791 was a busy one in the Georgetown area. Trees were cut to clear lots for building and for sale; more trees were dropped to lay out streets and avenues; foundations were dug; stone was quarried and piled high on the banks of the Potomac; brick kilns were constructed. The nation's Potomac Fever was rising with the spike of summer heat.

All the while L'Enfant busied himself with his most important task, the completion of a detailed city plan that would provide the basis for the sale of lots, come fall. Beyond that purpose, the production of such a document, engraved and easily reproduced and distributed, would mark a significant step in the evolution of the place toward reality. "What cannot be written is not truly known," goes the aphorism, and conversely, a well-mapped city might seem the next thing to the place itself.

The commissioners, meanwhile, placed advertisements of the upcoming sale in various newspapers around the country, and asked for bids on the conversion of the Tiber into a canal. And one other matter had surfaced for their attention.

Though L'Enfant had promised to look into the matter of whether the house that Daniel Carroll of Duddington was building encroached on what would be public land, no word had been forthcoming. Carroll approached his uncle in late July to demand a resolution to the matter—he had a foundation dug and he wanted to begin putting up the walls, especially now that his home would hold a handsome prospect over the nation's capital. Commissioner Carroll promised his nephew that he would track down L'Enfant and get an answer, once and for all, but L'Enfant was nowhere to be found. The younger Carroll—annoyed, and perhaps eager to establish a kind of squatter's rights—went ahead with his building.

Meanwhile, surveyor Ellicott and his men were hard at work marking out the city streets. By mid-August they were laying out the leg of New Jersey Avenue that ran southeastward on Jenkins Hill from the proposed site of the Capitol; its eastern boundary missed a newly constructed wall of Carroll's house by a scant seven feet. When Carroll protested to Ellicott, the surveyor promised to check with L'Enfant.

Not to worry, was the word Ellicott brought back to Carroll. L'Enfant had told the surveyor that the street would simply be reduced in width from 110 feet to 100, and the matter would thus be dispensed with—Carroll was to have no cause for concern.

But that was hardly the end of it. A letter from L'Enfant to the president, while only obliquely acknowledging the matter, suggests that a tempest was brewing. According to L'Enfant, the trees on Carroll's property that had been felled to make way for New Jersey Avenue had been left where they lay. Given the terms of the agreement the president had hammered out, the cleared timber remained the property of the landholder, and thus it was Carroll's responsibility to move it from what was now public property. Carroll's failure to do so was an obstacle—though only one of many—that was slowing the progress of the surveyors and impeding his efforts to complete a detailed plan, L'Enfant complained.

This was surely no welcome news for the president. The commissioners had already written in early August to inform him that the $120,000 promised by Virginia would not be forthcoming any time soon, as the treasury of that state held nothing in it. Furthermore, the Maryland legislature had announced that it would not be able to advance any of their promised $72,000 earlier than the first day of 1792. Though the commissioners had received a reasonable bid for the canal work, it now seemed that the only monies available for it or any other public building project would have to come from proceeds of the lot sale set for October 17.

But the prospect of a sale on that date, the commissioners lamented, seemed doubtful because of L'Enfant's slow progress on the preparation of his plan. The commissioners allowed that there were various reasons for the delay, and they passed along assurances from L'Enfant that he would be meeting with the president to explain it all "soon."

It must have been particularly distressing for Washington to consider such reports. After all, L'Enfant had completed the renovations of Federal Hall in a remarkably short time. Perhaps Carroll and other difficult proprietors like him, along with the daunting nature of the landscape, its isolation, the difficult summer weather, and any number of other unforeseeable factors accounted for L'Enfant's apparent difficulties.

On the other hand, Federal City development was facing a serious money crunch. Unless the sale of lots took place on schedule, progress on building the city would have to stop. Anyone ever faced with the specter of running completely out of cash can understand Washington's concern, and Thomas Jefferson's letter to L'Enfant on August 18: "Sir, the President had understood for some time past that you were coming to Philadelphia & New York and therefore has delayed mentioning to you some matters which have occurred to him. Will you be so good as to inform me . . . whether it is still your purpose to come this way and when?" Jefferson queried. "If you are detained by laying out this [*sic*] lots you had better not await that," the secretary added, "as a suggestion has been made here of arranging them in a particular manner which will probably make them more convenient to the purchasers, and more profitable to the sellers."

Jefferson did not elaborate on this strategy, but he did say that he thought L'Enfant a better choice than Ellicott to oversee the engraving of the map the president wanted, and closed by suggesting that the document be laid out on a square sheet of paper. "This is suggested merely for your consideration," Jefferson added politely.

If he had meant to reassure L'Enfant of Washington's continued support, however, Jefferson was not successful. L'Enfant snatched up a pencil and underscored Ellicott's name. At the bottom of Jefferson's letter, L'Enfant scrawled, "What right could this man have thereto?"

In any case, the letter produced the desired effect. L'Enfant was in Philadelphia a few days later, a copy of the plan in hand for Jefferson and the president to review, and accompanied by a lengthy "memorial" dated August 19, the day after Jefferson had written. L'Enfant began by thanking the president again for assigning him the project and went on to explain that "the business has proved more tedious than at first thought," owing to the difficulty of determining the acute angles and intersecting lines of streets with accuracy. It was a task complicated by all that "felled timber lying in every direction which the proprietors wish to preserve and are unwilling to remove," L'Enfant added.

While he claimed that the sites for the Capitol and the president's palace were already attracting crowds of visitors, he lamented that "the beauties of the locality are lost in a chaos of felled timber," and feared that prospective investors would not be able to visualize the magnificence to come, "even after inspecting a map."

Worse yet, from Washington's point of view, L'Enfant counseled that "a sale this fall is premature, for the land will not bring a tenth part of what it will later." He worried that until word spread more widely through the far-flung former colonies, interest would be confined to a relatively small number of speculators, "who will not be interested to improve the lots." He also feared that if a sale was held and very few showed up to buy, it would "rather disgrace the whole business."

That possibility played into the hands of "designing men" in Georgetown, L'Enfant argued, who had been dragging their feet in presenting him with accurate surveys of their individual properties, owing to their own petty boundary disputes, and who were far more interested in their own profit than in the development of the city. In L'Enfant's mind, once his basic design or "Plan" had been laid out— including streets, squares, and sites for major public buildings and monuments—then ancillary development would proceed in a natural and orderly fashion. Speculators and those who already owned property upon which the Plan would take shape were naturally opposed to such a process, for they were more interested in snatching up virgin lots at bargain prices or in withholding key properties from the government in hopes of fetching higher prices once development was under way. Certainly L'Enfant's concerns were sound, but they were not necessarily arguments that Washington wanted to hear—the nation's foremost man of action stymied by the artist's voice of reason.

L'Enfant went on to counsel Washington that they must not "confine the building idea to erecting a Congress House and a President's palace." To make the city a fact, L'Enfant wrote, "it will be indispensable to consider every part of the improvements proposed . . . as being a part most essential," adding that however unconnected any single feature might appear, it was important to "effect them at a same time and with a proportional degree of dispatch."

He also insisted that anything that would entice commercial interests to invest in the developing city should be a primary consideration, and central to that aim, he felt, was the development of the canal between the Potomac and the Eastern Branch. Not only would it encourage mercantile development, but the passageway would aid in the transportation of materials necessary to build "the two grand edifices" that were foremost in the president's mind.

L'Enfant went on to explain how important such a feature as the public walk that he envisioned leading down from the House of Congress to the Potomac and on to the palace, "an object which so ever trivial as it may appear to the eyes of many will be productive of as much advantage . . . in giving to the City . . . a superiority of agreements over most of the cities of the world."

Once the streets were properly laid out, L'Enfant argued—the grand avenues leveled and the public squares and parks made apparent—the lots would virtually sell themselves, and the accompanying rise in land values would surely make it worth the wait. And if all this were not enough, L'Enfant told the president, he had also hit upon the idea of distributing squares to each of the states, along with a donation of land to every major religious sect so that each might build a prominent house of worship within the city's bounds.

Though the latter were ideas intended to encourage immediate development by interest groups with the wherewithal to do so, L'Enfant acknowledged that the president might find his proposals farfetched. He said straight out that he expected that the notions would meet with Washington's opposition "and be much objected to" by others, but still, his belief that they were sound ideas dictated that he must put them forward.

Even with his recommended donations, L'Enfant said that 15,000 lots would remain for public offering. The road frontage of the lots would range from thirty-seven to sixty-six feet and sizes would range from four to seven lots per acre, accordingly. "The sum that will arise must be immense," L'Enfant declared, though he followed that with the warning, "only if cautiously managed." If the most valuable lots were snapped up at low prices, he pointed out, the foundation of the entire enterprise would be at risk.

"The whole matter should be contemplated coolly," he urged the president. He suggested that instead of rushing forward with a sale, funds be raised for building by obtaining loans on the property retained by the government. Furthermore, he counseled the adoption of a well-thought-out building plan that would add buildings to the list in an orderly procession and in accordance with the constraints of an annual budget.

L'Enfant closed his memorial with what might have sounded to the president dangerously like an ultimatum: "It is in this manner and in this manner only I conceive the business may be conducted to a certainty," he said, adding that it had always been his intention to produce "a plan wholly new," yet not beyond "your power to procure."

Certainly Washington did not quarrel with that final pronouncement. He remained in enthusiastic support of the physical details of the plan and believed himself capable of "procuring" it. But he was equally determined to keep the ball rolling. On August 28, after he, Jefferson, and Madison had reviewed L'Enfant's documents and heard him out on the means by which it would become a reality, Washington had Jefferson write to the District Commissioners.

The president had examined Major L'Enfant's design for the core of the new Federal City carefully, Jefferson informed them, and he had found it sound. Madison and Jefferson would soon arrive in Georgetown to help put its development in motion. But meanwhile there would indeed be a public sale of lots, and it would commence on October 17.

14

A Plan Wholly New

THE PLAN UNVEILED BY JEFFERSON AND MADISON BE-
fore the commissioners on September 8 was—despite L'Enfant's complaints about all the felled timber in his way—a
reasonably detailed map of a fifty-square-mile area ranging from the
Eastern Branch of the Potomac in the southeast to the land border-
ing Rock Creek and Georgetown in the northwest. In the accompanying memorial, L'Enfant asserted he had surveyed the "internal
content" of the district in the most "menutial" way, a process that
involved "the most laborious operations (which no ordinary surveyor
of land is called upon to understand)."

The principal features—the location of the Capitol, the president's
home, and the monument to Washington—remained more or less
unchanged from L'Enfant's June 22 report to the president. But in
this document he included a number of notes calling attention to what
he considered important components of the plan. He explained that
he had first chosen the sites for the principal buildings and public
squares, according to the prominence each should command in the
completed city. L'Enfant had Ellicott run a north-south meridian line
through the proposed site of the Capitol, then crossed it with another
line running east-west, making that point the anchor for the entire
plan. He also pointed out that streets had been laid out not only to
provide convenient travel between principal places, but to provide

sight lines between landmarks, thus adding to the sense of cohesiveness of the city as a whole.

"Every Grand traverse Avenue, and every principal divergent one, such as the communication from the President's House to the Congress House" was to be 160 feet wide, L'Enfant directed, and was to consist of a roadway eighty feet wide, flanked on each side by ten-foot sidewalks and thirty-foot graveled dividers, planted with trees. Other streets leading to major public buildings should be 130 feet wide, he advised, and no street (despite what he had supposedly conveyed to Proprietor Carroll) would be less than 110 feet in width. The walk from the President's House, L'Enfant counseled, would be particularly well suited for the location of foreign embassies.

In addition to the sites laid out for the Capitol and the president's home, L'Enfant called attention to a number of other principal features of the plan. Most important among them was the placement of the equestrian statue of Washington that had been authorized by the Continental Congress back in 1783, south of the president's home and directly east of the Capitol. He also created a spot for a National Church, to be "assigned to the special use of no particular Sect or denomination, but equally open to all." L'Enfant theorized that this edifice would be used for "national purposes" of prayer, thanksgiving, and funerals, and be also the proper repository for memorials honoring war heroes and special public servants. L'Enfant's argument for the national cathedral seems as reasonable as the need to finally designate a location for a statue honoring Washington, though both would end up among the most controversial elements of his plan. The equestrian statue originally planned for Washington became a political football that was tossed about for nearly a century; and the National Cathedral was not completed until 1990.

In addition, L'Enfant wanted to incorporate the natural beauty of the land into the Federal City and insisted on the inclusion of such features in his plan. Along with the designated parks, there would be at least five grand fountains in the city, which could be fed easily by the more than "25 good springs of excellent water" gushing within the city's borders, even in the driest seasons. He also mentioned the Grand Cascade pouring from the Tiber River into his proposed intracity canal, the designation of a lawn 1,200 feet on a side for the President's House, and the grand promenades that would connect both the houses of Congress and the president's home with the monument to Washington.

Fifteen yellow-colored squares—spaced more or less equally and connected by avenues—designated the proposed lots to be granted to the "several States of the Union, for each of them to improve, or subscribe a sum additional to the value of the land." He hoped that states might there erect "statues, monuments, or other ornaments" dedicated to war heroes and other worthy servants of the public. Such would, in L'Enfant's mind, "invite the youth of succeeding generations to tread in the paths of those sages, or heroes."

Colored in red were a number of sites for churches of various denominations, though he did declare that "no burying grounds are to be admitted within the limits of the City, an appropriation being intended for that purpose without." He also set aside a number of squares for colleges, academies, and learned societies "whose object is national."

All house fronts were to face the street before them squarely, L'Enfant added, even on the irregular lots formed by the "divergent" avenues. He had taken care that even those lots situated "on the most acute angle will not measure less than 56 feet and many will be above 140."

Though no notes were taken at the meeting at which all of this was presented to the District Commissioners, one might be forgiven for speculating that Jefferson urged those present to focus on the principal features of the plan and save debate on the smaller points for another time. After all, Jefferson's own preliminary "sketch" of the city shows he confined his vision for the city to the ground south of what is now Pennsylvania Avenue, and immediately southeast of Georgetown. Jefferson would have built the Capitol in the vicinity of Pennsylvania Avenue and Tenth Street, and the president's home near the old Naval Hospital, with the two connected by a short walk. So far as the rest of the District was concerned, Jefferson felt it could grow like Topsy, as it would, and without a planner's hand.

Whatever Jefferson might have said about the "plan" during the meeting, however, the commissioners apparently heard nothing worth announcing publicly. They wrote to L'Enfant on September 9 only that they had agreed to name the federal district the "Territory of Columbia" and had settled on the name of the Federal City as well—he was asked to title his document "A Map of the City of Washington." They also asked that he give numbers to the north-south streets and alphabetic designations to those running east to west. The commissioners authorized surveyor Ellicott to take soundings of the Eastern Branch to be included in the map, and asked that the location of the existing post road be added as well.

Ellicott also wrote to L'Enfant to say that Jefferson and Madison had departed the new "Territory of Columbia" apparently "well pleased with the plan of the city and the country which it concerns." He mentioned the matter of the soundings and reiterated the decision to press forward with a sale on October 17. As to that sale, he seemed to share some of L'Enfant's misgivings: "I expected some directions from them respecting the different places where the lots should be laid off," Ellicott said, "but received none, on that head I am at a loss."

Meanwhile, the commissioners had authorized L'Enfant to have 10,000 copies of the plan printed for distribution among the states and for other uses. During his August visit to Philadelphia to meet with Jefferson and Washington, L'Enfant had met with a French engraver, named Pigalle, to commission the engraving. All that remained, L'Enfant assumed, was to mark the few corrections that would be required on the copy of the document that he left in Philadelphia with his countryman.

However, when L'Enfant contacted Washington's secretary, Tobias Lean, to check on Pigalle's progress, he received a distressing reply. "To my great surprise and mortification," Lear wrote back, their artist had failed them. Pigalle explained to Lear that he had been unable to find any copper available before October 4 with which to execute the engraving. As a result, there could be no copies of the plan made before the end of the month. Pigalle claimed to have been misled by others who had assured him the copper was forthcoming, Lear said, though he added that—given the now unavoidable delay—the engraver requested that L'Enfant send along the larger draft of the plan so that a more detailed engraving could result.

In fact there were no copies of the plan available for distribution before or during the sale, and the president seemed satisfied that it had not been any fault of L'Enfant's, going so far as to write the commissioners to that effect. The commissioners might have accepted Washington's assessment of the matter had L'Enfant not complicated things by his behavior during the sale itself.

Tobias Lear had asked L'Enfant to purchase a choice lot on his behalf during the sale, and L'Enfant wrote back to Lear on October 19 to explain that he had been successful: "I gave charge to a friend of mine and your countryman, Mr. Cabott, to bid upon your account and am happy he has been able to obtain the lot I had pointed his attention upon at a much lower price than any of the like have sold for," L'Enfant said.

L'Enfant did not pass along other news to Lear: the architect himself had become a property owner in Washington. For "ninety-nine pounds Current Money of Maryland," he had purchased lot number 30 in square 127. Though any comment on the quality of the lot was absent from the commissioner's record, L'Enfant was surely happy with his purchase: the property lay at 17th and I streets, just to the northwest of the land reserved for the president's own home.

The architect told Lear he thought the sale had been "middling good" considering the bad weather, but he added, "I cannot say I am otherwise pleased with it." L'Enfant reiterated several of his concerns about having held the sale in the first place, including the fear that speculators would snap up the best lots early, but then mentioned that he had done his best to deter such activity by refusing to so much as exhibit his large copy of the plan during the sale.

It was a good thing he had been so clever, L'Enfant assured Lear, for otherwise buyers might have been able to actually see where the lots they were buying sat in relation to various future landmarks—and those "apparently more advantageous," in L'Enfant's words, "would have depreciated the value of those lots that sold the most high." Thus, L'Enfant hoped, the president would surely see the wisdom of his behavior, even if the commissioners themselves might misinterpret it as "resentment in my opposition to them to interest their selling."

L'Enfant closed the letter with the hope that Lear would explain his actions to the president's satisfaction, adding that he intended to travel back to Philadelphia soon to resurrect the matter of commissioning an engraving of the plan, though this time it would be one "worth sending abroad." In L'Enfant's eyes, this meant the end of Pigalle's involvement; he asked if Lear might be willing to "demand from the engraver every drawing he may have made and the copper plate he may have begun, to prevent his going forward."

On the same day, Commissioner Stuart wrote Washington to offer his view of the situation in the new district. Sales had not gone as well as they might have hoped, he said. The weather had been "much against us," and buyers complained that the prices seemed high. A total of thirty-one lots (of 15,000 available) were sold, at an average price of $265, totaling a bit more than $8,000 (a bit less than Walker's estimate of $10.5 million).

They might have done much better, said Stuart, "could we have been on the ground and exhibited a general plan." He closed by informing the president that they thought it best to discontinue the sale for the time being, though if anyone wanted to buy, "we should still be ready to receive their offers."

The president's reply suggested that Tobias Lear had not been as adept as L'Enfant might have hoped in explaining his behavior at the sale. On November 20 Washington wrote to tell Stuart that he had already heard what had happened—"with a degree of suprize & concern not easy to be expressed." The president seemed dumbfounded at L'Enfant's refusal to exhibit the plan, and could only speculate that men of an artistic temperament are often "possessed of some disqualification by which they plague all those with whom they are concerned."

Washington asserted that "for such employment as he is now engaged in, for projecting public works and carrying them into effect, he was better qualified than any one, who had come within my knowledge in this country, or indeed in any other." Given such qualifications, Washington said, it was understandable that L'Enfant would be quite protective of his plan, but it was inexcusable that he would go so far as to impede the sale and force prospective buyers into bidding on "a pig in a poke." Washington said he had told L'Enfant "that he must in future look to the commissioners for directions," and closed by assuring them that it would not be long before copies of an engraved plan were struck.

Whether or not he had previously found reason to privately consider L'Enfant headstrong or eccentric, with that letter Washington for the first time publicly criticized the man in whom he had placed his trust to bring the Federal City into being. Further reasons to shake his trust in the architect were not long in coming.

Just days later Washington received two letters that had been sent from Georgetown on November 21, crossing with his own of November 20 to Commissioner Stuart. One of the letters was written by L'Enfant, the other by Daniel Carroll of Duddington, the owner of the house that stood near the path of New Jersey Avenue as it ran southeastward down from the site of the Capitol. At issue was the fate of that house that Ellicott had assured him was safe. Carroll was convinced that it should be safe; L'Enfant was equally certain that it had to go.

On November 13, following his weekly meeting with the commissioners, L'Enfant approached Stuart, whom he knew had Washington's ear, and told him that he had sent off a letter to Carroll informing him that the house was in the public right-of-way and would have to come down.

It was not just that the foundations of the house lay too near the bounds of New Jersey Avenue, L'Enfant explained. In fact, the structure lay precisely in the middle of the square marked as "E" on the Grand Plan, where, in L'Enfant's mind, at least, there would someday rise "five grand fountains" with "constant spout of water." (The spring that L'Enfant envisioned as the source of that "constant spout" was in fact what had drawn Carroll to want to build his house there in the first place.)

When Stuart responded that he hoped L'Enfant had been appropriately politic about the matter, L'Enfant patted his pockets in a fruitless search for the letter to Carroll, but assured the commissioner that he had indeed been most accommodating. Stuart nodded, and advised L'Enfant to let the commissioners know at the next meeting if Carroll balked at pulling his house down.

Whatever the tone of L'Enfant's letter, its contents were enough to send Carroll riding off at breakneck speed to a judge in Annapolis, seeking a court order to protect his house. With a stop-work order secured and a summons issued for L'Enfant, Ellicott next sat down to pen his own outraged letter to the president.

With more on his mind than a dispute over an unoccupied house in the Maryland woods, Washington took a few days to answer. Finally, on November 28, he wrote to L'Enfant, advising restraint and the application of good judgment, just as David Stuart had: "As a similar case cannot happen again (Mr. Carroll's house having been begun before the Federal District was fixed upon) no precedent will be established by yielding a little in the present instance; and it will always be found sound policy to conciliate the good-will rather than provoke the enmity of any man, where it can be accomplished without much difficulty, inconvenience or loss."

Whether or not such counsel would have been effective, L'Enfant had already decided upon his course of action. On November 21 he had also written the commissioners: "In pursuance of the measure first taken and of which I took the liberty of informing you by last post respecting the house of Mr. Carroll of Duddington which may become necessary to have destroyed, he not having acquiesced . . . I directed yesterday forenoon a number of hands to the spot. . . . The roof is already down with part of the brickwork and the whole will I expect be leveled to the ground before the week is over."

Perhaps in the spirit of Stuart's appeal for civility, he asked that his demolition crew employ some of the men who helped to build the house "to the end that every possible attention be paid to the interests of the gentleman as shall be consistent in forwarding the public object."

While many historians consider the incident to be the defining moment when L'Enfant gained an unshakable reputation for being beyond the reach of reason, a close consideration of the facts suggests that he may have had a logical cause for his actions. While Carroll had in fact completed digging the foundations of his house prior to signing the proprietors' agreement in April of 1791, the terms of that agreement were quite clear: any improvements to the land begun before the agreement was signed that were found in the way of public improvement were subject to condemnation. Owners were entitled to compensation for any such improvements taken from them. But any improvements undertaken after the signing of the agreement were made at the owner's risk, and the government was not liable for any restitution.

Furthermore, as L'Enfant explained in his letter to the commissioners, he was under great pressure to complete such work as was necessary on the site so that construction on the President's House and the Capitol could begin in the spring, as Washington had promised Congress and investors. In addition, it was of the utmost concern to the president—and in everyone's best interest—that L'Enfant carry the single existing copy of his plan back to Philadelphia as soon as he possibly could, so that the engraving and printing process could go forward. Until the work of laying out the roads and public areas was complete, however, the plan would have to remain on-site so that work could be properly guided. From L'Enfant's perspective, then, he was entirely justified in removing what he considered a serious obstacle in the way of the greater goal of building a capital.

Of course, a political agenda lurked behind appearances. From the moment he was dispatched to the area with orders to begin his surveys on the Eastern Bank and to stir up competition between the competing groups of landowners, L'Enfant had been placed in a rather difficult position by Jefferson and Washington. L'Enfant was wise enough to see that the interests of all the property owners were not necessarily aligned with those of the president, who simply wanted to get his city built. On more than one occasion the planner had prefaced his advice to the president with such concerns.

Certainly, none of the proprietors wished to cede any more of their valuable land than was necessary, so that while L'Enfant's Grand Plan, with its broad avenues and capacious parks and squares, might have seemed breathtaking to an outsider, the proprietors viewed every designation of public land as money taken from their pockets.

Furthermore, the Carroll family, along with Notley Young and other proprietors with holdings on the Eastern Bank, had felt themselves at a disadvantage to the Georgetown interests from the beginning, suspecting that the very existence of an established commercial center there would carry the day for their opponents.

While the commissioners were dutiful in accepting every directive of the president at whose pleasure they served, they were themselves businessmen and residents of the area. Their practical considerations and family ties would have carried more weight with them than the aspirations and visions of an outsider and a foreigner, particularly when the man dared to destroy the property of one of their own.

On November 26, Commissioners David Stuart and Daniel Carroll (uncle of the aggrieved homeowner) drafted a letter to L'Enfant that began, "On our meeting this day we were equally surprised and concerned to find that you had proceeded to demolish Mr. Carroll's house. We were impelled by many considerations to give immediate directions to those acting in your absence to desist." (L'Enfant had sent his assistant, the engineer Isaac Roberdeau, and Benjamin Ellicott, brother of surveyor Andrew, to oversee the removal of the house while he traveled to Virginia to purchase a stone quarry at the commissioners' behest.)

And even though Stuart and Carroll admitted that the action might have been "absolutely necessary, and such an one as Mr. Carroll might be compelled to acquiesce in . . . still our opinion ought to have been previously taken on a subject so delicate and so interesting." In other words, the commissioners were scolding L'Enfant not so much for what he had done, but for not telling them what he had in mind beforehand.

A power struggle was brewing. The commissioners viewed L'Enfant, if not as their employee, then at least as subject to their direction. In executing the Grand Plan, however, L'Enfant recognized only the authority of the president. And as time went on, even that allegiance would seem questionable. In the mind of the planner, it may have been that the Plan itself was the true master.

15

All Things Reasonable and Proper

L'ENFANT WAS NOT THE ONLY ONE THE COMMISSION-
ers had written about the matter, of course. It is tempting to
imagine a scene in which Tobias Lear—tremulous and uncertain—approaches Washington to hand over a sheaf of letters sent
from an outraged Daniel Carroll of Duddington and an aggrieved
body of District Commissioners, and then starts at the look on the
president's face as he glances up after scanning those documents.

Not only had Washington spent time trying to reason with L'Enfant; he had also sent along a note to Carroll of Duddington suggesting two alternatives for remedy of this situation: Perhaps Mr. Carroll
might allow the commissioners to proceed with the demolition of the
house and then rebuild it the following spring, out of the way of any
public project. Or, alternatively, might Mr. Carroll wish to rebuild the
house at his own expense, with the understanding that he could occupy it for a period of six years before its final removal? If he chose the
latter course, he would be reimbursed for the value of the walls that
were torn down.

And after all his careful counsel to Major L'Enfant—"it will always be found sound policy to conciliate the good-will . . ."—L'Enfant
had gone ahead and *torn the house down*? What kind of conciliation
was that? For a moment the president must have wondered if he had
placed his trust in a madman.

Whatever his innermost thoughts, Washington dashed off a note to Jefferson for advice on the matter of their excitable planner. Washington gave over copies of the correspondence that had passed between himself and L'Enfant on the matter of the planner's failure to exhibit his map at the sale and asked Jefferson bluntly "to judge from the complexion of things how far he may be spoken to in decisive terms without losing his services; which in my opinion would be a serious misfortune."

Clearly the president still considered L'Enfant valuable, but, as he added to Jefferson, "at the same time he must know, there is a line beyond which he will not . . . go." Washington was uncertain of the cause of this trouble with his architect, but knew what needed to be done about it: "Whether it is zeal—an impetuous temper, or other motives . . . be it what it will, it must be checked; or we shall have no Commissioners."

While all this was going on in Philadelphia, L'Enfant returned from his quarry-purchasing expedition to Aquia, Virginia, happy to let the commissioners know that he had succeeded in carrying out their instructions on the matter. Then he turned his attention to the news that his orders for the demolition of Carroll's house had greatly distressed the body. Clearly he did not see what the fuss was about. If anything, he seemed taken aback by the commissioners' interference.

It was not his obligation to inform the commissioners of his orders to have the house removed, L'Enfant argued, for the owner had persisted in building upon the foundations in spite of two warnings L'Enfant insisted that he had issued. If the walls were not removed by the owner, L'Enfant had told Carroll repeatedly, then they would have to be removed *for* him. If Carroll objected, L'Enfant said, then *he* was the one who should have gone to the commissioners with a petition, adding, "It was not my business to call your attention on the matter."

Furthermore, since Commissioner Carroll had already told L'Enfant that he would have to disqualify himself from any ruling on this matter, and with Commissioner Johnson unavailable, that left only

Stuart to act—and thus no quorum was obtainable. Therefore, L'Enfant reasoned, "charged with the execution of the plan," he went ahead with orders to tear down the house, "with as much confidence as in directing a tree to be cut down or a rock to be removed."

He went on to suggest that part of the difficulty in this matter arose from the fact that Commissioner Carroll and Carroll of Duddington were related. While he assured the commissioners that they should "always find me disposed to respect the authority vested in you by law," L'Enfant added, "after mature consideration . . . I trust you will see the propriety of your never interfering with the process of execution, but in case when an appeal to you from individuals may be justly grounded."

The last must have had the commissioners pounding their desks. Never interfering? Who does he think he is?

But even if they were pounding, L'Enfant was oblivious. Ignorant as well of the firestorm he had set off at the president's mansion in Philadelphia, the planner went on to pen a blithe response to Washington's letter of November 28, in which all that careful counsel about patience and restraint had been laid out.

L'Enfant could see that Washington was unaware that he had already proceeded with the demolition of Carroll's house, and he regretted that he had not had the opportunity to explain beforehand why he was forced to move so quickly, "since I find that its being destroyed will in some respects oppose your paternal goodness." With that in mind, he went on to repeat a number of the arguments he had presented to the commissioners, and pointed out to the president that allowing Carroll's house to stand "would have afforded a dangerous precedent to others to contest every step of the people employed in laying off the city."

It was like "having grown a bush in the way of the people clearing the ground," L'Enfant insisted, adding that all the proprietors who had signed the agreement to build the Federal City "have evinced their satisfaction of the justice of my conduct"—excepting only "those connected with Daniel Carroll of Duddington," of course. (As to just how and where the others had evinced that satisfaction, L'Enfant was not clear.)

Meanwhile, Jefferson had responded to Washington's plea for advice with a draft letter of admonition to be sent to L'Enfant, which he admitted "may be too severe." But as the president had already attempted to rein in the planner with moderately phrased remarks, it seemed to Jefferson that L'Enfant "will not regard correction, unless it be pointed."

The president took Jefferson's advice to heart. On December 2—having not yet received L'Enfant's explanation of things—he began a letter to the planner as follows: "I have received with sincere concern the information from yourself as well as others that you have proceeded to demolish the house of Mr. Carroll of Duddington against his consent, and without authority from the Commissioners or any other person. In this you have laid yourself open to the Laws, and in a Country where they will have their course."

If that were not enough to sober L'Enfant, the next surely would: "In future I must strictly enjoin you to touch no man's property without his consent, or the previous order of the Commissioners. I wished you to be employed in the arrangements of the Federal City. I still wish it: but only on condition that you can conduct yourself in subordination to the authority of the Commissioners . . . and who stand between you and the President of the United States."

If L'Enfant had been assuring himself that he was serving the president as directly as a courtier commanded by the king at Versailles, then this statement of Washington's would have struck him like a slap. There was more to the letter, but readers can be forgiven if they imagine L'Enfant lifting his eyes from the document for a moment.

"Your precipitate conduct will, it is to be apprehended, give serious alarm, and produce disagreeable consequences," Washington continued in paragraphs he added to Jefferson's draft. "Having the beauty and regularity of your plan only in view, you pursue it as if every person & thing were *obliged* to yield to it. Whereas the Commissioners have many circumstances to attend to, some of which perhaps, may be unknown to you; which evinces . . . the propriety, the necessity, and the safety of your acting by their directions."

The president probably meant to soften the tone of the letter with his elaborations, and it is possible that the words had something of their intended effect. But it is just as fair to assume that the letter left L'Enfant reeling. Not only was his behavior called into question, but his *plan* was being demeaned, however obliquely.

The architect might well have scanned the final words of the president in a daze: "I have said, and I repeat to you again, that it is my firm belief, that the gentlemen now in Office have favourable dispositions towards you; and in all things reasonable and proper will receive and give full weight to your opinions;—and ascribing to your *Zeal* the mistakes that have happened—I persuade myself under this explanation of matters that nothing in future will intervene to obstruct the harmony which ought to prevail in so interesting a Work."

Throughout the dispute, it seems clear that Thomas Jefferson, serving as intermediary between the president and the situation on the ground in Georgetown, was not a disinterested party. Had Jefferson not found the scope of L'Enfant's Grand Plan distasteful from the very beginning, he might have opined to the president that Carroll of Duddington had acted unwisely, if not illegally, in attempting to build a house in direct contravention of an agreement he had signed. Or he might have reminded the president of the real objective: to keep the project moving. Did he want a group of self-interested landowners in charge of the development of the Federal City, or should the matter be left in the hands of a professional, even a somewhat single-minded and difficult professional?

In her 1929 biography of L'Enfant, Elizabeth Kite cites as an analogue the example of General George Washington Goethals, who was appointed by Theodore Roosevelt to be chief engineer in charge of building the Panama Canal. Legislation authorizing its construction, however, stipulated that a seven-man commission would oversee all the work. It was not long before Goethals sent word to Roosevelt that progress was virtually impossible owing to the interference of the commission. "I sent you down to build the canal," Kite reports Roosevelt as responding. "Do what you consider necessary to this end and report afterwards to the Commissioners."

In the end, however, Roosevelt solved the problem by appointing Goethals to the commission and declaring him its chairman. As a result, Goethals, answering only to the president and the secretary of war, assumed nearly unlimited power. According to his biographer, he became a man who might "command the removal of a mountain from the landscape, or of a man from his dominions, or of a salt-cellar from that man's table."

Had President Washington appointed L'Enfant to the commission in charge of the federal district—as the planner had served on the five-person panel while directing the rebuilding of Federal Hall—the contretemps he found himself facing might well have been avoided.

But that was not what Washington did. And, for all the kudos offered to Pierre Charles L'Enfant ("Peter" was a form employed principally by L'Enfant himself) for his talents, his achievements, and his Grand Plan, the architect found himself in this instance simply a man hired to do a job. The District Commissioners, and their nephews, and cousins, and the whole interlocking network of proprietors, constituted the nexus of power in the situation. In this view, there was surely more than one architect capable of designing a city; but there was, by this time, only one place where that city could be put.

On those terms, the final contest had begun.

16

Endgame

L'ENFANT HAD ENDED THE LETTER IN WHICH HE EX-
plained his actions to Washington with a rather poignant
by-the-way. "A respect for the law as well as a confidence in
the goodness of my cause has led me to the determination of submitting to the sheriff," L'Enfant told the president. "To this moment
however, I have neither seen him nor Mr. Carroll."

And in fact a letter of November 29, 1791, from Carroll of Duddington to James Madison states that the former had indeed been successful in obtaining a judge's order to stop the demolition, and in
summoning L'Enfant to appear before an Annapolis court in December. The summons was never served, but L'Enfant endured a stressful
period of anticipation.

When L'Enfant finally received the president's scolding letter of
December 2, he wrote back to try once again to defend his actions.
While that letter has been lost to history, Washington apparently
turned it over to Jefferson for advice, which the latter was quick to
give in a missive headed "Observations on Major L'Enfant's letter of
Dec. 7th . . . justifying the demolition."

In his reply to the president, Jefferson dismissed L'Enfant's claim
that Carroll had "erected his house partly on a main street," saying
that as the plan still had not been definitely determined when Carroll
began to build the walls of the house, there was no legal foundation

for L'Enfant's assertion. In case that point might seem sophistic, Jefferson went on at some length to disparage the planner's claim that pulling down a house was no different from cutting down a tree—anyone would understand the difference in the consequences of two such disparate actions, Jefferson said. Then he moved on to what he clearly considered the crux of the matter: "the style in which he writes the justification of his act, shows that a continuation of the same resentment renders him still unable to acquiesce under the authority [of the commissioners]."

Jefferson believed that the commissioners ought to supervise any and all "subordinate agents" in the undertaking before them, and though the president was certainly within his rights to remove L'Enfant from their direct control, it would be a grave error to do so and would "give him a line where he may meet with the Commissioners foot to foot, and chicane & raise opposition to their orders whenever he thinks that they pass his line."

"To render him useful, his temper must be subdued," Jefferson declared. "Submit him to the unlimited control of the Commissioners. We know the discretion & forbearance with which they will exercise it."

It was advice Washington must have received with a weary sigh. Obviously the president had not given up on L'Enfant or his ideas, for on December 13 he distributed copies of the L'Enfant plan to the two houses of Congress, under the heading of a memorandum from his office. But on the same day he also wrote L'Enfant to try to make the situation clear, once and for all.

"Sir, I have received your letter of the 7th," Washington began, "and can only once more, and now for all inform you, that every matter and thing which has relation to the federal district and the city within it, is committed to the Commissioners appointed." From the tone of it, one can imagine the stabbings of the presidential pen as each point was punctuated: "It is from them you are to derive your powers—and the line of demarcation is to be drawn by them." Though he closed with one more attempt to assure L'Enfant that the commissioners were surely disposed to listen to his suggestions, "to adopt your plans—and to support your authority for carrying the latter into effect," Washington seemed ready to end the discussion: "having said this in more instances than one it is rather painful to reiterate it."

In a final postscript, the president is almost plaintive in his hopes that quarreling could end and progress on his city might begin: "As you are well acquainted with mine, as well as the earnest wishes of the Commissioners, to have the work forwarded with all the dispatch the nature of it will admit, I persuade myself that nothing will be wanting on your part, or the part of Mr. Ellicott, to hasten the execution."

With that, the president apparently considered the matter closed. Convinced by L'Enfant's aside that only Carroll of Duddington and his cohorts were upset, Washington sent a note to Jefferson the very next day saying that he was happy "after all that has happened" that matters now stood so well between the commissioners and Major L'Enfant, though he was sorry to hear that work had not been progressing at the rate he would like.

As it turned out, Carroll had been appeased by the president's letter laying out the various options of redress open to him, and had decided that it would be just fine if the commissioners did as the president suggested—rebuild his house and let him live in it for the next six years. Though the commissioners would ultimately decide otherwise, for the time being the matter was resolved in the chief complainant's mind as well.

L'Enfant, meanwhile, seemed unchastened by the president's stern series of letters. He might have been unable to believe his old friend Washington sincerely meant to upbraid him. And, indeed, a comparison of the two documents—Jefferson's analysis of the L'Enfant/Carroll issue and Washington's final directives to his planner—shows where the disciplinary tone and the respectful pleas for civility and efficiency had originated.

The most striking distinction to be made between Jefferson's advice and Washington's ensuing letter is the clear attempt that the president made to lighten the blow that seemed required. In one lengthy passage, Washington refers to a delay in the original appointment of the elder Daniel Carroll to the Board of Commissioners—if that delay had not happened, Washington suggests, perhaps all his orders to L'Enfant would have been channeled properly to the planner through the board from the outset, and this unfortunate confusion might have been averted. Furthermore, it seems certain that had Washington relied solely on Jefferson for advice on how to deal with L'Enfant, there would have been no final paragraphs full of compliments and fond hopes for the future.

Perhaps L'Enfant had acquired enough of a politician's savvy to shrug off Washington's scolding as something urged on the president by Jefferson and others with agendas of their own. Or perhaps L'Enfant simply dismissed the matter altogether and returned his thoughts to the most important matter: the Grand Plan.

In a letter to his assistant Isaac Roberdeau, dated December 16, L'Enfant made no reference to the Carroll matter, discussing only a series of tasks that the assistant, who had come well recommended to L'Enfant from surveyor Ellicott, should handle over the winter while the architect was in Philadelphia overseeing the proper engraving of his plan.

First on the list was the building of a set of barracks near the two Aquia Creek quarries in Virginia that L'Enfant had bought as a source of stone for the upcoming spring building season. "The stone must be taken down as it comes and in as great quantity as the time will admit," L'Enfant told Roberdeau. Once he had established himself in Philadelphia, there would be time to send along requests that the workers find stones of particular dimensions for specific purposes, L'Enfant added, but meanwhile, "without waiting let the hands do the most they can." Given the size of the task before them, any rock that was free from stain and fracture was to be taken up and moved to Washington as quickly as possible.

As for the site itself, L'Enfant ordered Roberdeau to construct barracks at five locations convenient to the projects in the Federal City, each to be near a source of fresh water and sufficient to house six to eight hundred workers in all. One barracks should be near the site of the Capitol, with another close to the President's House. There should also be a smaller building near the mouth of Rock Creek, another to house those working on the Tiber canal, and a fifth placed near the market square to serve as a central storehouse.

L'Enfant assured Roberdeau that he had already made arrangements with a pair of local proprietors to supply the necessary timber, but he cautioned his assistant to be sure "no wasting of wood takes place." The clearing of right-of-way for the streets was to proceed quickly now that the survey lines were finished and the plan approved, L'Enfant said, and, where proprietors wished to keep the felled timber (as was their right), the trunks were to be laid "lengthly way on the side of the street so as to leave a free passage."

Diggers were to begin immediate excavations for the foundations of the Capitol building, a project that would require the manufacture of a number of wheelbarrows. As to payment for men and material, Roberdeau should send a list of what was needed to the commissioners, "but if they were absent or that in the execution of this order some delay should appear, let nothing interfere with the work; it must be pursued without interruption"—hardly the words of a chastened man sensitive to the desires of unpaid men or absent officials. It seems clear that L'Enfant was guided by one consideration, and one consideration alone: the unalloyed determination to see the city of Washington take shape.

Before leaving for Philadelphia, L'Enfant penned a note to the commissioners explaining that he had left Roberdeau in charge and saying that he trusted they would approve the hiring of twenty-five men for the quarries and another fifty to set to work in the city. He also called their attention to the "immediate necessity" of a hundred or more wheelbarrows, and hoped that the commissioners would be able to obtain them by the middle of March, when the weather would allow work to resume in earnest.

L'Enfant also took time to respond to the concerns of another pair of proprietors. To David Burnes, the owner of that "grubbed out" tobacco plantation that lay at the foot of Jenkins Hill, L'Enfant gave his blessing to commence work on a house he wished to build. The site would have a view of both the presidential palace and the grand park laid out before it, L'Enfant enthused. Given its grand location, he urged Burnes to erect an equally impressive home, reminding the proprietor that a "house of the proper dimension" was in his best interest. A grand design would, L'Enfant said, enable Burnes to "rent it or dispose of it to better advantage." And if Burnes found that he ran short of clay (normally taken from the excavations for a building's foundations), L'Enfant's letter was to stand as permission for Burnes to take as much as he needed from the Virginia Avenue right-of-way out front.

Regarding Notley Young, one of the most powerful Eastern Branch proprietors, L'Enfant sent a letter to the commissioners explaining that the final survey had, unfortunately, determined that Young's house was squarely in the way of one of the streets on the plan. "I see no necessity at present to proceed immediately to the removal," L'Enfant was quick to say, adding that the home lay at the far end of the street in question. He wished to leave it to the commissioners to contact Mr. Young and make the proper arrangements— perhaps Young would opt to remain in the house for seven years, or perhaps he would rather apply for immediate compensation for his property and build a new house "in a situation where the aspect may benefit the general improvement of the city."

L'Enfant, always looking for ways to encourage immediate development within the city's bounds, clearly favored the latter option. As he furthermore informed the commissioners in a postscript, he had been unable to keep himself from dropping a line to Young as well, "giving him my idea on what I conceive may be his interest," and offering advice on the best lots to choose from.

L'Enfant must have considered his letters on the issue tactful, given the lessons of the previous fiasco with Carroll of Duddington. Still, the commissioners could not have been happy to hear that yet another proprietor from the Eastern Branch interests was facing the condemnation of his property. And, worse, this was the same Notley Young who had been assured by L'Enfant at the unveiling of his plan that his house and grounds—valued at nearly $40,000—were probably safe.

Certainly Young did not find it welcome news, no matter how tactfully phrased, and never mind L'Enfant's offer of advice on new lots. In a letter to the commissioners dated January 7, 1792, Young complained vigorously: "I had as I thought a well grounded expectation that the Plan would be so ordered as to leave me in an eligible situation with respect to the spot I delighted in." He then invited the commissioners to share his dismay at the news that his home lay "entirely on" one of the streets L'Enfant and Ellicott had laid out.

By this time L'Enfant was back in Philadelphia, making the rounds of engravers and anxiously awaiting the arrival of a copy of the plan to be sent from Georgetown. Before leaving, he had asked Benjamin Ellicott, the chief surveyor's brother, to annotate the plan showing all work that had been accomplished since Washington unveiled it at Georgetown the previous spring, so that the copies would be more useful in encouraging sales.

That annotated plan seemed to be inexplicably delayed, however. And though L'Enfant might one day understand why, it is quite likely that he was oblivious to the strength of the storm he had left brewing.

17

Ditches in the Midst of Winter

As the new year dawned, L'Enfant's assistant Isaac Roberdeau was doing all he could to carry on with work on the site, in spite of the clamor raised by Notley Young and other landowners. The commissioners were subjected to continuous complaints from various interests fearful that any practical development in the city might detract from the value of their own holdings.

Roberdeau wrote to L'Enfant on January 2, 1792, to apologize for not yet having made his way down to the quarries in Virginia. He explained that word had reached him that the third commissioner, Thomas Johnson, had finally cleared his personal affairs and was now in Georgetown, ready to assume his duties. Thus, Roberdeau said, he had decided to stay on and meet with the full group to discuss the orders that L'Enfant had left behind.

Meanwhile, Roberdeau said, he had found what he believed to be a trustworthy source of wheelbarrows and had located a supplier of firewood and logs for barracks construction at a lower price than L'Enfant had expected. He had also found a few experienced quarrymen, though not as many as they would need. He planned to go before the commissioners the next day, and would report back on their opinions of the schedule L'Enfant had drawn up.

On January 7, Roberdeau wrote again—this time from Aquia,

where the quarries were located—to explain that the meeting of the commissioners had not in fact taken place as scheduled. He had left a copy of L'Enfant's orders with Commissioner Carroll, then had gone along to Virginia, where, he was happy to report, he had hired an experienced quarry foreman for about seventeen dollars a month and arranged for a crew to begin building the workers' barracks at both quarry locations.

There was some disconcerting news to pass along, however. On his way to Aquia, Roberdeau explained, he had met Commissioner David Stuart, who informed him that he had better return at once to Georgetown, because the commissioners were about to meet to discuss the work schedule that L'Enfant had proposed. Stuart led Roberdeau to understand that the schedule of activities outlined by L'Enfant had alarmed them all, and it was the opinion of the commissioners that all new hires, except the few men assigned to barracks-building, should be dismissed at once.

In a display of loyalty, Roberdeau continued, "Now most willingly I would have returned to Georgetown had the Doctor [Stuart] not mentioned the intention to discharge the men. A resolution of that kind I well knew it was impossible for me to prevent and being . . . determined . . . to adhere most strictly to your orders I came on to this place."

The next morning, a Sunday, Roberdeau had more disturbing news to pass along. Just moments earlier, he wrote to L'Enfant, he had encountered their commissary chief, a man named Boraff, who had arrived in Aquia after an all-night ride from Georgetown. Boraff told Roberdeau that the commissioners had delivered an edict that all the men in their employ were to be discharged, and that Roberdeau would be, in the words of the commissioners, "liable to prosecution should any of the tools be used until spring or their further orders."

He and Boraff discussed their options in light of the commission's actions, Roberdeau told L'Enfant, and their decision was unshakable: "[T]o follow implicitly your directions being my whole duty and my only aim I without hesitation gave my horse to Boraff and insisted upon his return to the city before morning that he might continue in service all the hands." L'Enfant should rest assured, Roberdeau continued, that "your orders will be attended to most punctually until they are countermanded by yourself." Meanwhile, Roberdeau would on Monday return by stage to Georgetown, where he would survey the situation for himself.

What he found was not encouraging. The commissioners had indeed discharged all the commissary workers, the foremen, and the work crews that Roberdeau had already put to work. What's more, Roberdeau found his own pink slip on his desk.

"I rushed into the commissioner's apartment and vindicated my conduct most strenuously," Roberdeau told L'Enfant. "Unfortunately I was thrown off my guard and insulted them in a public and indecent manner." Though Roberdeau did not provide the details of those insults, he did assure L'Enfant that the moment that he had been able to gain control of himself, he had apologized for his intemperance. Furthermore, he was to see the commissioners again in the morning, when he fully expected "to have their late resolution set aside."

"Should they not assent," Roberdeau said, "I shall take the most prudent steps to keep in employ your number of men, at all events until I hear from you." He went on to tell L'Enfant that "the country already rings" with the news of the firings, and he closed his letter with a touching appeal: "[A] single line from you would be most acceptable; but until that arrives your orders are fulfilled."

Even granting young Roberdeau a measure of naïveté and the necessity to write in a way pleasing to the man who employed him, his letters are a testament to the reputation that L'Enfant enjoyed for working well with those whom *he* employed, if not always with his own employers. While Jefferson and the commissioners would paint L'Enfant as vain, impractical, and ultimately impossible, it seems that his own men viewed him with great respect and were willing to go so far as to risk their own livelihoods in his defense.

As for that "single line" that Roberdeau wished to have from his superior, he would wait in vain. It is questionable whether or not

Roberdeau's posts ever reached L'Enfant, who had closeted himself for work on a detailed report to the president outlining a schedule for all public works to be undertaken over the next five years in the Federal City, including estimates for the necessary labor force and a budget, that he was to hand over on January 17.

Though he makes no specific reference to any of the troubles going on at the site, it seems very clear that L'Enfant had decided that he would never be able to work as the minion of the commissioners. He began his report to Washington by apologizing for bucking the chain of command: "Knowing you wished never to be applied to on the subject of business intrusted to the management of the Commissioners, I would decline troubling you at this moment," L'Enfant said, "were it not for the expectations" he was sure the president held for the imminent commencement of work in the spring and for L'Enfant's belief that Washington alone had the power to prevent a number of difficulties that now loomed.

Yet L'Enfant was ready to draw a line in the sand. "I feel a diffidence from the actual state of things to venture further in the work," he told the president, "unless adequate provisions are made." Wanting to get out from under the micromanaging purview of the commissioners, L'Enfant was banking everything on the belief that Washington would see the folly of the current arrangement, particularly if he backed his contentions up with a carefully considered progress report.

It was of dire importance at a time when serious work on the city was about to begin, L'Enfant said, "not to engage in it but with powerful means." And yet, as he pointed out, he had not been allowed to do any meaningful preparation. There was no supply system in place, no storehouse of tools and materials assembled, no employment office organized or authorized. And this vast and important project was being undertaken in a remote place far from any supporting infrastructure.

"These are the considerations which lead me to demand your particular attention to the enclosed statement of work," L'Enfant explained. And while he acknowledged the prodigious scope of the undertaking and the significant size of its budget, he hoped that the president would not be daunted. Perhaps he might consider the prospect of a loan "which is offered from Holland." Such a step would ensure the steady progress outlined in his document through the five-year period ending in 1796.

L'Enfant called for the hiring of more than 1,000 men: carpenters, masons, brickmakers, stonecutters, wheelwrights, blacksmiths, mechanics, pit sawyers, mule and oxen drivers, boatmen, a permanent commissary director, and 850 common laborers upon whose backs the principal burden of digging foundations, leveling sites, clearing rights-of-way, dragging trees, rolling boulders, and forming a miles-long canal with pick and shovel and wheelbarrow would be borne.

It would take 150 men to carry out the construction of the president's home and the Capitol alone, L'Enfant reckoned, and another three hundred for the canal and wharves associated with it. And then there was the operation of the quarries and lumber mills and the creation of a transportation system to haul all the necessary building materials from their origins to the various construction sites.

As to the cost of all this, L'Enfant had figured it down to the third part of a dollar for labor, housing and subsistence, lumber, furniture, rents, bellows, anvils, vises, grindstones, nails, spikes, cranes, gins, screws, capstans, blocks, tackles, cordage, and "instruments to be used at the quarries and at the bridge wharfs."

Even with all that, L'Enfant said, "no provision is made for the compensation, & subsistence of the following persons who ought to be placed on a permanent and fixed establishment." There was the need, he said, for a Director General (the reader can safely guess whom he had planned for that post), two assistant directors, one draftsman, one Surveyor of the City, one assistant surveyor, one head carpenter, and one head mason.

Clearly, the carving of a city worthy of the name of Washington out of a veritable wilderness was no simple matter. In addition to the roughly $200,000 promised by the state legislatures of Virginia and Maryland, the planner thought that another $1 million ought to be enough to carry on operations through the end of 1796. Not an insubstantial sum, he agreed, but it was a realistic assessment of the cost of progress on the city.

"The effect of this expenditure," he said, "will enhance the Value of Lots to such degree that a more considerable Sale may commence," and that sale would cover the interest on the million-dollar loan and provide a basis for future improvements as well. L'Enfant insisted that his all-or-nothing approach to the project was the only one that made sense: "[T]here is a necessity as well as an advantage in commencing each of the Objects at once—however as method and Sistem [*sic*] are absolutely necessary to be established in every branch of Employment." In essence, and as he had done in defense of the layout of the city itself, L'Enfant was calling for an organic approach to its construction. To do otherwise would be like creating a human being by first constructing a set of kidneys, then perhaps a lung, followed possibly by a heart—if there was money—and of course perhaps another lung and blood vessels and all the rest of it somewhere down the road. Efficiency was part of it, to be sure, but just as important was the strength and cohesiveness of an overall design.

While some of L'Enfant's letters and memorials might present him as a man out of touch with practical realities, his January 17 proposal belied that reputation, going so far as to lay out the components and the cost of a workman's daily rations. He recommended that each worker be allotted one pound of beef or pork, one of flour, a half-pound of corn meal, and, in the practice of the day, a half-pint of spirits. Beyond that, a man could expect a weekly bounty of a pound of rice, two ounces of chocolate, and four ounces of soap.

He did not expect the money to pay for all of this to tumble from the sky. Inquiries assured him that a twenty-year loan of a million dollars was obtainable from bankers on the Continent, at the rate of 5 percent, on an interest-only basis for the first five years. The principal would then be repaid in ten installments of $100,000. To guarantee the loan, L'Enfant suggested that individual states come on board as cosigners, with as many as three-quarters of the public lots offered as security. These should be the less desirable lots, farther away from the initial development sites, L'Enfant advised, leaving the most prominent to bring in a windfall of cash. If no state could be persuaded to participate as guarantor, perhaps the $200,000 promised by Virginia and Maryland could be pledged as security, or perhaps the newly formed Bank of the United States could secure the loan.

L'Enfant closed his report to the president by adding a note suggesting that Andrew Ellicott and his brother Benjamin were eminently qualified for the proposed executive posts, and by reiterating his certainty that his approach to the matter of building the city would stimulate development, "give confidence to those who are too disposed to adventure," and "prompt the well disposed to exert their means in improvement." The orderly plan of development he championed would, he believed, discourage idle speculators from snapping up choice properties at the lowest possible price, doing nothing to improve the property, and simply waiting to "flip" their holdings until values rose. "A prodigal disposal of the property at an early stage . . . would undoubtedly work a disipation [*sic*] of the means very detrimental to the attachment of the Grand Object," L'Enfant opined.

It would have taken a great deal of energy and attention to compose such a comprehensive document in a short time, but L'Enfant could well have viewed it as a last-ditch attempt to convince the president how impractical it was to allow the commissioners to interfere in such a complex organizational task. Once Washington could glimpse something of the day-to-day realities involved in bringing a vision to life, surely he would agree that L'Enfant must be free of niggling interference. The commissioners could confine themselves to matters of broad policy, not to the hiring of carpenters or the purchase of a hogshead of nails.

Whether L'Enfant handed his report to the president in a spirit of self-defense or simply passed it along as part of the due course of business cannot be known. Nor was it likely that he could have been aware that the president had already received another letter bearing on the matter, an alarming note from the commissioners dated January 9, the day that Roberdeau described bursting into their chambers with his "public and indecent" insults.

"From what we collect from the commissary of provisions [Mr. Boraff], there are about 75 laborers and their overseers in the city," the commissioners wrote, "and Major L'Enfant has ordered 25 of them to be withdrawn from thence to be employed in the stone quarry under the direction of Mr. I. Roberdeau. . . . We have reason to believe that he thus proceeded to avoid orders from us," the commissioners continued, though if the dates of the various letters involved are accurate, they had already met with Roberdeau to discuss the mass firings the commissioners had ordered. "Independent of this mortifying treatment," the commissioners went on, "we think it advisable, from the nature of the season, to put every thing for the present at least, on piece work, and to discharge the hands engaged." And while they might have agreed that a few men could be employed in digging for clay to be used for bricks, it did not seem prudent, they said, given that a final plan had not been prepared or adopted, "to warrant the digging of long, deep, wide ditches [foundation footings] in the midst of winter, which if necessary at all might be done much cheaper in any other seasons." Though they were hesitant to make a decision in Major L'Enfant's absence "which he might possibly think wanting in delicacy," the commissioners said, they had gone ahead and discharged all hands.

Nor was that all they had done. On January 16, L'Enfant had taken a moment away from work on his report to write to Roberdeau, asking that his assistant shoot the level of Jenkins Hill in preparation for work on the Capitol. Roberdeau would doubtless have been happy to follow L'Enfant's instructions had he been able. Unfortunately, however, the commissioners had already put him in jail.

18

Writ of Trespass

In *The Standard History of the City of Washington* from 1914, William Tindall offers an account of what transpired between the commissioners and Isaac Roberdeau following that fiery confrontation on January 9. As Roberdeau suggested in his somewhat shamefaced letter to L'Enfant, he did go to meet with the commissioners on the following day, January 10, whereupon he was informed that all work within the city was to be terminated immediately, the hands let go, and any public property in Roberdeau's possession turned over at once to their agent, Captain Elisha Williams. With that, the commissioners washed their hands of the matter and adjourned.

Roberdeau, however, remained true to his word to L'Enfant. On January 11, with the commissioners returned to their homes, Roberdeau rounded up his crews and took them back to work excavating foundations on Capitol Hill. When the commissioners were told what was going on, according to Tindall, they personally made their way to the site where Roberdeau was supervising diggers.

Accosted in a muddy clearing and asked what he thought he was doing, Roberdeau answered calmly that he was carrying out the orders of his superior, Major L'Enfant. He had received a letter from the planner in Philadelphia, he continued, telling him that it was not nearly so important to have clay turned up for bricks as to have these footings for the Capitol dug.

While Tindall does not record the apoplectic glances exchanged by the commissioners at that moment, it might be safely assumed that they were. As Tindall puts it, Roberdeau thus "held it necessary for his [L'Enfant's] justification to submit to an arrest, which the Commissioners proceeded to cause."

It is not clear whether Washington was aware that Roberdeau had actually been jailed, but on the same day that L'Enfant handed over his lengthy five-year plan, the president wrote to the commissioners to tell them he was in support of their decision to suspend work in the city for the time being. He went on, however, to support L'Enfant, who might yet, in the words of the president, "be an useful one, if he could be brought to reduce himself within those limits which your own responsibility obliges you to prescribe." Of course, Washington was quick to admit, "At present he does not appear to be in that temper."

In writing to the commissioners as he did, Washington was doing his best to serve political reality without sacrificing a man whose artistic talents he clearly valued. All chain-of-command issues aside, and despite the impressive detail contained within the body of L'Enfant's proposed schedule of construction, Washington had only to glance at the huge bottom line to realize the impracticality of L'Enfant's approach.

L'Enfant may have reckoned his figures carefully, but he had prepared his final tallies without the aid of the politician's slide rule. With no money in the national treasury and heated debates still raging about the disposition of the war debt, the very need for the existence of a national bank, and the wisdom of building a city in his own backyard, there was no earthly way the president could lead the charge for a million-dollar loan.

Meanwhile, yet another complaint against L'Enfant had reached the president, one that had him writing to Jefferson on January 18 for advice. What he had been told about "the conduct of Major L'Enfant and those employed under him astonishes me beyond measure," Washington told Jefferson. "When you are at your leisure, I should be glad to have a further conversation with you on this subject."

It seems that someone had told the president that, in retaliation against the commissioners, L'Enfant or someone employed by him had been visiting building lots in the Federal City surreptitiously and pulling up the surveyors' stakes marking their boundaries. It seems far-fetched to claim that L'Enfant would undermine the surveyors' efforts, given his well-documented zeal to see the "Grand Plan" take shape, but Jefferson was quick to take action. He wrote to Commissioner Daniel Carroll, cautioning him "to consider this letter as from one private individual to another," and suggesting that Carroll hire someone to hold the properties under surveillance, a charge that Carroll was happy to accept.

Meanwhile, Carroll wrote to James Madison to say that he had heard "a most infamous slander" going around, and to suggest that L'Enfant was spreading unflattering stories about the unsavory bargaining tactics of George Brent, owner of one of the Aquia quarries L'Enfant had been sent to acquire. It is not clear just how troubled Brent was by such "black calumny," as Carroll put it, but given that he was Commissioner Carroll's brother-in-law, and also the brother of Daniel Carroll of Duddington, he probably would have testified that he was feeling greatly injured indeed.

By this time Roberdeau had managed to get a letter out of his cell and back to L'Enfant, explaining why he had not been able to get over to Jenkins Hill and the matter of shooting its level. "My letters which have gone out with nearly every stage," Roberdeau wrote plaintively, "must have miscarried or you would not be ignorant of the lengths to which the Commissioners have proceeded against me."

On February 6, and though his assistant had been released by that time, L'Enfant wrote the president to express his dismay and outrage at Roberdeau's treatment and at the complete work stoppage. "The critical situation to which matters are now brought," he told the president, "testifying a disinclination in the Commissioners to facilitate the prosecution of the business," had led him to suggest his "new organization of the whole system." He followed that with a threat: "[F]eeling myself doubly interested in the success [of the undertaking] . . . enjoins me to renounce the pursuit unless the power of effecting the work with advantage to the public, and credit to myself is left me."

We can be forgiven for imagining the president pressing his hand to his forehead as he finished the letter. Perhaps, he told himself, this was really no crisis; L'Enfant was an excitable individual, and this might simply be one more agitated pronouncement. On the other hand, in order for any work to be done, the planner would simply have to stop this foolish stubbornness and learn to work within the hierarchy Washington had put in place.

As he considered the volatile state of affairs, it might have happened that Washington finally turned from L'Enfant's message to pick up another that bore on the matter, eight carefully considered pages just arrived from David Stuart, the man whom Washington trusted as his most reliable representative among all the commissioners. In that thick missive of Stuart's might lay the key that unlocked this dispute.

What he found, however, was only more evidence of profound discontent. Stuart told Washington that grave slanders against the commissioners were being spread about the Georgetown area, and repeated the charge of "malicious calumny" leveled against L'Enfant in the matter of the quarry negotiations. Stuart also said that L'Enfant and Roberdeau had gone so far as to call the commissioners "ignorant and unfit." This last information had been conveyed by trusted friends, Stuart assured the president—and while the trusted friends had not themselves heard L'Enfant or Roberdeau utter such slurs, it had been reported to the friends by a source that *they* considered reliable.

In addition to this irrefutable gossip, Stuart further wished to inform the president that he and the other commissioners were of a single mind that there were far too many open spaces provided for in the Plan, and that the extensive grounds surrounding the President's

House were particularly offensive. "It may suit the genius of a despotic government to cultivate an immense and gloomy wilderness in the midst of a thriving city," Stuart said, but "I cannot think it suitable in our situation."

In the end, Stuart said, the commissioners believed that the U.S. treasury was simply inadequate to fund the scope of the work that L'Enfant proposed. As a result, he declared, the three of them had determined to "give up their enviable offices" rather than continue to suffer the indignities and difficulties presented by the planner L'Enfant. Perhaps he would be happier working with another group, Stuart concluded graciously.

No one can say what expression might have found its way to Washington as he lay that letter aside, of course, but one longs to imagine it anyway. First L'Enfant threatens to resign, then the commissioners make the same petulant offer. What was a president to do?

Speculations aside, we do know that Washington had exercised great restraint throughout the course of the affair. We also know that he had stared down gun barrels and rallied troops so frozen and hungry that to win a battle with them seemed a miracle. This present engagement was scarcely life-and-death. But it *was* mightily important, and as was his wont when facing an important decision, he sought advice from a trusted source.

On the morning of February 7 he wrote a note to Jefferson covering the letters of Commissioner Stuart and L'Enfant. "The enclosed came to my hand yesterday evening. . . . I wish the business to which these letters relate was brought to an issue—an agreeable one is not, I perceive to be expected." The president was resigned: there would be no compromise between the planner and those who oversaw the plan. And he was asking Jefferson to resolve the dilemma.

When the secretary of state was slow to respond, Washington sent another, more urgent, letter two days later: "The President requests that Mr. J. would give the enclosed letters and papers a reading between this and dinner—and come an hour before it that he may have an opportunity of conversing with him on the subject." Furthermore,

Washington said, he had learned that George Walker, the original booster of the Georgetown site, was presently in Philadelphia. Perhaps Jefferson might want to confer with him and get a third party's perspective on this mess.

And, two days following that, the president wrote Jefferson yet again: "Dear Sir, If you and Mr. Madison could make it convenient to take a family dinner with me today—or if engagement prevent this—wd. come at any hour in the afternoon most convenient to yourselves, we would converse fully, and try and fix on some plan for carrying the affairs of the Federal City into execution . . . it is difficult, but it is nevertheless necessary to resolve on something."

The urgency is that of a man nearing his wits' end, and the letter that Jefferson prepared following his meeting with the president suggests that an irrevocable decision was indeed adopted. On February 22 the secretary of state wrote L'Enfant that "the circumstances which have lately happened have produced an uncertainty whether you may be disposed to continue your services [at the Federal City]." Jefferson went on that he had been charged by the president to say that while L'Enfant's services "would be desirable to him," at the same time he was required to add that "the law requires it should be in subordination to the Commissioners."

That body was to receive all propositions and plans from L'Enfant and pass them along to the president as necessary. "It is not pretended to stipulate here the mode in which they shall carry on the execution," Jefferson wrote. "They alone can do that."

If L'Enfant would simply agree to place himself within this chain of command, Jefferson said, it would "ensure an oblivion of whatever disagreeable may have arisen, heretofore." L'Enfant could begin with a clean slate, then, but he would have to swear allegiance to his lawful superiors. Jefferson closed with a blunt request: "I must beg the favor of your answer whether you will continue your services on the footing expressed in this letter."

The answer was not long in coming.

19

Purest Principles

L'ENFANT WAS WELL AWARE THAT CIRCUMSTANCES were deteriorating. Five days before Jefferson penned that ultimatum, the planner had written Washington's assistant Tobias Lear to say that it was the "last letter I propose to write interfering in matters relative to the city," at least until he heard from the president on just how all future business was to be conducted.

The overhaul of the "system" was not the primary concern of L'Enfant on this day, however. He was far more troubled by matters pertaining to the map he was trying to prepare for engraving. He told Lear of his last-minute request to Benjamin Ellicott for a careful delineation of all work that had been carried out in the city since the original unveiling of the plan. He had left the sketch that was to be the basis for the engraver with Ellicott, L'Enfant said, so that he could indicate the changes directly on the map in pencil. In turn, L'Enfant intended to complete the emendations himself, then turn the draft over to an engraver.

Imagine his surprise then, he told Lear, when he discovered that Benjamin Ellicott had apparently turned over the map to his brother Andrew, who claimed that Thomas Jefferson had given him the job of completing the map and finding an engraver for it. L'Enfant had believed that he would be called in to make final revisions, he told Lear, until he ran into a printer who informed him that plates of the city map were about to be struck carrying changes of which L'Enfant had no knowledge.

At this point L'Enfant hurried to the Philadelphia office of Andrew Ellicott, where, as he told Lear, he found the draft "unmercifully spoiled and altered from the original plan to a degree . . . tending to disgrace me and ridicule the very undertaking." As to what might have motivated the elder Ellicott to do such a thing, L'Enfant was at a loss—but whether it was due to carelessness or incompetence or the blandishments of others, the surveyor "has been induced to hazard opinions, and to engage himself more forward to effect objects, which besides the impossibility to accomplish, he ought not to have done."

L'Enfant had requested that Andrew Ellicott return the offending document to him, he told Lear, but Ellicott had declined. It left him with no recourse but to seek Lear's assistance in the matter.

Surely, if L'Enfant had begun to have doubts as to his standing with the president, such machinations would have been enough to nudge him toward paranoia. He had not had a direct communication from Washington since December 13, his assistant had been jailed, and his plan for the city had been stolen from him, most likely at the behest of the commissioners. With the president apparently put out with him, and the idea of applying to Jefferson unthinkable, L'Enfant had been reduced to pleading for help from the president's secretary. One might imagine his state of mind, then, when L'Enfant snatched up Jefferson's letter of February 22 and began to read.

It is unlikely that anything in what he saw there reflected Washington's own last-minute counsel to Jefferson. Lear had in fact passed along L'Enfant's complaint about the defilement of his plan, and the president had written to Jefferson that "the plan I think ought to appear as the work of L'Enfant. The one prepared for engraving not doing so is, I presume, one cause of his dissatisfaction." Washington went on to make it clear that he had not yet given up on the planner. "If he consents to act upon the conditions proposed . . . had he not better be gratified in the alterations?"

It must have seemed even to Washington to be a pretty big *if.* And

L'Enfant's reply to Jefferson seemed to settle the matter of his resignation once and for all. "I have received your favor of the 22nd," L'Enfant began, adding, "the sentiments therein expressed I have attentively considered."

He agreed wholeheartedly with Jefferson's observation that the building season was fast approaching and that preparations ought to have already begun. He had, after all, sent an urgent request on that very matter to the president several days before, and as he had pointed out there, it was the commissioners and not he himself who had caused the delays. He claimed to be "not a little surprised" that either Jefferson or the president would question his devotion to the cause— a glance at the document he had recently submitted would "evince most strongly how solicitously concerned I am in the success of it, and with what regret I should relinquish it."

L'Enfant insisted that he had always sought the "confidence and the friendship" of the commissioners. "I coveted it, I sincerely wished it," he said, "knowing that without a perfect good understanding between them and myself, whatever exertions I should make, would prove fruitless." However, as L'Enfant attempted to explain, the commissioners seemed predisposed to interfere in practical matters that they knew nothing about.

What he meant was that it should have been his decision whether a few workmen were better employed chopping out a foundation than turning up clay for bricks. And, indeed, the picture of a trio of prosperous businessmen roused from their homes to gallop across a rugged, wintry landscape in pursuit of an obstreperous shovel-wielder might strike anyone as ludicrous.

Instead of soliciting his advice and acting in accordance with it, L'Enfant said, he had come to count on the fact that whatever he suggested to the commissioners would produce the very opposite effect. He enumerated several examples of their interference and intransigence: their insistence that a boundary line be moved so that Benjamin Stoddert could keep his spring; their rejection of Robert Peters's request to be allowed to build a series of wharves nearer

Georgetown because it would upset the Eastern Branch interests; their refusal to begin work on the canal because that would have upset the Georgetown interests; and on and on.

In the end, then, while it pained him exceedingly to do so—"to renounce the pursuit of that fame, which the success of the undertaking must procure"—he would nonetheless withdraw his service. "If therefore the law absolutely requires without any equivocation that my continuance shall depend upon an appointment from the Commissioners," he told Jefferson, "I cannot nor would I upon any consideration submit myself to it."

L'Enfant's reply apparently reached Jefferson on the same day that it was written. The secretary of state dutifully passed it along to the president, who dashed off a note back at four o'clock that same day. "A final decision thereupon must be had," Washington said, though it might have seemed to anyone else that there was little deciding to be done. Still, he wanted Madison called in, along with Attorney General Edmund Randolph, before the matter was finalized. The four of them would meet at half past eight on the following morning, Washington declared.

Meanwhile, in a last-ditch attempt to stave off L'Enfant's resignation, the president sent Tobias Lear to try to reason with him concerning his "unfounded suspicions" toward the commissioners. Another person might have been moved at the gesture, but L'Enfant had become an "all or nothing" man. He told an astonished Lear "that he had already heard enough of the matter," veritably slamming the door in the secretary's face. When Lear returned with news of the encounter, Washington was incensed.

The summit meeting held the following morning of February 27 lasted only moments, and the note that Jefferson sent to L'Enfant was accordingly terse: "[I]t is understood you absolutely decline acting under the authority of the present Commissioners," Jefferson said. "[I]f this understanding of your meaning be right, I am instructed by the President to inform you that notwithstanding the desire he has entertained to preserve your agency in the business, the condition upon which it is to be done is inadmissible & your services must be at an end."

While many of L'Enfant's own letters tended toward the verbose, the one he sent that day to the president was succinct. "By the letter of Mr. Jefferson . . . I perceive that all my services are at an end," he told Washington. "Seeing things are so—let me now earnestly request you to believe that it is with the regret the most sincere I see the termination of all pursuits in which so lately I was engaged, and that my every view throughout was incited by the warmest wishes for the advancement of your favorite object, and that all my abilities were united to insure its success."

20

Least Obedient Servant

L'ENFANT'S REPLY MIGHT HAVE ENDED HIS INVOLVE-
ment with the building of the Federal City, but as history suggests, final curtains rarely drop in actual life. Scarcely had
Washington read L'Enfant's glum missive than he was jotting one of
his own to Jefferson, wondering if they had done the right thing after
all. "Would it be advisable to let L'Enfant alter the plan if he will do
it in a certain given time . . . ? Should Mr. Ellicott be again asked in
strong and explicit terms if the plan exhibited by him is conformable
to the actual state of things on the ground and agreeable to the design
of Majr. L'Enfant?"

To L'Enfant he sent a formal letter in which he accepted the planner's resignation, and suggested that it was L'Enfant's demand that
the commissioners be ousted that forced his hand. He went on to
scold L'Enfant for not moving more quickly to secure an engraving of
the plan for printing, and for his failure to prepare detailed plans for
the president's home and the Capitol.

The president wrote a draft of the message in his own hand, in
which he decided to strike out two paragraphs, including one suggesting that it likely would have done no good even if he had replaced
the three commissioners: "The same cause will produce like effects,"
Washington said in his draft, "and it is feared that you would [submit
to] the control of no one."

Apparently no longer willing to soften the impact of his letters with explanations and qualifications, the president thought it best to keep his final communication with L'Enfant short and to the point. After he marked his cuts and edits, the final version was probably copied out by Lear. A note penciled in by L'Enfant suggests that it might have been better to have sent along the original: "The President could not have written this with his own hand," the planner wrote. "I question if he read it before signing his name."

At the end of the paragraph where Washington took him to task for failing to engrave the plan, L'Enfant jotted, "See letter to Mr. Lear of February 17"—the note in which he told Lear that Ellicott had refused to return the map. And at the bottom of Washington's letter L'Enfant lamented that the president's reproof was "all the more singular in that the Commissioners had since the month of January—arrested the survey I wanted for completion of the plan."

It is possible to see these marginalia as the mutterings of a malcontent, of course, and for years L'Enfant suffered that characterization ascribed to him by Jefferson and the commissioners in the wake of his dismissal. On March 1 the secretary of state wrote to George Walker to say he was sorry that they had not been able to meet concerning the L'Enfant matter during Walker's sojourn in Philadelphia. But Walker should not concern himself—given L'Enfant's insistence that the commissioners be replaced or he be made independent of them, there was only one way to resolve the matter: "[T]he latter being impossible under the law and the former too arrogant to be answered, he was notified that his services were at an end."

"I think you have seen enough of his temper to satisfy yourself that he never could have acted under any control," Jefferson added, "not even that of the President himself." He concluded with the observation that the building of the city could now proceed smoothly, and, more important, prudently: "as fast and no faster than it can pay." On that same day, Jefferson wrote to Daniel Carroll with the news of L'Enfant's dismissal, explaining that while much time was spent in trying to "reduce" the major in "proper subordination to the Commissioners," the planner was intractable.

A few days later Washington himself wrote the commissioners to say that though he had a strong desire to retain L'Enfant, "the condition of his submission to their authority" had made his continuing employment impossible. Jefferson wrote a letter to accompany that declaration, reiterating that it had been "found impracticable to employ Majr Lenfant about the Federal City, in that degree of subordination which was lawful and proper, [and] he has been notified that his services are at an end."

Given such pronouncements from the president and the secretary of state, it is no wonder that many simply accepted it as fact that the temperamental Frenchman had stamped his foot one too many times. And, given the record, it is difficult to imagine that L'Enfant ever could have agreed to receive his orders from anyone but Washington himself. While Jefferson's contention that not even the president could have controlled L'Enfant is less credible (L'Enfant, of Versailles, was building a "palace" for his employer, after all), it would have required a great deal of Washington's time to oversee the enthusiastic planner.

It seems clear, though, that the commissioners were as sensitive to the political pressures attendant on the project as they were to practical considerations and careful planning. In their eyes, L'Enfant was, finally, a nuisance. He might have been the most brilliant city planner ever to walk the wilds of the Potomac, and he might have had logic on his side when he counseled the need for a well-coordinated approach to the building of the Federal City. But they had too many incidental political battles to fight—managing the strategy of a "Grand Plan" simply seemed impractical, and, given his own philosophical and aesthetic differences with the architect, Jefferson was pleased to concur.

In his letter of March 6 to the commissioners, Jefferson brought up the need to make some payment to Lenfant (the secretary always dropped the apostrophe from the major's name—whether it was a calculated slap at a perceived affectation is a matter of conjecture), and he passed along the president's recommendation that the amount be somewhere in the range of $2,500 to $3,000. More important, he warned the commissioners, opponents of the Federal City were likely to seize upon L'Enfant's departure as an excuse to scuttle the entire project.

In fact, Jefferson told them—quite confidentially—that they might give serious consideration to securing a loan to underwrite construction until land sales were able to provide the necessary monies. It was a suggestion that would have had L'Enfant penning apoplectic notes about plagiarism in the margins, had he seen a copy. Jefferson also passed along a copy of the detailed budget that L'Enfant had submitted with his building plan to the president on January 17. Some of the notes contained the views of L'Enfant, Jefferson admitted, and he added rather halfheartedly, "If you find anything good in them, you may convert it to some account."

Nor was the president above attempts at damage control on behalf of the Federal City project. On March 8 he wrote to his friend Commissioner Stuart what he called at the outset a "private letter," in which he counseled Stuart that "[e]very advantage will be taken of the Major's dereliction. A vigorous contradiction therefore is essential." As part of his planned counteroffensive, Washington had begun to rethink the size of the payment to the planner. Instead of the $2,500 to $3,000 mentioned before, "suppose five hundred guineas [a little less than $2,500], and a Lot in a good part of the City be substituted?"

While this was taking place, L'Enfant had mounted something of a campaign of his own. On March 10 he wrote a letter to the proprietors who had signed on to the agreement to provide the land for the Federal City. He began by reminding them of his relentless efforts on behalf of the Potomac site and also of the many obstacles that he had managed to sidestep—their own squabbles not least among them—in his efforts to see the city take shape there.

But of all the impediments, said L'Enfant, the most difficult was the obstinacy of the commissioners. When added to the task of transforming a wilderness into a city within a period of months, "in a country devoid of internal resources . . . distant from materials and necessities," their opposition had turned difficulty into impossibility. Whatever the motivations of that august body, L'Enfant said, he simply was writing to counsel the proprietors to be realistic in their hopes for a speedy appreciation in the value of their holdings. "Your property may not rise with that rapidity which has been your expectations," he told them bluntly.

But he was not counseling a fire sale, either. "My intention is not to depreciate your property nor to advise you to part with it at the low price that may suit the convenience of petty speculators. . . . Your interest is to moderate your prices . . . in proportion to the advantages to be derived from the improvements the purchaser may engage to make thereon." L'Enfant went on to suggest that proprietors might reduce their prices on a certain number of their lots where purchasers were willing to improve the lots immediately, for that would ensure a run-up in the value of the lots that were kept back.

In short, he hoped that the proprietors would see the wisdom of the coordinated development of the city that he had been calling for all along, and he also warned them that an "erroneous map" of the city was about to be published, with his original design "mangled and altered in a shameful manner."

The proprietors, of course, were well aware of the situation. George Walker had returned to Georgetown to find Jefferson's terse letter regarding L'Enfant's ouster waiting for him, and he wasted no name in rallying support for the planner among his constituency. He wrote to Jefferson to say that "the dismission of Major L'Enfant has given great alarm to the Proprietors, and all those interested in the City of Washington." In talking with his colleagues, Walker said, he was "sorry to discover such a want of confidence in the ability of the Commissioners, and am afraid the affairs of the City will come into public investigation if means cannot be adopted by which Major L'Enfant may yet be continued."

Along with his letter, Walker included a petition signed by thirteen of the proprietors (Carroll of Duddington and Notley Young were not among them, of course) asking the president to reconsider. While they were willing to admit that L'Enfant might at times exhibit a "warmth of temper" and exert a degree of firmness that was "improper," his talents, zeal, and impartiality were unmatched. If he were to see this proof of the confidence of the majority of the proprietors, Walker speculated, perhaps he would be willing to "stand less on punctilio than he has hitherto done." To that end, Walker sent a copy of the petition to L'Enfant on the same day that it was posted to Jefferson, but that copy was apparently lost in the mails.

The original did make its way through Jefferson to Washington, however, and the president—clearly miffed that the architect had refused his many efforts at conciliation—minced no words in his reply. "No farther movement of the part of Government can ever be made towards Majr L'Enfant without prostration," he said, "which will not be done." He went on to explain that he felt himself "insulted," still smarting from L'Enfant's sharp reply to Tobias Lear "that he had already heard enough of this matter."

If L'Enfant was willing to go before the commissioners himself and seek reinstatement, the president would not stand in his way. But the proprietors were to understand: "No fa[r]ther overtures will ever be made to this gentleman by the Government."

Jefferson wrote back to Walker as well, echoing the president's sentiments, and adding (in direct contradiction of his letters to the commissioners), "The retirement of Majr. Lenfant has been his own act." Furthermore, Jefferson speculated, L'Enfant's value was being overblown: "[I]t was believed he might have been useful . . . but that the success of the enterprise depended on his employment is impossible to believe."

On March 14, the commissioners wrote L'Enfant themselves, saying that they had been notified that they were "no longer to consider you as engaged in the business of the Federal City." They wanted him to know, however, that his past services would not go without recompense. "You will therefore receive from Messrs. Cunningham and Nesbit of Philadelphia five hundred guineas, whenever it may suit you to apply for it. Besides the above sum, we will make you over a lot in the City of Washington, near the President's house or the Capitol as you may chuse."

To L'Enfant, it was an insult. "Without enquiring of the principle upon which you rest this offer," he responded in his characteristically convoluted way, "I shall only here testify my surprise thereupon, as also my intention to decline accepting of it."

That response would not sever L'Enfant's connection with the president entirely, but it was certainly the last time he would deal with Stuart, Carroll, and Johnson. A few weeks later, after finally seeing a copy of the petition that the proprietors had sent to the president on his behalf, he wrote George Walker to express his gratitude and ask that his feelings be passed along to the rest of the proprietors who had taken his part:

"You may assure them and with confidence, that in my objection I do not stand upon punctilio, nor am actuated by motives of pride or disregard or of enmity . . . but that I have been wholly determined from a conviction of an impossibility to effect the undertaking . . . under a system of direction which must perpetuate misunderstanding amongst the parties concerned."

And with that, the nation's preeminent architect and planner withdrew.

PART TWO

On the Potowmack

21

In This Great Castle

WHEN THE NATION'S SECOND PRESIDENT, JOHN ADAMS, came down to the City of Washington in June of 1800 following the last session of Congress to be held in Philadelphia, he might have expected to find something grander awaiting him. Nearly eight years had passed since the cornerstone was laid for the president's home, after all, and instructions in the Residence Act of 1790 were quite clear: "Prior to the first Monday in December, in the year one thousand eight hundred," the Commissioners of the District were to have ready "suitable buildings for the accommodation of Congress, and of the President, and for the public offices of the government of the United States."

What Adams found in June, then, could not have greatly inspired him. The Congress House on Jenkins Hill had only its north wing under construction (the process would actually continue until 1916), the plaster and the paint in the unfurnished president's residence were still wet and cattle grazing on the treeless lawn outside, and of all the new government offices, only the Treasury Building, just to the east of his new home, was substantially complete. Space for the Departments of State, War, the Navy, and the Post Office would have to be rented from among the owners of the 368 brick and wood buildings deemed habitable that had risen within the confines of the city. The Department of War, for instance, would occupy a stone warehouse on G Street at the Potomac River, owned by none other than Tobias Lear, the former secretary to Washington.

A virtual map of Washington in 1800, constructed by the historical cartographer Don A. Hawkins, shows about six hundred structures of all types within the district, many of them clustered in the area east of the president's home between H Street and Pennsylvania Avenue, with another grouping just east of the Congress House and trailing along New Jersey Avenue down toward the Eastern Branch of the Potomac. Pennsylvania Avenue itself was a broad but unpaved track—dusty in good weather, a near-impassable quagmire when it rained—and sidewalks were still a dream.

Compared with New York, with its 60,000 citizens, Philadelphia with 41,000, and Baltimore and Boston with about 25,000 apiece, Washington City with its 3,210 souls in residence was the antithesis of a thriving metropolis. Even early capital contender Lancaster, Pennsylvania, with its 4,200 residents, could boast an actual city center, broad avenues, tree-lined sidewalks, and an imposing courthouse that the city fathers had offered for the use of Congress.

Drawings of Washington at the time, including William R. Birch's watercolor of the partially completed Congress House, now housed in the Library of Congress, suggest a decidedly rural landscape, the vistas dotted with cottages, while here and there an occasional behemoth of an unfinished public building rises incongruously on a barren hillside. While cartographer Hawkins locates areas where trees still stood, he points out that by 1800 most of the native forest had been cleared for lumber and fuel. Furthermore, the haphazard and scarcely regulated building process had left its scars: abandoned brick kilns, eroded hillsides, piles of rock, and forgotten quarries turned into stagnant ponds punctuated the landscape. Livestock wandered freely, and hay wagons and tobacco carts constituted the main traffic on local roads.

It might have struck Adams as a bit mad that the entire government would have to be moved from Philadelphia, described by the British diplomat Augustus Foster as the "best city in the New World," to this veritable wilderness within a few short weeks, but on the other hand he could not help but understand the significant role he was playing in history. He would be the first president to reside in what had been decreed to be the permanent home of the United States government, and he was not about to reopen debate on the matter, not with himself and the nation embroiled in a presidential election process so acrimonious that it is sometimes called the "Revolution of 1800." The voting season would last from April to October, and would only be partially decided in December, when the ballots from South Carolina were finally counted.

In May, in the midst of the uncertainty, Adams issued a directive to his department heads and advisers "to make the most prudent and economical arrangements for the removal of the public offices, clerks and papers . . . that the public offices may be opened in the city of Washington by the 15th of June." It was an order that affected the grand total of 136 individuals working for the federal government at the time, all of whom set about dutifully preparing for the move.

And it was more than an affair of state, preparing for such a move. As Abigail Adams wrote poignantly to her sister Mary Cranch on the eve of her departure from Philadelphia, "I arrived in this City last Evening & came to the old House. . . . Tho the furniture and arrangment of the House is changed I feel more at home here than I should any where else in the city, and when sitting with my son & other friends who call to see me, I can scarcely persuade myself that tomorrow I must quit it, for an unknown & and unseen abode."

Abigail might have been the more colorful writer of the pair, but John Adams, who had gone to Washington a bit ahead of his wife, was not without his own rhetorical gifts. He wrote to her from their new home, "I pray heaven to bestow the best of blessings on this house, and all that shall hereafter inhabit it. May none but honest and wise men ever rule under this roof."

With those lofty sentiments penned and posted, he might have strolled once more about the cavernous, dimly lit rooms of his unfinished residence, wondering just how Abigail might take to life here. She was a trouper, and had even braved an ocean voyage to join him during his sojourns as minister to Paris during the war, but they had been young then.

And, furthermore, he was the president now, and she the president's wife. Yet there wasn't even a proper stairway that led to the second floor of this "palace." To get to their bedchambers required climbing up a rickety service passage. There was no plaster on the bare brick walls of the East Room, and Adams's footsteps echoed as he paced beneath its twenty-two-foot-high, and leaking, ceilings.

Adams had witnessed a great deal in his twenty-five years of political service, and, knowing his residency in the new presidential palace might well be limited by the long-awaited election results, he was surely philosophical about small inconveniences. But still, as he gazed about his unfinished home, or out the windows at the nearly empty landscape of Washington City, it must have caused him to wonder just what had been going on here since 1792.

22

Revolving Door

A REGULAR OCCURRENCE IN THE FEDERAL CITY DURING the years following L'Enfant's dismissal was the periodic firing or resignation of his successors. Andrew Ellicott was appointed to replace L'Enfant, but the arrangement was plagued by the same sorts of bickering that marred the relationship of L'Enfant and the supervisors. Once again, Washington made public statements in support of the commissioners, but urged them privately to let the superintendent superintend. His attempts to mediate were no more successful this time, and within a year an equally exasperated Ellicott, having been publicly reviled by his employers as careless in his work and prone to the abuse of drink, angrily resigned.

After Ellicott came Samuel Blodget of Massachusetts, a lot salesman, speculator, and erstwhile builder, who was named as City Superintendent for "the expediting of construction." What was mainly expedited by Blodget—a man very nearly as passionate as L'Enfant about the future of a Potomac capital and particularly interested in founding a national university within the city—was his own falling-out with his supervisors.

More practically, an announcement was made of an open competition for the design of the home of the president and for the "Congress House." On March 14, 1792, immediately following the termination of L'Enfant's services, the commissioners authorized a prize of $500 (or a gold medal of the same value) for the winning entries, and Jefferson drew up an advertisement that was published in newspapers around the country.

Jefferson himself had strong ideas about the proper design of the president's home. He entered the competition secretly and signed the plans he submitted with the initials "A.Z.," leading to much speculation among the commissioners as to the mysterious architect's identity. Another renaissance man of the time, Dr. William Thornton—a West Indian–born physician, inventor, painter, and self-styled architect— sent in a plan that excited comment among the commissioners.

When the winning entry was announced in July, however, it proved to be the work of neither front-runner, but that of James Hoban, an Irish immigrant architect who had actual training in his field from the Dublin Society School. Hoban, born in Kilkenny in 1758, immigrated to Philadelphia in 1785 and later moved to Charleston, South Carolina, where he was hired to design the State House. Intrigued by the national competition, he submitted a set of preliminary drawings for the president's home, then sailed up the coast to survey the site that Washington and L'Enfant had chosen. It was during that visit that Hoban was informed the job was his, a decision that would keep him in the Federal City for the remainder of his life.

Hoban's original design, based on the Georgian-style home of the Duke of Leinster in Dublin (now the Irish Parliament), was a steep-roofed, three-story structure that, while built to a modest scale, would allow for wings to be added as the need for growth arose. Even with such practical features, commissioners still reckoned that it would cost about $400,000 (including a supervisor's fee of $1,500 to Hoban) to bring the design to fruition.

And there was one other problem: the home he had designed did not come close to filling the grandiose plot of land that L'Enfant had conceived of as right and proper for the new American ruler. As a result, the commissioners wondered if Hoban mightn't be willing to lop off the third story of his design so that the dimensions of the building's footprint could expand by about 20 percent.

In early August, Washington journeyed up to the city from Mount Vernon to make certain that Hoban's design aligned properly with the actual building site he had picked out more than a year earlier. The smaller size of the new design might have meant slightly shifting the axis of Pennsylvania Avenue to maintain a perfect sightline between the residence and "Congress House," but that would have entailed significant alterations to the original L'Enfant grid. It took Washington almost no time to make his decision: L'Enfant's plan would stand. The location of the president's home could shift accordingly.

Hoban went quickly to work on the design changes, and on October 13, 1792, the cornerstone for what would one day be known as the White House was laid in a ceremony attended by the commissioners, townspeople, and a contingent of Freemasons from Georgetown. Afterwards the party retired to Suter's Fountain Inn in Georgetown, where it is reported that sixteen toasts were raised, including one to the fifteen states (Vermont had joined the union in 1791, and Kentucky on June 1, 1792), as well as to the president, the new city, the Marquis de Lafayette, the fair daughters of America, and—quite likely—all things great and small.

At first, progress on the building of the president's home was extraordinary, by Washington City standards. A master stoneworker from England named George Blagden came down from Philadelphia to join the contingent headed by Scots mason Collen Williamson working on the erection of the walls; soon they had persuaded the commissioners to forgo the brick facing they had planned for the interior walls. Given the excellent quality of the materials and the careful workmanship ongoing, brick was simply superfluous, the masons pointed out, and the parsimonious commissioners were only too happy to agree.

In a letter of May 30, 1793, a skeptical Isaac Roberdeau wrote to L'Enfant that stone for the first story of the house had risen at a surprising rate, to "almost above ground." The letter reached L'Enfant in the newly founded city of Paterson, New Jersey, where he had found employment through the efforts of his old friend and patron, Secretary of the Treasury Alexander Hamilton.

Over the past several years, while Washington and L'Enfant had been immersed in planning the Federal City, Hamilton had thrown himself into his own pet project, the preparation of an ambitious "Report on Manufactures" authorized by the House of Representatives in January of 1790. The aim was the development of a strategic plan by which the United States could increase its manufacturing capacities and render itself "independent of foreign nations for military and other essential supplies." Hamilton's lengthy report, submitted to the House on December 5, 1791, called for government support of agriculture, commercial trading, and manufacturing if a healthy economy was to be maintained.

Also included in the report was Hamilton's announcement that "a society is forming with a capital which is expected to be extended to at least a million dollars, on behalf of which measures are already in train for prosecuting on a large scale, the making and printing of cotton goods." In fact, Hamilton had encouraged a group of wealthy New Jersey businessmen to form an organization called the Society for Establishing Useful Manufactures, which purchased a six-square-mile tract of land adjacent to the Great Falls of the Passaic River in northeastern New Jersey, where their various enterprises would be headquartered. William Paterson, New Jersey's governor and a framer of the Constitution, lent significant credibility to the project by pledging $10,000 of state funds toward stock in the new company, and, as a result, the board of directors of S.U.M., as it came to be called, christened their new city Paterson.

If Washington City was to be the political capital of the new nation, Paterson would be its industrial showplace, Hamilton and the S.U.M. directors believed. And if Pierre Charles L'Enfant had been the president's choice to design the Capital on the Potomac—as Hamilton pointed out to his associates—who else should they consider to design their own new metropolis?

Surely Hamilton downplayed L'Enfant's difficulties with the commissioners of the federal district. After all, he was no stranger to the practicalities of politics, and furthermore, his opinion of the three anti-

Federalists Washington had placed in power over the District of Columbia could not have been high. And given his immersion in difficult matters far from Washington City, it is possible that he foresaw only good things ahead for L'Enfant and the development of Paterson.

The city, he wrote, would soon have facilities in place for the manufacture of wallpaper, newsprint, and book papers; cotton thread; shoes and other leather goods; straw and felt hats; woolens; pottery; and bricks. And there would be homes constructed for the people who would work in these enterprises as well. Homes, schools, streets, mills, businesses—all to be laid out in a harmonious design by Major L'Enfant, whose incomparable services could be obtained for $1,500 per annum, not inconsiderable at the time, but modest for a man of such talent.

Given Hamilton's enthusiasm, and the heady optimism surrounding the utopian enterprise itself, why would the directors of S.U.M. hesitate for even a moment? Soon L'Enfant was on board and on-site and offering interviews with local reporters. "Paterson would be a city that would far surpass anything yet seen in this country," one writer observed dutifully, following a session with L'Enfant.

Paterson was to be laid out much as Washington City had been, the whole centered atop a rise known as Colt's Hill, with a network of two-hundred-foot-wide streets and avenues cut across rather rugged terrain to strategic future locations in the new "National Manufactory." L'Enfant further envisioned a kind of superhighway, connecting Paterson to Newark and on to New York City. Yes, stone might be rising "almost above ground" down in Washington City, but in Paterson, fifty homes were under construction, and magnificent possibilities were taking shape.

WORK ON THE president's home might have been moving along quickly, and Paterson might have seemed a promising island of industry about to rise to prominence from nothing, but the Congress House had not progressed nearly so well. Jefferson's advertisement for the competition called for the design of a modest brick building containing a Senate chamber of 1,200 square feet; a representatives' chamber that could seat up to three hundred people, with an adjoining conference room of equal size; and lobbies for both legislative chambers. In addition, there were to be a dozen rooms of six hundred square feet for committee meetings. Compared with the building that housed Congress in Philadelphia—with no conference room, no lobbies, and just four meeting rooms—it was a spacious design, much more on the scale of Federal Hall in New York, though doubtless modest in comparison to what L'Enfant might have come up with had he been given the chance.

Although Jefferson had earlier opined to L'Enfant that the design for the Congress House should be informed by "one of the models of antiquity," he made no suggestion of architectural style in the competition advertisement he placed. He did, however, record his ideas on the matter in a drawing now held by the Massachusetts Historical Society, in which he proposes a "spherical temple" based on the Roman Pantheon for the housing of Congress and the Supreme Court. While ultimately impractical, the sketch conveys Jefferson's strong commitment to the symbolic importance of the building. Both he and Washington were agreed that—as no other building—the Capitol should embody the might and the philosophical principles that had carried the Union into being.

Jefferson did not formally submit his design, though it is a matter of some contention just how many submissions were presented to the commissioners by the July 15 deadline. Eighteen designs by ten different individuals survive, none of which found the favor of Washington or Jefferson. Most were submitted by self-taught amateurs; only one came from a professional architect—that of Etienne (Stephen) Hallet, a Frenchman who had come to the United States in 1790 and who had worked briefly for L'Enfant as a draftsman.

In 1791, Hallet had drawn up a rough plan for the Congress House, a neoclassical model that Jefferson had seen and approved of. The commissioners were also familiar with this earlier plan, and though they found it too elaborately "French" for their tastes, they encouraged him to simplify the document and resubmit it in the competition. (Whether or not Hallet's original plan was too ornate for American tastes, the very existence of such a plan, circulated by a L'Enfant employee long before difficulties with the architect came to a head, certainly calls into question the charge that no progress had been made on design of the principal buildings for the city.)

Washington's response to the submissions was tepid, though he did approve of certain elements of an entry that had come in from George Turner, a self-styled architect earning his living as a judge in the far-flung Northwest Territory. Turner had called for a dome above the central conference room, which, Washington opined, "would, in my opinion, give beauty & grandeur to the pile; and might be useful for the reception of a Clock—Bell &c." While the president admitted that he was no expert in such matters, he wondered if it might be possible that "such a plan as Judge Turner's be surrounded with Columns and a colonnade like that which was presented to you by Monsr. Hallet." If such a marriage could be managed, Washington added, "it would in my judgment, be a noble and desirable structure."

Meanwhile, with Ellicott still laboring dawn to dusk trying to complete the laying out of the district, the commissioners announced a second public sale for October of 1792. They hoped that this year the clear progress on the President's House and some desultory work on the Congress House site might spur more interest among the public. The October 8 event—with still no finished city plan to display— brought in about $20,000 for two squares and forty-five separate lots at an average price of $244. It was not enough to qualify the sale as a stampede, but at least the prices of individual lots had held firm, several of the purchasers were men of means from Boston and elsewhere in the Northeast, and the $5,000 gathered in down payments would help keep work going.

The pace of that work, however, even at the site of the President's House, had slowed. Skilled labor was difficult to find, and the shortage was exacerbated by the revolution in France and an economic upswing in England and on the Continent that slowed the rate of emigration to the New World. Hoban was short not only on help but also on materials. He complained to the commissioners that once the first-story stone walls of the president's home were up, he was going to need timber and planking—plenty of it, and of a decent grade: "clear plank . . . not three knots in a plank large as a man can cover with his thumb, which is the quality I . . . expect to get."

Hallet, meanwhile, had gone on to complete a second, a third, and—following a conference with the president himself—a fourth revision of his design for the Capitol. From the first, his concept presaged the shape the building would finally take, with a central domed structure flanked by two wings that would house the legislative chambers. Conscious of the building's prominence over its surroundings, he had also proposed a winding staircase leading to a viewing platform at the base of the dome, which would afford "a Magnificent prospect Surrounded with Hills that terminate the horizon very Pittoreskly [*sic*] for almost the whole Semi Circle."

Yet for all the favor that Hallet's design found with the president, the architect had failed to take into account the same practical factor that had doomed his former employer. As the commissioners put it in a letter to Washington, "In our Idea the Capitol ought in point of propriety to be on a grand Scale . . . yet under the uncertain State of our funds . . . we cannot but feel a degree of anxiety for the Event of Expensive undertakings."

While Hallet labored to bring his designs into harmony with both the tastes of the president and the budget of the commissioners, another amateur architect entered the fray, long after the official closing date of the competition. Dr. William Thornton of Tortola—who had submitted an unsuccessful design for the White House and whose previous principal claim to notoriety had to do with the creation of an organization formed to send slaves back to freedom in Africa—was well aware of the competition for the Congress House and had gone so far as to complete a drawing of a grand, Georgian-style edifice that would have outdone Hallet's in terms of expense. Perhaps wisely, he had not submitted the drawing to the commissioners.

In November of 1792, aware that no design for the Capitol had yet been selected, Thornton made his way to Philadelphia, where he met with both Washington and Jefferson and was allowed to examine a number of the losing designs. In January, having gained some sense of the practical considerations surrounding the matter, Thornton presented Washington with a revised and much simplified version of his original concept, which featured north and south wings joined by a low-domed rotunda building. Thornton also appended a large semicircular conference room on the west side of the rotunda and designed a grand entryway affording a view of the planned centerpiece beneath the dome, a statue of Washington.

How much the latter feature (along with an office for the president and the crypt for Washington's remains proposed for the basement below) may have had to do with Washington's enthusiastic response cannot be known, but on February 1, 1793, Jefferson wrote the commissioners that he and the president were recommending the Thornton design for the reasons that it was "simple, noble, beautiful, excellently distributed, and" (perhaps as important as anything else) "moderate in size." Washington affirmed his admiration for "the simplicity and beauty of the exterior, the propriety with which the apartments are distributed," and, of course, noting the "economy in the whole mass of the structure." The commissioners, happy to have the matter settled, concurred readily.

On March 11 they announced Thornton as the official winner of the competition, though in recognition of Hallet's significant service, they awarded him, the only trained architect in the competition, the sum of $500 and an additional premium equal to the value of a city lot. Furthermore, the commissioners declared, given Hallet's formal training, *he* would be placed in charge of actually constructing Thornton's winning plan.

We can only imagine what L'Enfant's reaction might have been had he received such news, but perhaps Hallet had learned a few lessons in practicality from his time under the planner's tutelage. Instead of refusing the prize out of pique, Hallet promptly sat down and drafted a *fifth* redesign of his own, which he presented to Jefferson on March 15.

History does not record whether or not Jefferson noted the almost uncanny resemblance of Hallet's new plan to Thornton's winning entry (the two differ primarily in a recess that Hallet set in the east façade), though it has been suggested that the dueling designs actually embodied the bitter political divide that had opened up between Washington and Jefferson. The historian C. M. Harris has pointed out that all of the Washington-specific features in Thornton's design—placement of the equestrian statue under the rotunda, the basement crypt, the chief executive's office—were likely added to the design at the behest of the president. And all of those features would have been particularly odious to Jefferson, who suspected Washington, Hamilton, and their Federalist cohorts of promoting a near-monarchical form of central government.

While Jefferson did not want to wage a public battle over these objectionable designs—since, after all, the Congress itself had mandated a monument to the popular leader more than a decade ago—he was determined that the very symbol of the nation's government would not turn into a monument to an individual. Thus, he engineered the elegant solution of reinvigorating Hallet's proposals and publicizing comments by the formally trained architect that Thornton's plan was full of an amateur's flaws.

Washington was apparently oblivious to Jefferson's tactics. In response to his secretary's urgings, the president authorized a July 15 meeting in Philadelphia at which a compromise was hammered out by Jefferson, Hallet, Hoban, and new construction supervisor Blodget. After a thorough excoriation of the structural faults and impracticalities to be found in the winning proposal, it was determined that Thornton's elevations for the exteriors would remain, but Hallet's building plans would guide the actual construction, with the addition of an eastward-projecting portico to balance the westward weight of the rotunda.

In a conclusion that would have found favor with L'Enfant, Hallet promptly declared himself the winner of the competition. Furthermore, at the commissioners' behest, he stayed on as superintending designer, and when the building's cornerstone was laid on September 18, his name was chiseled thereupon as its architect.

23

Plague

I F THINGS SEEMED BACK ON TRACK IN THE FEDERAL CITY,
a serious derailment loomed in Paterson, where L'Enfant found
himself once again at odds with his governing board of directors.
The issue, as was often the case in the cash-strapped new republic,
was money.

While the Society for Establishing Useful Manufactures had been
buoyed by the governor's pledge of state involvement in the enterprise
and the promises of major investors soon to join, the dollars had
flowed in far more slowly than anticipated. With a total of $60,000 in
their coffers, the directors were alarmed by some of L'Enfant's plans.
They agreed, for instance, that there was an immediate need to construct a spillway that would divert the waters of the Passaic River and
furnish power for the proposed millworks in the new city. The directors thought that something along the lines of a big ditch might do,
but L'Enfant had something more ambitious in mind. To carry this
torrent of water, he proposed constructing an elevated aqueduct that
would have made a Roman emperor's heart swell, one to be built of
stone and supported by seven miles of graceful arches.

Hamilton stepped in when the S.U.M. directors considered placing L'Enfant under the control of iron manufacturer Samuel Ogden,
giving the latter the title of project building superintendent. Hamilton protested that the notoriously opinionated Ogden would drive

L'Enfant off the project instantly. Ogden had already declared publicly that L'Enfant knew nothing whatever of waterworks, a charge that was patently false, said Hamilton. As he pointed out to the directors, L'Enfant was "what is called in France a civil Engineer . . . an Artist acquainted with Mechanics generally [but] . . . in reference to Architecture Aqueducts Canals &c &c including necessarily a knowledge of Hydraulics."

Whether or not the directors were moved by such assurances, they still doubted there were funds available for L'Enfant's aqueduct. When the architect got wind of the fact that the board might indeed endorse Ogden's pared-down spillway plan and hire him as superintendent, he dismissed all the workers under his command and informed the directors that they would have to choose between him and Ogden.

Peter Colt, who had been employed by the board as superintendent of factories for the project (and whose grandson Samuel would one day manufacture pistols in Paterson) tried to intervene with Hamilton. L'Enfant should confine "his views to those things which are essential instead of what is ornamental," Colt said.

But it was all to no avail. In early June of 1793 the directors sent L'Enfant a brief message, the substance of which can be surmised by his response: "Your extraordinary communication of the 8th instant, the shortness of which in evidencing the hurry of your proceedings of that day . . . make it Indispensable I should call for more particulars . . . wishing to know the reason which have determined you to direct all the operation in which I am concerned at Patterson to cease."

L'Enfant claimed to find his dismissal baffling, "as I know of no circumstance that could exist which can justify it." Given that he had employed fewer than half of the workers the directors had authorized and that no materials had been purchased that were not approved by the directors, L'Enfant was unable to comprehend the statement "that the funds of the society are altogether inadequate to the support of the expense of the plans." He closed his letter with the hope that further explanation would be shortly forthcoming from the board, though that was another hope destined to go wanting.

MEANWHILE, IN PHILADELPHIA, a force far more formidable than politics and money threatened to interpose itself in the governmental process. Yellow fever—aided by an unusually thriving mosquito population and a wave of political refugees from the Caribbean bearing the disease—was already sweeping through the city. The death rate soared from ten per week in July to one hundred a day by early October, as victims turned a sickly yellow before they began to vomit black clots of blood and die. No one understood how the frightful disease spread, though they suspected that filth on the streets and in the poor quarters of the city contributed to the contagion, and physicians— even the august Benjamin Rush—were helpless to alleviate the suffering of their patients. "Flee the city" was the operative advice, and with 4,000 of the city's 28,000 dead, even Washington hastened his scheduled departure for Mount Vernon by a week.

With medical knowledge so limited, some worried that the plague might sweep through the infant nation the way bubonic plague had decimated Europe. But the federal district commissioners were not among the wary. Fearful that a panic would create a ghost town where it was already difficult to attract investors and workmen, the commissioners actually took out newspaper advertisements proclaiming that Washington City was "remarkably healthy," and inviting visitors to attend the ceremony for the laying of the Capitol cornerstone and the upcoming sale of public lots.

Fortunately the new capital was spared the ravages of the plague, and though certain of the more ghoulish Washington City residents thought that Philadelphia's misfortune would only redound to the federal district's benefit, others feared that the epidemic would force Congress to move its upcoming session elsewhere—to Lancaster, perhaps, or even back to New York City. If that happened, the debate about Congress's permanent location might be reopened by die-hard opponents of the Potomac.

As it happened, nature intervened. The onset of hard frosts in

Philadelphia put an end to the mosquito hatch, and though the city had lost more than 15 percent of its population, by the beginning of November no new cases of fever were being reported. As medical men like Rush tried to pinpoint the cause and treatment of the disease and the city government pledged to build a waterworks to bring clean water in for drinking and street cleaning, those who had survived took a deep breath and soldiered on.

HOBAN, MEANWHILE, WAS forging ahead with his work on the President's House, hurrying to get as much done as possible before he would have to pack the porous stones away beneath straw and dirt for protection from the winter storms. The basement walls were completed by September, though the floors there were still packed earth. Some of the piers and vaults that would support the weight of the massive structure above had also been put in place.

Still, labor issues continued to plague Hoban's progress. He and head mason Collen Williamson—who did not get on well with his men and who considered his boss a know-nothing amateur—clashed frequently. The commissioners, who got on with Williamson no better, might have sent him packing sooner had the shortage of skilled labor not been so acute, especially in the stonecutting and stonemason trades. Their desperation led them finally to send proprietor George Walker off to Edinburgh in the late fall of 1793, with orders to recruit as many as one hundred skilled men.

Walker spread the word that workers would have expenses for their transatlantic passage advanced, and could expect to earn about $1.25 a day. While single men were preferred, the commissioners allowed that where it was absolutely necessary, they would advance the funds for a married man to bring his wife along. Although the offer was a reasonably attractive one, there was little need for a skilled workman to risk a perilous sea voyage (and the possibility of impressment by British and French warships alike) when employment was plentiful at home. In the end, Walker left Scotland having persuaded only seven men to leave the protection of their local guild houses for the unpredictable life of a federal district employee. That small group, along with Williamson, would be responsible for the building of what was to become one of the world's most notable structures.

At the same time, work was finally under way at the site of the Capitol on Jenkins Hill, a project that the commissioners hoped would lend credibility to their undertaking—and promote much-needed land sales. In fact, the desire of the commissioners to boost public confidence in the future of Washington City might have led to their interference in the design competition and to the imposition of an unacknowledged influence on both winning architects Thornton and Hallet: Pierre L'Enfant.

Thornton had enjoyed what could be called an unfair advantage by being allowed to see the unsuccessful proposals from Hallet and others before he submitted his own plans, a leg-up that led to his selection. But Hallet likewise benefited from prior knowledge of Thornton's winning design when he submitted his own, quite similar, revision that convinced the commissioners they should name him the architect for the project. Even though Jefferson's exasperation with L'Enfant was due to the planner's failure to produce plans for the public buildings—"He says he has them . . . in his *head*," Jefferson once muttered to Commissioner Stuart—the footprint of the Capitol building had in fact been drawn on the plan that was engraved and circulated following L'Enfant's dismissal. Furthermore, it was this footprint that had guided the original foundation excavations led by Roberdeau and aborted by the commissioners after their frantic winter's day gallop to the site.

The architectural historian Pamela Scott theorizes that it was actually L'Enfant's outline that influenced both Thornton and Hallet, pointing out that the Capitol's final plan resembled at least in outline the building depicted on the published city plans. According to this view, the commissioners may well have guided the selection process in such a way that would promote confidence in what was still viewed as a shaky enterprise, the plans being the only tangible suggestions of what was to come for bidders during land auctions. If the suggestion is true, it would mean that the commissioners had ended up in the thrall of a design they had once dismissed as wildly ambitious. Certainly, it is a contention that would have warmed L'Enfant's heart.

By the fall of 1793, the former district planner had quit Paterson and returned to Philadelphia, drawn by a job offer that may have contributed to his cavalier behavior with the directors of the Society of Useful Manufactures. On May 9, as relations between L'Enfant and his New Jersey employers were fraying, but well before his ultimate dismissal, the architect received a note from former U.S. superintendent of finance Robert Morris. "I had like to have stopped [work on] my house for fear of wanting money," Morris wrote from Philadelphia. He went on to dismiss rumors of any financial embarrassment, however. The real reason he had put work on hold was "for want of Major L'Enfant."

The summons must have appeared as a godsend to L'Enfant. Instead of remaining at the beck and call of a group of businessmen indifferent to the demands and the greater callings of his craft, he would enjoy the sort of relationship that had always seemed most comfortable to him: that of an artist in service to his liege. His father had served the kings of France, and—in his own eyes—L'Enfant had enjoyed the same relationship with the first president of the nation.

Morris, a confidant of Alexander Hamilton and a wealthy trader from Philadelphia who was a central figure in securing the financing to support the Revolutionary War, had amassed the largest private fortune in that city and wanted to build a house that would advertise the fact. When L'Enfant remarked to Morris at a dinner party that he could build such a house for $60,000, Morris did not blink. He owned a number of properties in the city, including the house in which the president was staying, and Morris reckoned he could raise that much and $20,000 more by selling his holdings. The letter he sent along to L'Enfant on May 9 confirmed the deal.

"This note pursuant to previous invitation caused me to quit the Paterson business," L'Enfant wrote, and soon he was out of New Jersey and hard at work on a mighty marble and red-brick mansion at Eighth and Chestnut streets in Philadelphia. Though the building's facing was typical for an edifice of prominence in the city, L'Enfant added a mansard roof constructed of iron plates, perhaps the first such instance in the United States, and soon the city was abuzz with word of the project, even drawing noted artist William Birch to compose a view of admiring gentry watching the building's progress.

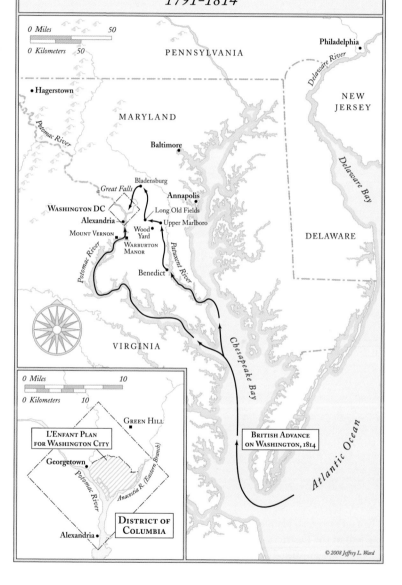

WASHINGTON ON THE POTOWMACK
1791–1814

0 Miles 50
0 Kilometers 50

PENNSYLVANIA

Philadelphia

Delaware River

NEW JERSEY

• Hagerstown

Potomac River

MARYLAND

Baltimore

Delaware Bay

Bladensburg
Great Falls
WASHINGTON DC
Annapolis
Long Old Fields
Alexandria
Upper Marlboro
MOUNT VERNON
Wood Yard
WARBURTON MANOR
Patuxent River

DELAWARE

Benedict

Potomac River

VIRGINIA

Chesapeake Bay

BRITISH ADVANCE ON WASHINGTON, 1814

Atlantic Ocean

0 Miles 10
0 Kilometers 10

GREEN HILL

L'ENFANT PLAN FOR WASHINGTON CITY

Georgetown

Anacostia R. (Eastern Branch)

Potomac River

DISTRICT OF COLUMBIA

Alexandria •

© 2008 Jeffrey L. Ward

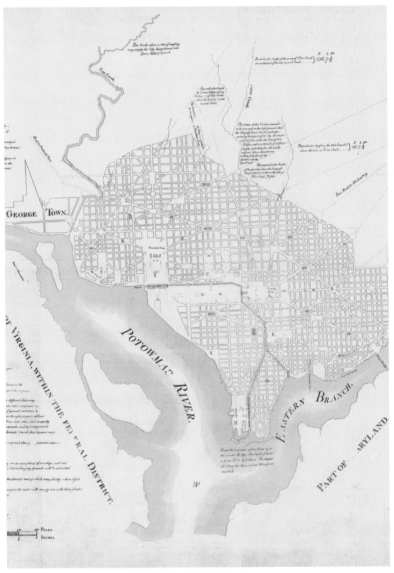

L'Enfant's original plan for the city of Washington, D.C., covered about one half of the District's 100 square miles. Despite the controversy his elaborate design stirred in the nascent republic, history has borne out the validity of the planner's vision. *Library of Congress, Geography and Map Division*

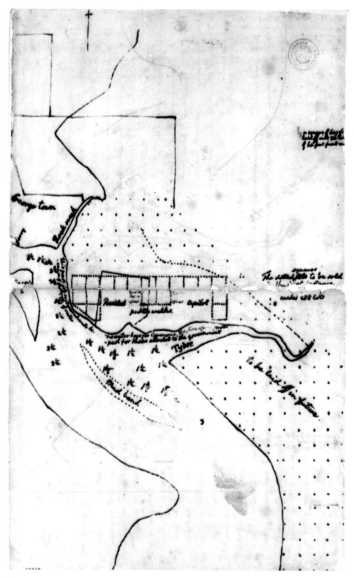

In stark contrast to L'Enfant's concept of a grand capital that would embody a new "empire," Jefferson's modest plan for a Federal City, which he sketched out in March of 1791, consisted of a few square blocks hugging the banks of the Potomac—with no mention of a memorial to the first president. *Thomas Jefferson Papers, Library of Congress, Manuscript Division*

The only authenticated likeness of Pierre Charles L'Enfant to survive is this silhouette executed by New Jersey artist Sara DeHart circa 1785. Such profiles, which predate the advent of photography in the 1840s, were the snapshots of their day. *Courtesy U.S. Department of State*

This conjectural portrait of L'Enfant was created by Colorado-based artist Bryan Leister in 1990, based on the DeHart silhouette as well as a contemporary portrait of L'Enfant's father. *Bryan Leister and the Historical Society of Washington, D.C.*

L'Enfant's Arlington Cemetery tomb, engraved with an image of his "Grand Plan," provides a fitting vantage point for a sweeping view of contemporary Washington, D.C. *Library of Congress, Prints and Photographs Division*

Below: This 1790 engraving by Amos Doolittle of New York's Federal Hall—the first U.S. Capitol building—conveys something of L'Enfant's vision for a new American architecture. The last known public building that the architect and planner saw to completion, it was razed in 1812. *Library of Congress, Prints and Photographs Division*

Above: The insignia of the Society of the Cincinnati, designed by L'Enfant in 1783 for French and American officers who served at least three years in the Continental Army or Navy. *Society of the Cincinnati, Washington, D.C.*

William Birch's 1800 engraving of the never-finished Philadelphia home immortalized in local lore as "Morris's Folly" gives an inkling of L'Enfant's original, if extravagant, architectural notions. Robert Morris was once America's richest man. *Independence National Historic Park*

The famed portrait of Washington saved from fire by Dolley Madison in 1814 still hangs in the East Room of the White House and is generally credited to Gilbert Stuart circa 1797. It is the last in a series of four similar renderings, known as the Lansdowne paintings, though its authenticity has been challenged by some art historians. *White House Historical Association (White House Collection)*

This so-called "Edgehill" portrait of Jefferson was a favorite of the president and his family. Rendered by Gilbert Stuart in 1805, it derives its designation from the family estate where it was hung for many years. Though it has its own murky provenance, the portrait has become the prototype for the contemporary image of its subject. *Monticello/Thomas Jefferson Foundation, Inc.*

This 1931 oil by Garnet W. Jex depicts a vivid if fanciful gathering in which Commissioners David Stuart, Thomas Johnson, and Daniel Carroll (at left) convene with Capitol architect William Thornton, planner Pierre L'Enfant, George Washington, Andrew Ellicott, and (at far right) the often-overlooked astronomer and surveyor's assistant Benjamin Banneker, to lay out the future capital city. *The George Washington University, 2002; George Washington University Permanent Collection, Courtesy of the Luther Brady Art Gallery*

This engraving, executed in 1816 by Benjamin Latrobe, portrays a still-bucolic capital, with the designer's just-completed St. John's Episcopal Church (the "Church of the Presidents," at today's 16th and H Streets) in the foreground, looking southward toward a White House that still shows the effects of the British assault. *Library of Congress, Prints and Photographs Division*

Though it takes some liberties with geography, this 1814 woodcut published in London shortly after the assault on Washington, D.C., provided what one presumes was a stirring collage of destruction for its pre-daguerreotype audience. A burning "Presidential Palace" is depicted in the upper-right center, with the "Senate House" ablaze just below and to the left. *Library of Congress, Prints and Photographs Division*

Flyglarna of Capitolen i Washington år 1819.

This Swedish 1824 aquatint engraving, probably by Carl Frederik Axrell, offers a somewhat more photographic depiction of the aftermath of the destruction of the Capitol—the Senate chamber completely gutted, the roof of the House damaged, the temporary central section obliterated altogether. *From the collection of U.S. Rep. John L. Mica*

24

No Match for the Rogues

WHILE L'ENFANT MOVED AHEAD ON THE MORRIS house in Philadelphia, difficulty and controversy remained the order of the day in Washington City. The labor shortage and the cold and rainy winter weather stalled significant work on the president's home through the end of 1794 and early 1795; furthermore, Hallet and Thornton found themselves locked in combat over just whose concept of the Capitol was going to take shape atop Jenkins Hill.

In September, Washington exacerbated matters by appointing Thornton to the District Commission, replacing David Stuart. It might have seemed an unusual miscalculation on the part of the president, or perhaps evidence that—with the winding down of a second term that he had not especially desired in the first place—he was beginning to tire of the endless balancing of fragile egos on the district grounds. But the likely truth is that after finally finding time to inspect the progress on the Capitol foundations, Washington realized the extent of Jefferson's manipulation of the design competition for his own political ends. The office of the president, set just off the conference room chambers in Thornton's original plan, had been relegated to the distant reaches of the east portico in the Hallet design that Jefferson sanctioned. And the ceremonial rotunda that would house the glorious equestrian statue was nowhere to be found.

The president's response constitutes one of the more adroit parries in the annals of early U.S. politics. There would be no public confrontation between chief executive and secretary of state, no embarrassing call for the restoration of architectural amenities more pleasing to a president's pride, no muttering asides about the lack of loyalty in one's own cabinet. No, there would simply be a new appointment to the Board of Commissioners. And could the fact that this new member happened to be William Thornton be a matter of mere coincidence?

With Thornton now supervising the man who had been hired as superintendent of construction for their joint design of the Capitol, it was not long before matters came to a head. On November 15, Hallet was formally dismissed, because, as Thornton wrote, "he had altered the intended Dome in the center." Hallet stayed on, though, until early the following year, when James Hoban, still busy at the president's home, took over as acting architect. A permanent successor—or one intended to be so—was hired in October of 1795.

Thirty-two-year-old George Hadfield, who had been trained at the Royal Academy in London, would survive for three years as the supervisor at the Capitol, though his inexperience led him into political missteps almost immediately. He suggested lowering the whole building by half a story, eliminating the projecting basement. He also wanted to diminish the prominent eastward-facing portico that Thornton had designed, and even went so far as to suggest that the north and south wings of the building be joined by an unadorned cube, topped with a low, saucerlike dome that would spread almost to the edges of that central structure. Although these all might have been reasonable suggestions, they not only diverged significantly from the original designs, but seemed to diminish the grandeur of the enterprise.

As Benjamin Latrobe, Hadfield's eventual successor, would one day point out, this young architect was motivated primarily by good taste and impeccable training, qualities that might have served him well in another, less politically fraught situation. "Too young to possess experience and educated more in the room of design, than in the practical execution of great works," Latrobe wrote in his journal, "he was no match for the rogues then employed in the construction of the public buildings, or for the charlatans of architecture who had designed them." As a result, Hadfield "lost the most precious period of his life, and loiters here, ruined in fortune, in temper, and in reputation. Nor will his irritable pride and neglected studies ever permit him to take the station in the Art, which his elegant taste, and excellent talents ought to have obtained."

IRRITABLE PRIDE AND temper were not confined to the architects of Washington City. In Philadelphia, those once-sanguine relations between P. Charles L'Enfant and his newfound patron were rapidly deteriorating as well. On September 24, 1795, more than two years after L'Enfant had left Paterson, Morris was writing the architect to explain why he was feeling more than a bit impatient for the completion of his home. "My sole motive for being urgent proceeds from an anxiety to get a roof over the West Wing of the House," Morris said. "I am now paying about [$5,000] p. ann. Rent, and having sold the House I live in, the owner may want it before I have a place to go. You gave me assurance six weeks ago that the House should be covered this Fall. If I am to pay, I am entitled to every information I may think proper to ask, and I have an unquestionable right to expedite my building and lessen my expense if I choose to do so."

He had made up his mind, Morris declared. "I am therefore determined to have the Roof put on the West Wing as early this Fall as possible." And furthermore, as for all that marble L'Enfant had talked him into, "an inclination to indulge your genius induced me to permit so much of it." However, Morris pointed out, "had you executed my intentions instead of your own, my family would now have inhabited the House instead of being liable to be turned out of Doors."

Morris was willing to be reasonable, though L'Enfant was not to misunderstand the urgency of this communication: "After all, I prefer that . . . the whole building should go on under your directions but with this proviso, that you will positively have it covered this Fall . . . if you agree, follow it up & get the thing done."

But if Morris had visions of a chastened L'Enfant folding up his letter with a tearful vow to set things right, he was bound to be disappointed. Indeed, in the architect's mind this matter had already been settled the very day before, when a blustering Morris had appeared at the building site, demanding that the house be covered up before wintertime. When all in attendance had pointed out to Morris that such a thing was not possible, the owner then insisted that at least the west wing be secured. At which point the major had explained patiently that without the brick facing in place, that too would be impossible. And, while it was regrettable that the installation of the brick facing could not be completed until the marble window frames were in place—well, he and Morris had long ago agreed that such a house as the banker had in mind demanded accoutrements of the greatest distinction. An undertaking of this magnitude would have to be done properly, or it should not be done at all.

Morris might be forgiven his naïveté when it came to managing L'Enfant. After all, his connection to L'Enfant was through Hamilton, not Jefferson or even Washington. And given Hamilton's mild description of difficulties in the federal district, the former finance minister would have had little sense of what had actually transpired between the architect and the commissioners. As for L'Enfant's rocky relationship with the board of the Society for Establishing Useful Manufactures, Morris had stolen L'Enfant away, not gone to them seeking a recommendation.

In any event, Morris's letter clearly failed to light the intended fire under his architect. In fact, nearly a year later, in August of 1796, Morris was writing in yet another near-apoplectic frenzy upon discovering that L'Enfant had actually taken down some of the already installed facing so that *more* marble could be added to the home's façade. Such a two-step-forward, one-step-back approach was "intolerable," Morris warned. He had already been subjected to the ridicule of his friends and neighbors, and if he could not get into his house soon, the ever-mounting expenses would force him to stop work.

Still, L'Enfant was somehow able to mollify his patron, and work on the house continued into the following year. As it turned out, however, Morris's references to his diminishing financial capacities were no mere ploy. The story that L'Enfant's excess sent one of the country's richest men to the poorhouse in 1797 makes for colorful lore, but the truth is that the collapse of a land speculation scheme involving 6 million acres of land, much of it in the wilderness beyond the Appalachians, was the real cause of Morris's financial undoing.

L'Enfant had himself invested in Morris's North American Land Company and had also loaned the banker several shares of his own Bank of the United States stock. As the land venture slid toward bankruptcy, L'Enfant asked for his stock back, but Morris was unable to comply. "I am in as great need as you are," he wrote L'Enfant, on October 18, 1797, "and [am] equally desirous of acquiring relief for both [of us]." That should not take long, Morris continued, for "my endeavors shall be increasing and the moment I secure it shall be announced to you with joy and satisfaction."

The truth was that Morris's "endeavors" were about to morph into a three-year term in debtor's prison, but if it seems a stretch that he sincerely wished to maintain cordial relations with L'Enfant, a letter to an associate suggests that despite everything that had happened between the two, Morris not only honored his debt but their friendship as well: "[H]e lent me thirteen shares of bank stock disinterestedly," Morris said, "and on this point I feel the greatest anxiety that he should get the same number of shares with dividends, for want of which he has suffered grave distress." In the end, Morris signed L'Enfant's name to a lien on shares of stock he owned in a New York State land development as compensation.

Work on the Philadelphia house stopped in 1797, but it remained a point of interest. Isaac Weld, a traveler from England who passed through the city, mentioned that of all the grand houses he saw there, "the most spacious and most remarkable among them stands in

Chestnut Street, but it is not yet quite finished. . . . At present it appears a huge mass of red brick and pale blue marble, which bids defiance to simplicity and elegance . . . and stands as a monument of the increasing luxury of the city of Philadelphia."

Undoubtedly, L'Enfant would have appreciated such words. And while once again he had failed to carry out a project of magnificence to its conclusion (the unfinished house—which became known as Morris's Folly—was pulled down in 1801, leaving Birch's rendering in the city's public library as the sole tangible reminder of the enterprise), he could point out that it was hardly his fault that his patron had mismanaged his money and landed himself in a debtor's prison.

IN THE FEDERAL City, meantime, another development had taken place. In the summer of 1794, in addition to the appointment to the board of commissioners of William Thornton, who stepped in to replace a weary David Stuart, the president was also forced to replace Thomas Johnson, who had himself tired of the demands of the job and wished to return home to care for his ailing wife. Finally, mindful of the years of inertia and intrigue among the proprietors, Washington decided to replace Daniel Carroll as well, the last of the commissioners who had so tormented L'Enfant. Perhaps with a clean sweep, the pace of progress might pick up.

As Johnson's replacement, the president chose a Baltimore attorney named Gustavus Scott, and for Daniel Carroll, he named an old friend and former representative from Virginia, Alexander White—thus assuring Washington of keeping an "inside man" on the panel. Furthermore, the job was to be recognized more formally as such. Commissioners would now draw a salary of $1,600 per annum, and they would be required to live in the district so that the monthly meeting schedule could be replaced by gatherings twice a week. In this way, progress could at last be made, the president felt—and indeed he might have been right, had there been any money in the treasury to fund the work.

The hopes of the commissioners and the president had been buoyed by an agreement with the Boston merchant James Greenleaf (partnered with Robert Morris and John Nicholson of Philadelphia) for the purchase of 6,000 lots—almost 42 percent of the total—for $480,000, or eighty dollars per lot, an amount to be forthcoming in seven annual payments, at no interest. The commissioners had agreed to the terms on the condition that Greenleaf and his partners would accept a strict timetable for development of the parcels, a step that would, theoretically at least, drive up prices on what property remained in the public holdings.

Greenleaf, U.S. envoy to Holland and married to a Dutch baroness, had been successful in raising foreign capital for other major undertakings in the former colonies, and it was assumed that he would have no trouble in this instance either. However, as instability triggered by the French Revolution spread through Europe, Dutch capitalists withdrew their support. Greenleaf, who had hoped to raise $1.2 million from among his sources on the Continent, came home from his scouting trip with less than a quarter of that. As a result, the syndicate he had formed with Morris and Nicholson was unable to make its second payment on the properties, a signal that the entire enterprise had been nothing more than the sort of cynical exercise in speculation that L'Enfant had warned against from the beginning.

It was a profound blow for the president and the commissioners, who were left with no choice but to appeal to Congress for funds. In early 1796, with the concerted efforts of district commissioner and former House member Alexander White, the House and Senate took up debate on a measure that would authorize up to $300,000 in loans, all of which were to be secured by lots.

As debate raged in Philadelphia, White reported back to his colleagues in Washington City that feeling was running high in the House that a great deal of money could be saved if the commissioners would agree to drop plans for a separate building and simply convert a sizable portion of the proposed Capitol building for the use of the Supreme Court. Others from Jefferson's anti-Federalist ranks objected to the size and grandeur of the major buildings already under way. One representative from North Carolina said that he would vote in favor of any amount that was necessary to pull down what was built of the President's House and replace it with something "on a proper scale."

Finally, however, the plans for the Capitol and the House were approved and the necessary loans were authorized, with the added proviso that every expenditure of the commissioners would be rigorously reviewed by Congress. If Major L'Enfant had been dismayed by the necessity of reporting to the commissioners, the commissioners would have been similarly outraged by this new arrangement.

25

Raise High the Roof Beams

THOUGH THE VALUE OF LOTS IN WASHINGTON HAD taken a blow with the failure of Greenleaf's syndicate, some development nonetheless was under way by the spring of 1795. James Barry, a Baltimore merchant and trader, purchased a tract on the Eastern Branch and set about building a wharf. William Duncanson, another merchant who had prospered in the trade with the East Indies, laid out the site for a mansion just above Barry's site. But, generally speaking, these private efforts didn't constitute a boom.

Samuel Moodey, a British craftsman, disembarked in Alexandria about that time with a chest of tools and "one trunk, one bag wearing apparel, one hat box, [and] one bed and bedding." He wrote back to describe his new home as a veritable den of iniquity that included "cockfighting [and] horse racing, with every other species of gambling and cheating." As to the stories circulating about the Continent of a fabulous new paradise springing up on the banks of the Potomac, it was, from his perspective, spun from the same stuff as tales regarding a fountain of youth. "It is all a mere fabrication," Moodey declared, noting dryly that there were not forty houses to be found in the entire "extensive metropolis."

Work was proceeding on the President's House and on the Capitol, however. Pleased with his ability to drive a project forward, the commissioners placed James Hoban in charge of all masons at work on public projects in the city. One of the first things the architect did was to dismiss prickly master mason Collen Williamson—who was publicly anti-Irish, anti-Catholic, and above all, anti-brick. Why would anyone use such a despicable material, Williamson wanted to know, when there was a wealth of perfectly good stone available to be chiseled directly from the earth? Though Williamson protested that Hoban was nothing more than an Irish carpenter, and that next they'd be asking him to make some shoes as well, the commissioners backed their architect.

Succeeding Williamson was the Englishman George Blagden, who had been working under the Scotsman for almost three years, carrying on the process of transforming the designer's elevations of the President's House into actual walls. In the master mason's shed, Blagden created (as had Williamson before him) a makeshift table, atop which he laid a six-foot-by-six-foot paper, created from smaller sheets pasted together on a linen backing. On that sizable canvas, he would then create his own rendition of one of the walls on Hoban's blueprint using a pencil for his first draft. Every stone in the wall would be drawn and numbered, the dimensions figured down to the very thickness of the mortar joints. Once he was sure that his calculations matched up with the architect's intentions, the lines on the mason's drawing would be traced over in permanent ink, and the process of stonecutting could begin. Blagden would travel to the sandstone quarry at Aquia, inspect the blocks that had been cut from the earth, and designate each one for its eventual place in the walls, miles away. It was a practical art form, in which the mason arranges stone after stone in a painstaking, pointillist fashion, until that moment when the façade of the White House blooms into focus.

When each stone arrived at the site, it would have what is called a quarry-cut finish, its dimensions a few inches larger than the plan called for. This allowed the masons to shape the stones with precision, first gouging away the extra inches, leaving a series of coarse furrows in the stone, then "tooth tooling" the foundation and basement stones somewhat more finely, and finally flattening and sanding the "finish" stones for use in the façade walls and interiors.

Once the stones were finished and any decorative features added, they would be numbered and carted to an outdoor storage area to "cure." Not until its natural moisture had evaporated and the sandstone was sufficiently hardened to bear weight could it be lifted into its place in the giant assemblage. As any mason would point out, once all the stones had been set in place, the building would stand perfectly well on its own. Any mortar added was simply to produce a flat finish (and perhaps keep the drafts out)—by no means would the stones be "glued" together.

Washington toured the site often, and while he still found the design and its execution pleasing, he worried that some of the masons were getting carried away with their work. The soft Aquia stone allowed for relatively easy carving, and the president wrote to the commissioners they might call for restraint on all the decoration, especially on the exterior, as it was "not so much the taste now as formerly."

And while he had originally managed the affairs of the new city with a jeweler's eye for detail, as his second term wound to an end, the president began to leave more and more up to the commissioners to decide. While he understood the importance of this building, he also knew he would never live in it. And perhaps the never-ending controversy had begun to wear on him as well.

Critics, including Massachusetts representative Henry Dearborn, had suggested that since construction was moving ahead on the building relatively well, and since it was clearly far larger than any one person or couple needed as a domicile, perhaps *it* should be turned over to Congress when it was finished. Another bill was introduced to designate the president's home for use by the Supreme Court. Even the commissioners began to fret. Perhaps, they wrote Washington, they should quickly roof the president's home over, then send all hands at work there on to the Capitol, so that Congress should certainly have its home by 1800.

Washington might have been weary by this time, but he was not beaten down. The commissioners had made certain alterations to the house in the interests of economy—the stone central staircase changed to wood, the lead roof to slate, mahogany paneling on the second floor switched to pine—and he had not complained. But as to this suggestion, he was adamant. He wrote back immediately to say that both the Capitol *and* the president's home were to be ready in time for the removal of government to the Federal City: "I require it."

Another controversy had arisen that required the president's intervention. Buildings for the Departments of the Treasury and of War ought to be readied by the time of the government's removal to the Federal City, Congress determined, and certain anti-Federalists thought that the structures should be placed in close proximity to the Capitol so that representatives and senators might keep a close eye on the doings within. Washington responded by pointing out that the residents of the Congress house would be in the Federal City only periodically. It was the Chief Executive who was always *in situ*, and thus the department offices should be in close proximity to that residence.

To resolve the matter, Washington traveled to the city in October of 1796, and personally laid out the sites of the two buildings, choosing lots to the east and west of the president's home, "to which," as he wrote the commissioners, "they will appear as wings." The land Washington selected for the War and Treasury Departments had, in fact, already been set aside by L'Enfant, though he had envisioned using the space for a grander, monarchical residence there. Yet while the spectacle of the surveyor-turned-president tramping the pastures and pounding building stakes for such purposes would have likely dismayed the former planner, it was apparently enough to put an end to any indecision as to where the two departments would reside.

WITH THIS MATTER behind him, and wearying of the demands of his office, Washington resolved not to run for a third term in 1796. Shortly after the election results were in, confirming John Adams as the second president in early 1797, the commissioners diverted George Hadfield from his work on the Capitol long enough to complete designs for the two new department buildings. While they would be constructed of red brick, they featured sandstone porticoes and other stone trimmings that would connect them visually to Hoban's design for the president's home. The foundations for the two buildings would be laid out as soon as possible, the commissioners told Washington, but they were quick to assure him that no substantive effort would be directed there until the president's home had been essentially finished.

Meanwhile, Commissioner White had delivered a report to Congress detailing progress on the Capitol. As of March 11, 1796, the foundation of the building was completed. The walls of the north wing, which was considered large enough to accommodate both houses of Congress temporarily, had begun to rise, averaging three and one-half feet in height, and White estimated that it would take about $75,000 to bring that wing to completion. The south and central sections of the building would rise in due time, White said, adding that the final design of a central dome had still not been settled. Even without that expense, White estimated that it would take yet another $400,000 to finish the building, though he stopped short of asking for an actual appropriation.

Work on the north wing of the Capitol continued at a relatively brisk pace throughout the remainder of the 1796 building season, with carpenters cutting the floor joists and rafters for placement as soon as the mortar in the walls had dried. By the end of the year the walls had risen to the bottom of the second-story windows, and prospects looked good for "drying in" (adding the roof and windows) during the following year.

On March 4, Federalist John Adams, who had served as Washington's vice president, was inaugurated as the second President of the United States amid deteriorating relations with the country's formerly staunch ally, France. Because of unresolved quirks in the Electoral College voting system, Adams's Democratic-Republican opponent,

Thomas Jefferson, received the second-highest number of votes cast by the electors and thus was named vice president, instead of Adams's running mate, Thomas Pinckney.

There was considerable acrimony between Adams and Jefferson, of course: among other things, Federalists blamed Jefferson and his fellow Republicans for exacerbating the mounting disarray in France—even that great patriot Lafayette now languished in a French prison, accused of treason by zealots; on the other hand, Republicans accused Federalists of a secret alliance with the archfiend Great Britain. To prove it, said they, took only a glance at the spineless Jay Treaty, which granted their former oppressors most-favored-nation status without addressing such lingering outrages as the continued and regular impressments of American sailors into the Royal Navy.

Much of all that was lost on the American public, however, who simply mourned the departure of their beloved general, the only democratic leader they had ever known. Washington drafted his farewell address in the form of a public letter that decried the rise of partisan politics, which had so bedeviled the union in its early years, and urged that the United States restrain itself most assiduously from any entanglements with foreign nations. "Every day the increasing weight of years admonishes me more and more that the shade of retirement is as necessary to me as it will be welcome," Washington began, though concern for the welfare of the country prompted him not to depart without a reminder that the goal was union above all else—the interests of North and South, Atlantic and Western were one.

Just as important was the principle of neutrality, said Washington: "The great rule of conduct for us in regard to foreign nations is, in extending our commercial relations to have with them as little political connection as possible. So far as we have already formed engagements let them be fulfilled with perfect good faith. Here let us stop."

The address, which went on to explain why the interests of Europe and the United States were so divergent, stirred its audience so deeply that for years it was read annually in both houses of Congress. It was reprinted in children's textbooks, woven into tapestries, engraved on jewelry, and cited as the final word on every American political debate that hinged in the slightest on questions of foreign entanglement. The legacy of this thinking was powerful enough to doom the League of Nations following the First World War and complicate the formation of the United Nations in the wake of the Second. In fact, the United States did not sign a treaty of foreign alliance until the NATO agreement of 1949.

The president closed with the admission that he had surely made mistakes in the course of a forty-five-year career as a public servant, but noted that none had been intentional, and prayed that he might be forgiven for any "incompetent abilities." In the end, he said, he was looking forward to his retirement and to "the sweet enjoyment of partaking in the midst of my fellow-citizens the benign influence of good laws under a free government—the ever-favorite object of my heart, and the happy reward, as I trust, of our mutual cares, labors, and dangers."

On March 14, then, the former president and his wife passed through Washington City on their way home to Mount Vernon, accompanied by seventeen-year-old George Washington Lafayette, the son of the French general, whom they had taken in during his parents' imprisonment. The *Washington Gazette* reported the next day that supporters had arranged a private banquet near the Capitol to honor the former Chief Executive, after which the party proceeded down Pennsylvania Avenue on a chill and blustery day to view the status of the president's home.

The roof beams were in place on that day, but still uncovered, the windows gaping for want of glass and frame. Crowds swarmed the grounds and clambered atop unfinished walls to catch a glimpse of the man who had freed them from foreign rule and created a nation they could call their own. James Hoban presided over the ceremony as the Washington Artillery Company fired a sixteen-gun salute.

Who can say what thoughts ran through Washington's mind as echoes of the gunfire drifted away and the cheers rattled off the rough walls of the half-done residence before him? Great divisions threatened the fragile union, and his central place in the national drama was gone. Yet he had willed that unfinished home into being—along with the bits of a city around it—as surely as his actions had helped galvanized a disparate band of colonies into a republic.

He would never live in the president's home, and he would never see the rugged landscape about him transformed into the magnificent cityscape that he and that impossible Frenchman L'Enfant had long ago envisioned. But surely he understood that he had started something here. And how could that have failed to give him comfort as he and his wife turned to make their way toward home?

26

Race to the Finish

ITH WASHINGTON GONE, MUCH OF THE FORCE driving development within the Federal City went with him. Adams was largely indifferent to the progress on the White House, and a shortage of cash plagued both its development and that of the Capitol as well.

Still, slate was delivered for the roof of the President's House in 1797, and, with stone and brick work largely completed, roofers installed it during the summer of 1798. Floors were laid and the interior walls erected at about the same time, though the finish carpentry would continue up to the point when Abigail Adams came bustling through the front door in 1800.

In accordance with the plan that they had not dared to carry out with George Washington watching over them, the commissioners shifted teams of workmen off the President's House and on to other projects, and managed to complete the principal construction of the Treasury Building by July of 1798. When the stonecutters still on the payroll at the President's House objected to a cut in their salaries, the commissioners were only too happy to trim the budget further and fired the lot of them.

In short order, the commissioners turned their attention to work at the Capitol, and after determining that progress was moving too slowly, they dismissed George Hadfield, the young architect who had come over from England to replace Hallet back in 1795. Hadfield was certainly a young man of taste, the commissioners allowed in a letter of explanation to President Adams, but he was "deficient in practical knowledge of architecture." In the aftermath of Hadfield's dismissal, James Hoban was given a hefty raise and authority over the construction of the Capitol, in addition to his duties at the President's House. Moreover, with Washington out of the picture, Hoban was not to labor under any misconception: priority number one was the completion of the north wing of the Capitol.

Fortunately, Hoban was not only the perfect company man, but an able one as well. He dashed back and forth from the Capitol to the president's home to the Treasury Building, goading his workmen forward on all the projects, spurred by a deadline that seemed to have shrunk too rapidly from ten long years down to two.

By the end of the building season of 1798, Hoban reported to the commissioners that the roof of the Capitol had been finished and its gutters in place and sealed. Most of the ceiling and flooring joists were in place, and during the following season the planks could be laid and the interior walls plastered. Plenty of clear pine was on hand for flooring and interior trim, but Hoban asked for—and received—the commissioners' approval to order sufficient lath and plaster, including 1,000 bushels of hog and horse hair (at a cost of $279), to help bind the coatings for the walls and ceilings.

Hoban's relationship with his employers, though largely positive, was not without incident. Stirred by the complaints of a group of workmen, who might well have been organized by the disgruntled mason Collen Williamson, the commissioners called a hearing toward the end of the 1798 building season to consider charges that, among other things, Hoban had forced his men to serve in the Washington Artillery as a condition of their employment and that he had often hired vagrants and "Irish vagabonds" while plenty of skilled workmen were going unemployed.

Taking a page out of L'Enfant's book, Hoban wrote the commissioners rather archly that the charges were not worth the breath it would take to repudiate them, and that furthermore the commissioners were ill-advised in calling the hearing in the first place. Given the history between the commission and its primary employees, Hoban might well have let the letter lay awhile before thrusting it into the post.

In short order the commissioners reminded him of the natural order of things in Washington City: "Your letter to the board . . . made up of very indecent & even impudent language, & such as they are by no means disposed to suffer from you or any other person . . . it will give us much pleasure to find you able to clear up every doubt & to prove that your conduct has been as economical & careful as we believe it to have been," they informed him. A contrite Hoban complied, and ultimately the commissioners let bygones be bygones, even going so far as to reward him with a new house for him and his bride in celebration of his wedding.

By April of 1799, John Kearney, a contractor from Baltimore, had set his crews to work applying twenty tons of plaster to the interior walls and ceilings of the Capitol building, a laborious process that was ameliorated somewhat when the commissioners allotted each workman a half-pint of whiskey each day. Down Pennsylvania Avenue, plaster was also being boiled up at the president's home, where a man named Smallwood watched over the mixing of great vats of pulverized gypsum, animal hair, and water until the stew reached its proper pasty consistency.

As the primary contours of the Capitol's interior took shape, Hoban realized that he had no detailed drawings of its finish, including the design of staircases and the decoration of its rooms. When he contacted William Thornton, co-winner of the design competition with the long-departed Hallet, Thornton responded by saying that such details were hardly within his purview. He would be happy to send along some verbal descriptions of what might do, but surely Hoban would understand that any drawings would be his own responsibility. Whether he "understood" or not, it was the last time Hoban would ask Thornton for any drafting help.

The doctor did provide a few suggestions for Hoban to consider, however. He had run across some amazing new doodads being manufactured by a man named George Andrews in Baltimore: ready-made architectural ornaments, molded of plaster and reinforced with wire. These prefabricated moldings no doubt were beneath the contempt of the master carpenters and stone carvers whose work they were intended to supplant, but given the press of time and the ever-meager state of the treasury, the commissioners quickly authorized Hoban and Thornton to do business with Andrews.

They also hired another plasterer named Densley, and set him at work troweling the walls of the president's home as quickly as Mr. Smallwood could boil up his mix. Densley started in the basement, but soon the commissioners realigned their priorities—with the president due to arrive in little more than a year, the basement walls could wait. Densley was ordered up to the main parlors, and by fall the first-floor walls were finished, with the exception of the great East Room. On to the upstairs private rooms Densley marched, though there, the commissioners ordered, he was to confine himself to the half of the chambers that might absolutely be required by fall of 1800. The other rooms, along with the attic, could simply wait.

As fall approached, the basement walls were whitewashed and the wood trim was painted white, its hallways paved with orange brick tiles. Some of the windows in the building held glass, while others stood open to the elements. Two tons of white lead were purchased to form the base for paint, and brass and gilded knobs, hinges, and pulls came down by the boxload from merchants in Baltimore. A debate began among the commissioners on whether French wallpaper (the gold standard) or its British counterpart (serviceable but inferior) should be used to cover the most important rooms in the home.

By August 11, chief carpenter William Lovell had driven his last nail, and the final coats of whitewash had been added to the building's façade. Given its solitary aspect (since the commissioners had banned the construction of any ancillary outbuildings) and its prominence atop the gentle rise overlooking the Potomac, it is likely that the building picked up its now-mythic epithet almost immediately, though it would be more than a decade before it found its way into print, and even longer still before the term took on its politically charged connotations. Still, who can doubt that residents would have referred to their new city's greatest landmark with the simplest description: "the president's white house"?

As for the building's intended tenant, John Adams had long professed no interest in taking up residence there. He claimed he would as soon rent quarters in a row house close to the Capitol. But then there came a development that in all likelihood changed his mind.

On Thursday, December 12, 1799, the retired George Washington was caught in a sleet storm as he rode about the farms of his Mount Vernon estate. The following day he complained of a sore throat to his faithful secretary Tobias Lear, who suggested he take something for it before he went to bed.

"No," Washington replied. "You know I never take anything for a cold. Let it go as it came."

That night the former president woke his wife to tell her he was feeling poorly indeed. She did her best to comfort him, but by Saturday morning he could barely speak. She sent for Lear and explained that the president wished to be bled, in hopes that it might do some good. Lear in turn sent for one of the plantation overseers, a man named Rawlins who was experienced in the process, and he also sent another rider to Alexandria to fetch Dr. James Craik, the president's longtime physician.

Rawlins approached his task gingerly, making an incision that the president deemed insufficient. "The orifice is not big enough," he told Lear, but the blood poured freely. "More, more," Washington called to Lear, until they had taken nearly a half a pint.

Dr. Craik arrived shortly after, and, after a brief examination of the president, was joined by two other physicians whom Craik considered specialists. Ointments were applied to Washington's throat, more blood was drawn, potions poured down his throat that choked and nearly suffocated him. After some hours of this, the former president called Dr. Craik to his bedside to deliver his own prognosis.

"Doctor," he said, gripping Craik's hand, "I die hard, but I am not afraid to go."

Craik did not patronize his patient. He and his associates applied soothing wheat poultices to the president's hands and feet, then Craik sat down by the fire to wrestle with his grief.

During the evening, Lear went often to Washington's side, to bathe his face, turn him, or raise him to a more comfortable position. When Washington protested that he was surely being too great a trouble, Lear replied that his only wish was to give him ease.

"Well, it is a debt we must pay each other," Washington managed. "I hope when you want aid of this kind you will find it."

About ten o'clock that evening, Washington called Lear to his bedside to let him know that it was time. He asked his secretary that he be buried decently, then added, "Do not let my body be put into the vault in less than three days after I am dead."

Lear, unable to speak, simply nodded.

"Do you understand me?" Washington demanded.

Lear met his gaze, finally. "Yes."

"'Tis well," Washington replied. And that was all.

THERE WAS NO removal of Washington's body to what he doggedly called, up to the last days of his life, the Federal City. Nor any grand processional down Pennsylvania Avenue. No entombment in a marble crypt beneath a Capitol's soaring dome. George Washington was laid to rest at Mount Vernon, and despite periodic talk of grander graves, his body has remained there ever since.

Something of that great loss seems to have influenced John Adams's feelings about the president's home. In the summer of 1800, mindful of the nation's vast sorrow, Adams decided to make a trip down to Washington, just to have a look at the house that Washington intended for his successors.

The coach in which he rode with his personal secretary, William Shaw, tossed over the rutted roads like a rudderless boat in rapids.

When they finally pulled up before the White House, workers explained somewhat apologetically that they would have to enter through the basement.

Inside, Adams found Densley hard at work with his plasterer's trowel while assistants hurriedly glued the prefabricated ornaments to doorframes and mantels. When Adams took exception to some of the figurines applied on one of the mantelpieces, Hoban winced inwardly, wondering if all of those clever time- and money-saving decorations would have to go in favor of articles of old-fashioned American craftsmanship.

But craftsmanship was not the issue at all. Adams objected only to the fact that some of those molded cherubs were a little too nude. Naked statuary might pass muster in Paris, but it was hardly appropriate for the U.S. president's home, not so far as John Adams was concerned.

Nonetheless, though doors still leaned against walls, awaiting their hinges and latches to be hung, and though freshly plastered walls would have to cure before the favored French wallpaper might be applied, Adams had apparently bought into the idea that he would live in this house after all, and not in some row house off Jenkins Hill.

Other than the replacement of those cherubs, the second president asked only two things of Hoban: the addition of bells to call servants about the vast reaches of a house where a carriage and four could easily pass down the main halls; and—for the outside—the addition of a vegetable garden. For this practical-minded New Englander, the concept of a home without a vegetable garden was as impractical as a ship without its canvas sails.

The commissioners must have been beside themselves to have gotten off so easily. They wrote off quickly in search of cord-, crank-, and bell-hangers. And Dr. Thornton himself brought hoe and spade to the northeast side of the White House, where he began turning up earth for a garden at once.

Adams, meanwhile, had issued the executive order for all departments to prepare for a removal to Washington City as soon as possible following the final Philadelphia session on May 14, 1800. All the records of the government would have to be packed and shipped, as would the furniture in the president's domicile, the Congress Hall, and the ancillary government offices. Nor could the employees themselves—along with their families and their worldly goods—be forgotten.

According to a tally made by the historian Pamela Scott in an article called "Temporary Inconveniences and Privations," the moving of the Treasury Department, with its six divisions and sixty-nine employees, cost $6,157.05 for staff expenses and $2,222.58 for office furniture and records. Congress had twelve staff members at the time, and the bill to move them was a bit more than $1,000, or about half of what it took to relocate their counterparts in the Senate. The grand total for the entire move was just short of $79,000.

Primary responsibility for resituating all the records and preparing all the offices as well as the White House and the Capitol fell upon a man named Thomas Claxton, doorkeeper of the House of Representatives, who arrived in Washington on May 24 with a staff of six. They would labor day and night to prepare for the move, plagued by the heat, the unpaved streets, and the lack of the most basic supplies in the still-remote outpost.

At the Capitol, the builders' preparations for the arrival of the government were frenzied as well. Though a ground-floor chamber had been completed for the use of the Senate and a slightly smaller room on the second floor prepared for the House, a serious winter storm had damaged the building's new roof and gutters, and the resulting leaks caused much of the newly applied plaster to fall. While repairs were made, workmen warned that painting and papering of those portions would have to wait for the better part of a year to allow for proper curing. Latches and locks for many doors were still missing, and by August, seventy boxes of window glass were still awaiting arrival from the manufacturer in Boston.

To permit some semblance of normal travel between the White House and the Capitol, Congress made a special $10,000 allocation to the commissioners for the paving of sidewalks along Pennsylvania Avenue. And not to be overlooked was the matter of the congressional privy adjacent to the Capitol: at seventy feet long, eight feet wide, and with a roof thirteen feet high, it was completed at the beginning of October, say commissioners' records, at a cost of $324. The architect of this structure was not named.

27

A Residence Not to Be Changed

O N NOVEMBER 1, 1800, PRESIDENT JOHN ADAMS RE-
turned to Washington City with surprisingly little fanfare.
According to a note in her diary, the wife of Dr. Thornton
was shopping at a silversmith's with her mother when she glanced
out a window to see "the President, with his Secretary Mr. Shaw,
passed bye in his Chariot & four, no retinue only one Servant on
horseback."

Indeed, Adams would take possession of the president's home on
the very schedule that Congress had stipulated ten years before,
though a few details needed attending to. Thornton's kitchen garden
had been planted and in fact harvested, but piles of rubble were still
strewn about the weed-choked grounds. There was a wooden walkway
bridging a gully in front of the north entrance, and on the south side
of the building, a temporary wooden balcony had been hastily thrown
up outside the windows of the Oval Room where one day a spacious
porch would overlook the Potomac in the distance.

Inside, only half of the thirty-six rooms had been completed, and
work continued on the two main staircases, leaving only the narrow
service steps to connect the basement and the two main floors. The
oval room had acquired its fine new wallpaper, but whether it would
stick was a matter of conjecture. A workman kept the fireplaces in the

building going day and night in hopes of hastening the curing process in the rooms that had received their plaster.

Claxton and his men had placed the furniture that had arrived from the president's home in Philadelphia, but the few worn and mismatched sticks looked lost and forlorn in their vast new surroundings. The only item that truly measured up was the sole work of art to be found in the home, the impressive, full-length portrait of George Washington executed by Gilbert Stuart in Philadelphia in 1797. Aside from the likeness that adorns the U.S. one-dollar bill, the painting is perhaps the best known of the more than 106 portraits that the artist executed of his most famous subject, and it attracted the general approbation of the day for its size and regal connotations, if nothing else.

Though many who beheld the painting exclaimed that it was the next thing to being in the same room with the man himself, Dr. Thornton sniffed that it did not look like Washington at all. Stuart reported that Washington had been an unenthusiastic model from the beginning, and that at the first instant of every sitting, "an apathy seemed to seize him, and a vacuity spread over his countenance, most appalling to paint."

Most vexing, however, was the fact that those cherubim were still flouting their nakedness on the presidential mantelpieces. The very day that Adams moved in, the appalled commissioners wrote George Andrews in Baltimore that he was to come down to Washington at once and remove every figure in the President's House "intended to represent man or beast." He could replace the offending items with urns or rosettes or any other feature he wished, they told him, but the naked angels would have to go.

The concern of the commissioners apparently mollified Adams. He unpacked his bags, spent the remainder of the day receiving visitors, and at nightfall wound his way up the servants' staircase to his upstairs chambers by candlelight—presumably averting his gaze from the mantelpiece all the while. The following morning he sat down to pen that famous benediction to his wife, praying that "none but honest and wise men" would ever follow in his footsteps.

IN THE DAYS following Adams's arrival, members of the House and Senate made their way to Washington, scrambling to find quarters in the few completed buildings in the city, or in Georgetown, before the Congress convened in the finally readied north wing of the Capitol building on November 17. As Treasury Secretary Oliver Wolcott wrote to his wife, "I do not perceive how the members of Congress can possibly secure lodgings, unless they will consent to live like scholars in a college or monks in a monastery, crowded ten or twenty in one house."

There were plenty of complaints that echoed Abigail Adams's difficulty in even finding the city: "Having lost my way in the woods on Saturday in going from Baltimore, we took the road to Frederick and got nine miles out of our road . . . wandering more than two hours in the woods in different paths, holding down & breaking bows of trees which we could not pass."

But some of the grumbling in the new city was balanced by relief at having dodged the yellow fever epidemic that had ravaged Philadelphia. And with Washington's passing still fresh in the communal memory, his passion for the place seemed to hang palpably in the air, auguring against the usual rancor directed at the site on the Potomac. On November 22, Adams appeared before a joint session of Congress, speaking enthusiastically of "a residence not to be changed." While he admitted to privations in the new city, they were only temporary, Adams asserted, adding a reminder to his colleagues of the importance of this place: "May this Territory be the residence of virtue and happiness!" he exhorted, asking that the wisdom and magnanimity that characterized the man for whom the city was named be ever venerated, and adding the hope that "here, and throughout our country, may simple manners, pure morals and true religion, flourish forever."

That language might have seemed a bit overblown to some in the audience who would have more likely seconded Mrs. Adams's sentiments to her sister. Washington was isolated and underdeveloped, she said, and as for neighboring Georgetown, she found it "the very dirtiest Hole I ever saw for a place of any trace, or respectability of inhabitants. It is only one mile from me but a quagmire after every rain."

They were living nearly two miles away from the Capitol, she told Mary Cranch, and while she allowed that her new home had indeed been "built for the ages to come," she longed for a simpler, more comfortable abode. "I had much rather live in the house at Philadelphia," she told her sister. "Not one room or chamber is finished of the whole. It is habitable by fires in every part, thirteen of which we obliged to keep daily, or sleep in wet and damp places."

Of course, the Adamses' stay in the president's home was to be brief. Beset with a popular backlash against the Alien and Sedition Acts (which the Federalist Party had pushed through Congress in 1798 in an attempt to stem the tide of pro-Republican Irish and French immigration), Adams and his running mate, Charles Pinckney of South Carolina, were defeated in the popular election by Thomas Jefferson and Aaron Burr. The victory was made all the more significant by Jefferson's dear-to-agrarians platform, in which he argued eloquently against anything smacking of monarchy, and for a return to a "simple and frugal" federal government.

The final outcome of the election was delayed, however, when the Electoral College reached a deadlock on February 11, 1801, between Jefferson and his running mate, Burr. The Republicans had intended for one of their electors to vote for Jefferson but not for Burr, giving Jefferson the majority of votes, but the plan was bungled and the vote was tied. According to law, the winner of the most electoral votes would be named president, with the runner-up becoming vice president, regardless of the proclaimed aspirations of each during the election itself. Now the House of Representatives would have to break the tie.

Debate was acrimonious, with most Federalists in the House casting their votes against Jefferson more than for the controversial Burr, whose election to the New York Senate delegation in 1791 had displaced Alexander Hamilton's father-in-law, a staunch Federalist. Representatives of the sixteen states (Tennessee had joined the Union in

1796) voted en bloc, with a majority of nine required to decide the matter. Thirty-five votes were taken between February 11 and 17, with none producing a majority, until Alexander Hamilton finally stood up to throw his support to Jefferson, who, though a Republican, was in Hamilton's eyes "by far not so dangerous a man" as Burr (an epithet that would prove eerily prescient, given the results of the famed 1804 duel between the two). With that, the Maryland and Vermont delegations went over to Jefferson, who was finally declared the victor just a few days before the inauguration.

The results were revolutionary for the Federalists, who had held power in the United States from the beginning. With Washington dead and Adams out, their influence was waning. "Jacobins," Jefferson and his adherents had been called during the mudfest of an election, while Republicans referred to Adams as "the Duke of Braintree," and a "monarchist" at residence in his "palace." Indeed, Jefferson would later describe his victory as the "second 1776."

An aging and disappointed Adams is reported to have snapped at Jefferson, "You have put me out!" when the two first met in the election's aftermath, though they parted finally on friendly terms. But if Adams's departure from the president's home could indeed be viewed as the ignominious decampment of a deposed monarch, no one would have been more disconsolate than a certain Frenchman, who had only recently made his way back to the city of his dreams.

28

A Concurrence of Disastrous Events

THOUGH MAJOR P. C. L'ENFANT HAD EXHIBITED A nearly uncanny knack for landing on his feet after every disaster, luck—or, perhaps more accurately, the patience of his admirers—had begun to desert him in the aftermath of the Society of Useful Manufactures and Morris House debacles. In fact, he began to seem less a miracle worker and more a man with a problem for every solution.

In 1794, for instance, having just begun his work for Morris, L'Enfant received a commission from Secretary of War Henry Knox, who named him (at Washington's suggestion) a temporary engineer in charge of upgrading the fortifications protecting the ports of Philadelphia and Wilmington, Delaware. He had a budget of about $12,000 for Fort Mifflin on Mud Island in the Delaware, about seven miles south of the Philadelphia city center; and for Wilmington there was another $3,000. "The proportions of expense therefore must not be exceeded," Knox declared, though it is doubtful that even screaming capitals and double underscores would have caught L'Enfant's attention.

Given those budgetary constraints, Knox advised L'Enfant should devise earthen parapets for the walls of the forts, though he would leave it to the engineer to lay out the positions and design of the firing batteries. He was also to provide shelter for a garrison of at least five hundred men, and a powder storage magazine protected by a timber roof no less than seven feet thick, as well as to design a "reverberatory furnace, of the best construction, in order to heat balls red hot," for each of the cannon batteries.

"These are general ideas," Knox told L'Enfant, "but are not to constrain your own judgment, excepting as to the limitation of the expense." He closed by reminding the engineer of the need to file weekly reports on his progress.

Sixteen days later, L'Enfant wrote back to Knox that following a passage of time that had allowed him "to mature my ideas on the subject," he had come to realize what a "grand system of defence the protection of a fort on Mud Island will require." A fort on Mud Island might not be a bad idea, L'Enfant allowed, but to his way of thinking "a fort standing alone may easily be passed" by a determined invader. Perhaps Mud Island was not the best possible choice, he thought; but if it had to constitute the principal line of defense, Knox should surely see the wisdom of erecting a second fort on the opposite bank of the river.

To help Knox visualize, L'Enfant provided a rough sketch, which showed the proposed fort at Mud Island being point "A," and the proposed second fort at point "C," as well as additional fortifications at points "D," "E," "F," "G," and "H." With this, L'Enfant concluded in a typical flourish, "the greatest possible security would be ensured to the city of Philadelphia."

One longs to see the eyes of Secretary Knox widen as they flick from one letter of the alphabet on to the next and hear the clatter of gold eagles required by each in his mind. All he had intended was the piling up of a bit of earth around some old fort walls there on Mud Island, and the addition of the barest few buildings required to house a garrison and keep the powder dry—should it ever be required, of course.

Furthermore, he had been perfectly clear about the constraints of budget: $11,913.82 for Mud Island, and not a penny more. And in response . . . *this*? What did the man envision in their future, another invasion by the British?

Perhaps that was exactly what L'Enfant envisioned. After all, the fall of Mud Island's Fort Mifflin during the Revolution had forced George Washington's retreat to Valley Forge in the winter of 1777. And since L'Enfant had seen the results of that failure firsthand, he might well have understood something that Knox could not.

"Far remote from the sea as that situation is, it is certain that no attack will ever be made, unless it is a very determined one," L'Enfant continued in his report. And as to the possibility of making any use of those old fort walls that remained from the days of the Revolution, it was out of the question. While they might go ahead and build the new fort without bothering with the old walls for the time being, L'Enfant said, the moment his men were finished, those ill-conceived fortifications would have to be removed.

Was Knox fuming at this point, or was he chortling at the absurdity of it all? There'd been no detailed plans for a point "B" explained. What might this man have in mind there, a remake of the Colossus of Rhodes? By the time L'Enfant concluded his letter—with the observation that the entire mucky expanse of Mud Island just might have to have its elevation raised via the application of a giant lattice-platform of logs—Knox might have held his head gripped tightly in his hands.

No record survives of Knox's response, if there was one, but on September 15, L'Enfant wrote his friend Hamilton at the U.S. Treasury to complain that unless more support was forthcoming, he would have to "relent of the progress" at Mud Island. Since he had not heard from Knox, L'Enfant had taken it upon himself to approach the governor of Pennsylvania for help. He had been promised $6,000 by the governor, L'Enfant said, but unfortunately the state legislature had adjourned without approving the measure. As a result, he told Hamilton, "the prosecution of the business solely now depend on what you can do."

Ultimately, Hamilton could—or would—do little. L'Enfant would have to carry the fight on his own. And thus, after grudgingly embanking some of the original walls of the fort and (here records are inconclusive) possibly constructing the commandant's house in the style of a French chateau, L'Enfant quit the project in frustration and returned to his desultory work on the Morris house in Philadelphia, leaving behind plans that would be completed by others, toward the end of the decade.

At the time—and very likely from the first days of his decampment from work on the Federal City—L'Enfant was living in a Philadelphia boardinghouse where he and a close friend named Richard Soderstrom had agreed to share the rent. Soderstrom was a member of a well-to-do family of merchants from Sweden who came to the United States in 1781. He prospered in the trade of grain and tobacco with Europe, and, following the conclusion of the Revolutionary War, secured the commission of the Swedish king as a trade consul to the United States. Soderstrom and L'Enfant met and became friends— and perhaps more—sometime during the architect's halcyon days in New York City.

Despite his refusal to honor claims against his trading partners in Sweden, and a subsequent stint in debtor's prison in New York in 1790, Soderstrom emerged from his difficulties to be named Sweden's consul general to the United States. He also became involved in Robert Morris's ill-fated North American Land Company and served as the financial liaison between L'Enfant and Morris, setting up the loan of the architect's bank stock to Morris, and collecting Morris's payments to L'Enfant as well.

The financial relationship between Soderstrom and L'Enfant was a fluid one, with L'Enfant lending money to Soderstrom as his circumstances allowed, and Soderstrom responding likewise when L'Enfant found himself in need. By 1798, however, with Morris's house abandoned and the man himself in debtor's prison, L'Enfant found himself very much in need, so much so that he prevailed upon Soderstrom to approach his old friend Alexander Hamilton to see if he might finally realize some compensation for his work on Federal Hall, nearly a decade before.

Soderstrom was willing to give it a try, but he returned from a meeting with Hamilton in New York City bearing news that stunned L'Enfant. The former treasury secretary could not be bothered to intervene on behalf of an individual who had behaved so irresponsibly with his employers as had L'Enfant. Furthermore, Hamilton intimated to Soderstrom that it was his opinion that L'Enfant remained in the service of the government of France, and should probably look to that increasingly suspect quarter if he wanted for assistance. With such friends as Hamilton, Soderstrom advised, L'Enfant clearly had no need of enemies.

L'Enfant was so outraged that he wrote to Hamilton at once, demanding that he affirm or deny such heinous remarks, the preparatory step in an "affair of honor." Hamilton, apparently taken aback at the prospect of a duel with L'Enfant, wrote back quickly to say that he had simply assumed that the major *was* in the employ of the French government, and, if so, could not legally be formally engaged by the United States. If the logic of the reply seemed specious, the fact that an explanation was proffered at all seemed to satisfy L'Enfant. If the architect had indeed taken his pistol from its case, it was returned without incident.

Still, the financial exigencies that had prompted L'Enfant to petition Hamilton in the first place had not vanished. And if dignity and some self-imposed sense of honor had prevented L'Enfant from pressing a claim against the commissioners of the Federal District for his services while Washington was alive, the great man's death changed things dramatically.

On August 30, 1800, L'Enfant, still living in Philadelphia, broke his silence on the matter at long last and sent the commissioners a lengthy memorial requesting proper remuneration for his work. In that document, L'Enfant begins, cogently enough, with an explanation for the tardiness of his appeal, blaming it on "a concurrence of disastrous events rendering my position so difficult as to be no longer possible to withstand unless speedy relief be obtained by collecting what yet remains my due."

While Washington was alive, L'Enfant was content to withhold an application, he told the commissioners, but with the "American Chief" departed, it was impossible to "any longer forbear claiming Redress for Injury." He had been driven out of the city too soon for the merit of his labor to have "been made perceptible to vulgar Senses," L'Enfant said, but now that the plan had begun to take shape, if only in a few of its principal features, perhaps it was time for him to receive his due.

He had derived no profit from the transformation of the city into a rich corporation, L'Enfant pointed out, even though "the immediate result to others has been a great Increase of their wealth." Furthermore, he lost his standing with the original commissioners owing to his opposition to a piecemeal plan of development that would result in lower property values and a retarded pace of development—prophecies that, he wished to remind his present audience, had proved true.

From there, L'Enfant proceeded to a list of more-specific injuries that began with the complaint that his direct line of communication with Washington had been disrupted by the "underhand" influence of others in government, leading to "an unshakened disturbancy" regarding his position. More to the point, L'Enfant complained that his original engraving of the city plan had been stolen and secretly reproduced without his consent—and without credit—and that others had thereby profited from the fruits of his own unrecompensed labor.

Furthermore, L'Enfant wanted to make it clear that he had never "resigned." He had been offered terms of employment that he did not find acceptable, and his suggestions for a basis upon which he could continue simply "remained unanswered." The pittance of $2,500 that the commissioners offered him at the time of his dismissal was hardly adequate, and he had been compelled to refuse it, L'Enfant said.

But by then, he had reached the paragraph that began "12thly" in his litany of complaint and even he realized that it might be time to shorten "the disgraceful Catalogue." His attempts to do so were fruitless, however, for the memorial continued on for page upon unpunctuated page, with only an occasional phrase of coherent expression rising up from a nearly incomprehensible tangle of lament and self-approbation.

By sheer force of will, it seems, L'Enfant sought to bring his letter back to bear on practical matters. He opined that he was due a salary "commensurate with the magnitude of the Object and of the Affairs managed" and, second, "payment of the delineation of the City Plan on an estimation expected such as the Sentiment of a work of [genius] alone can suggest"; also, he was due a part of the proceeds derived from the printing of the City Plan, he contended, and, as well, some consideration for the "great additional perquisites necessarily to have devolved" had he remained in his post as chief architect of the city. What those additional perks might have amounted to was difficult to say, but he pointed out that he had already been shown proposals for buildings amounting to more than $1 million before he was driven from his office, and that he might have made as much as $50,000 had he accepted those commissions, never mind whatever else was sure to come in their wake.

This reckoning might have had more force if the author had been content to end his appeal at that point, but L'Enfant could not contain himself, and rambled on for several pages more about his years of selfless service, Washington's esteem of those efforts, and . . . well, it was sometimes difficult to make out what, just exactly, he *was* trying to say. In the end, the document exhibits all the earmarks of a man who, if he had not lost his grip altogether on reality, was certainly feeling it slipping from his grasp.

It is true that even at his best, L'Enfant's command of English was spotty and his various enthusiasms often overcame careful reasoning. But the missive that he posted to the commissioners in August of 1800 would have been bewildering to the most attentive reader. To a group of businessmen beset with the ever more pressing demands of a city that would soon house the whole of the nation's government, it would have been maddening in its vagueness and circumlocutions.

In September, L'Enfant and Soderstrom followed in the wake of the migration of the government from Philadelphia to Washington, taking quarters at Stelly and Barney's Tavern. Once there, and having heard nothing from the commissioners concerning his appeals, L'Enfant turned his efforts toward Congress.

In a memorial addressed to both houses of Congress, dated December 7, 1800, L'Enfant did his best to put a firm number to his desires, though it was obviously very difficult for him to come directly to the point. He began by reminding his listeners that he had served the country long and honorably during the Revolutionary War and that he had been wounded and held as a prisoner of war during that time. Following this, he launched into a lengthy rehash of his engagement and eventual disappointment in the design and construction of the Federal City.

Toward the end of the first section of this pages-long missive, L'Enfant managed to convey something of the true pathos of his position: "If they be but disinterested men, will all agree that the Success of the City of Washington was first Insured by the reputation which I gained to the enterprise—by the quick Conception of the properties of its locale—by exertions and Combinations uncommon to my professional line and—by the devotedness with which, whilst I Suffering a great reverse in my family fortion [sic] I still persevered in unprofitable labour and at the end resolved, the Sacrifice also of my prospects in that Enterprise to a reconciliation and harmonising of parties and Interests that opposed the progress."

In his eyes, he had worked gratis in the service of Washington's dream and had been willing to step aside for the same reasons. In the end, he could only pray that Congress would respond to his mortifying position and make him whole again.

At the end of this preamble, L'Enfant attached a fanciful set of interrogatories in which he responded to a series of practical-minded questions posed to himself, including: "Q. 6 Did the commissioners not in a surreptitious manner procure and cause my plan to be engraved at Phildelphia? A. They did so. . . . Q. 8 Was I not justly entitled to expect from them the price for those 10,000 copies that I might have got by a sale to others? A. I believe there can be no doubt of it." And so on, through fifteen such concocted exchanges.

L'Enfant does his best to specify his losses, but it would be difficult for any accountant to translate his complaints into a dollar figure. He laments the "injury done to my fame as an Artist," and the forfeit of the sale proceeds of "upward of 15,000 copies" of his plan for the city. He also blames the commissioners for having lured him from a successful position in New York and for the loss of income from the sale of the lots he had been promised there "through contrivance of some malevolent avaricious men amongst the Corporation of that City who made me appear as having renounced the grant." But it was not long before the thrust of his petition wandered away again into dense thickets of abstraction with dependent clause tacked onto dependent clause, and sentences rambling on for paragraphs at a time.

Following an attempt to lobby members of Congress on L'Enfant's behalf, Soderstrom returned to advise his good friend that the congressmen he had spoken to found his memorials far too lengthy and full of vague generalizations. L'Enfant should get down to brass tacks, Soderstrom advised. The men he was appealing to did not appreciate eloquence or philosophy, but they could reckon figures with the best of them. L'Enfant should sit down and draw up a clear schedule of days worked, salary due, and specific expenses to be reimbursed. To do otherwise was a waste of time.

In a petition dated January 1801, the architect did his best to follow Soderstrom's counsel. He asked Congress pointedly for $8,000 for his work on the survey and design of the Federal City; for $37,500 as lost income from the unauthorized sale of copies of his plan; and for an additional $50,000 as recompense for commissions lost as a result of his removal. When Congress still did not respond, L'Enfant finally penned a lengthy letter to President Thomas Jefferson.

"I now with great dependence on your goodness beg your consideration," he began, describing himself as a "dupe and victim" of "Jealousies and machinations," before going on to invoke, among other familiar recitations of his service, the mission to France that he had undertaken on behalf of the Society of the Cincinnati "at a great personal cost to me . . . [that] embarrassed my affairs and never has been redeemed." Perhaps he should have remained silent on that final score, for it could only have reminded Jefferson of those howling creditors of L'Enfant's whom he had faced upon arriving in Paris lo those many years before. In any case, Jefferson did not respond to L'Enfant's entreaty.

On March 12, 1802, L'Enfant wrote the president again, begging for some word. This time Jefferson found time for a terse response. He had no authority to intervene in this matter, so he had forwarded L'Enfant's requests to the authorities involved—the commissioners of the District of Columbia. "For anything else," Jefferson wrote, "the powers of the legislature are alone competent, and therefore your application to them was the only measure by which it could be obtained. Accept my respects and best wishes."

It was the sort of bureaucratic circle-spinning that foreshadowed the work of Kafka. L'Enfant would have been reeling. Such a dodge from the president would have been a devastating blow to anyone.

Whether Jefferson truly saw himself as a simple servant of protocol or had taken perverse pleasure in dropping this petitioner down the rabbit hole of bureaucracy, the outcome was the same to L'Enfant. His patron and the father of his country had died. His place among the movers and shakers of a nation was no more. He was destitute and at the mercy of forces he scarcely understood.

How strange it must have seemed, then, to wander the streets of Washington for years to come, one thick petition after another clutched in hand, lost in a landscape that he himself had designed.

PART THREE

Forged by Fire

29

Destroy and Lay Waste

GIVEN THE LOW ESTEEM IN WHICH WASHINGTON City had been held by so many Americans from the days of its founding, it would be no exaggeration to say that the entourage that made its way along Old Fields Road on the morning of August 24, 1814, was the most eager and intent group ever to have contemplated an arrival in the U.S. capital. It is equally unfortunate, of course, that the band also happened to comprise a well-armed and highly trained army of invasion.

There were actually two detachments marching together on that blisteringly hot morning: a veteran British Army artillery and infantry force of about 4,000, under the deliberate and highly respected Major General Robert Ross; and another five hundred or so marines and sailors under the command of the fearsome Rear Admiral George Cockburn, a warrior who had delighted in a number of predatory raids on isolated American settlements over the previous several months, and who had been described as "rough, overbearing, vain, and capricious." It was indeed something of an unusual alliance, but even more ironic was the fact that the troops were there at all.

It is true that despite the indifference of many Americans to their own capital, Vice Admiral Alexander Cochrane, commander of British troops in North America, had theorized that the capture of

Washington would provide him with a significant advantage in his ultimate plan to put an end to this troublesome conflict with the former colonies. With Washington under British control, the area could be used as a supply port and staging area for ground assaults on nearby Baltimore and Annapolis, where the surrounding shallow waters prevented proper naval assaults.

Once Washington and then Baltimore fell, Philadelphia would be next, and then New York and Boston, the latter to be pincered by simultaneous ground and naval attacks. Cochrane further reasoned that his attacks on Washington and Baltimore would divert U.S. forces from making any incursions into Canada, and away as well from New Orleans, through which Cochrane planned to sail his fleet up the Mississippi for the final, western stage of his campaign.

The first steps in the plan were taken on August 18, when Cochrane led his fleet, carrying Cockburn and General Ross's troops, up the Patuxent River, which parallels the course of the Potomac, running through rural Maryland some fifteen to twenty miles to the east. At the hamlet of Benedict, about twenty miles upstream, General Ross and his troops debarked and began to march northward by land toward the capital. While Cochrane remained at Benedict, Cockburn took a contingent on up the Patuxent to search for a flotilla of tiny gunboats commanded by an American sailor named Joshua Barney, whose harassing guerrilla tactics had constituted the only meaningful obstacle to the British presence in Chesapeake Bay.

Ross encountered no resistance to speak of during his march on land. On August 22, Cockburn finally overtook Barney's sixteen gunboats up the eastern branch of the Patuxent. The American commander promptly blew up his own boats to prevent their capture by the British, and retreated with his men over land. Cockburn left a few of his marines and artillery men to secure the site of that victory and marched overland to join Ross, who had established a camp at the village of Upper Marlboro, near the head of the western branch of the Patuxent and less than a day's march from Washington City. There the two commanders congratulated themselves on the ease with which their mission had progressed—it was surely a harbinger of things to come at Washington City, they agreed.

But hardly had their backslapping ended and the two retired for the night when a rider burst into the camp on a lathered horse, calling for the commanders. Ross and Cockburn struggled out of bed at the commotion to find Lieutenant James Scott, Cockburn's aide, bearing an urgent message from Vice Admiral Cochrane. Ross read the message first, then handed it over to Cockburn, who scanned it and turned his gaze upward in disbelief.

They were to leave their position and return to their ships at Benedict at once, Cochrane ordered. Having had time to consider things properly, he had decided that the invasion of Washington was too risky. There were not enough troops to ensure the success of the mission, no means of securing their supply lines, no certainty of escape along the narrow roads snaking through the otherwise impenetrable woods between Washington and the Patuxent. Ross and Cockburn had already "effected more than England could have expected" with their limited resources. Meanwhile, they were "on no account to proceed one mile farther."

Ross, the consummate military man, was philosophical at this turn of events. If that was what their commander had decided, then that was that. He would issue the order for a return to the ships at Benedict at daybreak.

There Cockburn put out a hand to stop him. To come this far and with such ease and not proceed on to their objective was unthinkable. It would be worse than a defeat, he argued. British troops would be ridiculed, their morale sapped and that of the U.S. troops transformed.

Furthermore, he had absolute faith in the intelligence that had been provided him—there was nothing standing in the way of glorious triumph for their cause. A ragtag militia such as the Americans had mustered would never stand in the face of an advance by Ross's veteran troops. "If we proceed," Cockburn declared, "I'll pledge everything that is dear to me as an officer that we will succeed."

With their combined forces on land, Ross now outranked Cockburn and could have simply dismissed such objections. But the general wavered. Protocol might have demanded an immediate end to the mission, but everything in his warrior's heart responded to Cockburn's argument. The debate went on throughout the night, while Lieutenant Scott watched, unsure what it might mean to his career if the orders he carried from Admiral Cochrane were ignored.

Finally, near dawn, as Cockburn begged that they at least carry on for a few more miles to test the enemy's strength, Ross held up a hand to stop the impassioned flow of words. He walked to the edge of the firelit clearing where their debate had raged, and stared out into the darkness in the direction of Washington City. Finally he gave his forehead a blow with the heel of his hand and turned back to Cockburn.

"Well, be it so!" he told his comrade. "We will proceed."

In moments the word spread to the soldiers in the camp, most of whom had been as distressed as Cockburn at the prospect of an unforced retreat. But now the admiral vowed to conquer Washington or die, it was said, and a mighty cheer rose in response.

THAT A SIZABLE force was contemplating an invasion within a few hours' hard ride of Washington unbeknownst to its citizenry might seem impossible, though at the same time it was not a total surprise that a contingent of British troops had ventured onto U.S. soil. The two countries had been at war for more than two years, locked in a low-grade but often deadly contest (featuring some raids along the coastline by British naval forces) over long-standing issues of free trade with Europe, regular impressments of American sailors from their ships by agents of the king, and the bloody raids of British-supported Indian tribes along the western frontier of the United States, all of which had lingered on unresolved for decades following the so-called British surrender at Yorktown.

On June 18, 1812, President James Madison, who had served as Jefferson's vice president, declared war on the British for a second time, and many in the United States responded not with fear and trembling but with a huffy "What's taken so long?" It was widely felt that from the first days of the republic, the British had not truly recognized the former colonies as an independent and coequal nation. If they had, then why were American seamen still being dragged from their ships to serve in the British navy, and why were American ships being forced to stop in Great Britain and pay an onerous tariff before visiting any European ports?

Pundits had been calling for a declaration of war for several years. With Great Britain weakened and preoccupied with Napoleon's threat, the time was ripe for the United States to assert itself and, while at it, lay claim to the bountiful and sparsely populated lands of Canada. (There were 500,000 Canadians at the time, and 7,500,000 residents of the United States.) Demonstrating that arguments for war persist over centuries, a number of orators and editors assured Americans that the people of Canada would welcome invading U.S. troops as liberators. The governor of New York predicted that fully half of the Canadian militia would throw down their arms and join the American forces. Even Thomas Jefferson declared that the conquest of Canada would be "a mere matter of marching."

Of course, the war did not proceed quite according to plan. The initial American invasion of Canada resulted in dismal failures at Detroit and at various sites along the Niagara River and at Lake Champlain; and operations along the western and northern frontiers quickly devolved into a series of thrusts and counterthrusts, with neither side able to gain a permanent foothold. U.S. naval forces managed better than expected against "the nation that ruled the seas," however, often giving as good as they got in encounters on the Great Lakes and the Atlantic—the sinking of HMS *Guerrière* and HMS *Java* by the USS *Constitution* ("Old Ironsides") were to go down as among the most inspiring victories in American military history.

But despite the successful showing of the U.S. Navy, the conflict along the eastern shores of the country was as indecisive as elsewhere. There had been regular depredations up and down the U.S. coastline by British troops deposited briefly from their men-of-war, but there had been no permanent advantage gained and no serious ground campaign launched against any American target of note. Once Napoleon abdicated power in France in April of 1814, however, all began to change.

With the "scourge of Europe" exiled to Elba, Great Britain, though war-weary, was able to divert a significant number of experienced ground forces and supplies from the Continent to the conflict across the Atlantic. Speculation naturally abounded in the United States as to where these troops might be headed: Boston, perhaps; New York, more likely; Baltimore was an outside prospect. Despite the blockade that the British fleet had imposed on American shipping and regular depredations along Chesapeake Bay by Cockburn's British squadron dating back to April of 1813, the Federal City of Washington did not even warrant a mention by most pundits. Some of their reasoning was based on bravado; but others assumed that with the city's esteem so low in the eyes of its own citizens, the British could scarcely find it a worthwhile target.

"What though the enemy has taken possession of some islands in the Chesapeake?" crowed Joseph Gales, editor of the *National Intelligencer* in May of 1814. "As to his near approach to the Capital, which has been hinted at, we have no idea of his attempting to reach this vicinity; and if he does, we have no doubt he will meet such a reception as he did at Craney Island [where a British assault on the Norfolk shipyards was spectacularly repulsed in 1813]. The enemy knows better what he is about than to trust himself abreast or on this side of Fort Washington [the lone military installation guarding the city, about 10 miles down the Potomac]."

Brave words indeed! And even when, on August 18, a great number of newly arrived British ships were observed to join Cockburn's flotilla in Chesapeake Bay, no one feared for Washington City. Though this news was quickly relayed to Washington by a rider from an army observation post at the mouth of the Potomac, Secretary of War John Armstrong, unpopular and generally considered incompetent, dismissed it out of hand. The British "certainly will not come here," Armstrong assured Major General John P. Van Ness, commander of the Washington militia, who was sitting in Armstrong's office when the breathless rider burst in. "No! No! Baltimore is the place, sir," Armstrong assured Van Ness as he shooed the messenger out of his chambers.

Not everyone in the government was as blockheaded as Armstrong, of course. Although he agreed that Baltimore was the more likely military target, President Madison had no desire to stand defenseless if the British should come marching his way. In consultation with Secretary of State James Monroe, Madison had earlier that year established the 10th Military District, charged with the defense of the entire Baltimore-Washington area.

Though it might have been a good idea in theory, the actual execution of the plan for the 10th Military District left something to be desired. There was little money to arm or provision this force, and at its command, Madison had in July of 1814 named Brigadier General William Henry Winder, a Baltimore lawyer with only a smattering of field experience. While Winder was happy to accept his commission, he discovered that there would be few permanent troops at his disposal. "Upon the spur of the occasion," Armstrong told Winder, he was to call up the Maryland militia, though no one seemed to understand exactly how to reach those forces. Promised 3,000 men from Maryland, Winder found that 250 actually arrived in answer to his summons. Some of them had rifles, but most did not. And while many had shoes on their feet, there were a good number lacking those as well.

Thus, when a functionary from the War Department showed up in Winder's office on the afternoon of August 18 to voice his concerns about what he had just overheard in Armstrong's office, Winder was flummoxed. Like most everyone, he feared more for such potential targets as Baltimore or the nearby Chesapeake port of Annapolis than for Washington City, but all of the area was his responsibility, and with a total of five hundred regular troops at his disposal, how on earth was he supposed to prepare for an invasion by the British Army when he didn't even know where they intended to attack?

While Winder dithered and sent out frantic appeals for reinforcements, Secretary Monroe visited Madison at his office to voice his personal concern that Washington City was indeed the intended target of the British. After all, Monroe reasoned, Washington might still be a veritable "sheep meadow," with no trade or economic importance and with barely 6,000 residents, but it was nonetheless the capital city of the nation. Furthermore, there had been significant public outcry in Great Britain when on April 27, 1813, U.S. forces invaded York (now Toronto), the capital of Upper Canada, and, after finding an American scalp tacked to the wall behind the Speaker's table, burned its Houses of Parliament to the ground.

British Commander Cochrane had already given George Cockburn blanket orders "to destroy and lay waste such towns and districts upon the coast as you may find assailable," and to spare only the lives of unarmed citizens he encountered along the Chesapeake shores, a task that he had undertaken with enthusiasm and dispatch. It was quite possible, then, that the British intended an even more brutal reprisal in Washington City, whatever else they had in mind for the rest of the country.

At the very least, Monroe suggested to Madison, why shouldn't he round up a few men and ride down to the mouth of the Potomac, where the British fleet had gathered? Perhaps he could turn up some information of value. They certainly couldn't trust Armstrong to do anything useful, and Winder had enough on his plate as it was.

Madison, who, as president of a country at war, wore on his chest the biggest bull's-eye of anyone, was not about to discourage Monroe—a decorated veteran who had served alongside Washington in the Revolution—from his scouting mission. By the following afternoon, August 19, the secretary of state freed himself from the normal demands of a Cabinet position and became an army scout, riding on horseback toward enemy lines with an escort of twenty-five men.

All the debate and theorizing needed to come to an end, Monroe knew. Someone had to find out exactly what the British were up to.

30

The Little Malice of Fools

I**T IS ENTIRELY POSSIBLE, GIVEN** L'E**NFANT'S TROUBLED** times in the early 1800s, that the designer of the still-nascent city of Washington might have glanced up from the shade of one of the poplars Thomas Jefferson had planted along Pennsylvania Avenue to see Monroe and his retinue thundering off toward the Chesapeake on that August day. L'Enfant had become a familiar sight on the streets of Washington City since his return at the beginning of the century, though his once-dashing image had undergone a considerable transformation.

"Daily through the city stalks the picture of famine, L'Enfant and his dog," wrote Benjamin Latrobe. "He is too proud to receive any assistance, and it is very doubtful in what manner he exists." Indeed, the intervening years had been less than kind to L'Enfant. Following his unsuccessful pleas to Congress for payment for his work on the Federal City, the architect turned his attention back to New York in 1801, renewing his claim for payment for his renovation of Federal Hall.

His old friend and former client Robert Morris agreed to exert his influence upon the New York City Council and asked his son Thomas, an attorney and member of the House of Representatives from that state, to lend a hand as well. The ten acres originally offered to L'Enfant by the city in 1791 had long since been divided into lots and sold for about $1,500. A preliminary response from the council suggested that the matter might be easily resolved, and after some debate, they voted to offer L'Enfant $750. In keeping with his long-standing belief that anything less than his just due was unacceptable, L'Enfant refused the city's offer.

When he was unsuccessful in persuading the city to reconsider the matter, L'Enfant asked Thomas Morris to enlist the aid of his old sponsor Alexander Hamilton, but Hamilton proved reluctant to intercede with the council—perhaps mindful that the last time he had gotten involved with L'Enfant's affairs, it had nearly ended in an affair of honor.

L'Enfant was not one to give up easily, however. He wrote Hamilton directly on the matter several times, though the former secretary remained unmoved right up to the moment in 1804 that Vice President Aaron Burr fatally shot him on the dueling field. One can't help wondering, if it didn't occur to Hamilton as he lay dying, that at least he wouldn't have to read any more of those endless pleading letters from L'Enfant.

Following the collapse of his appeals to New York City, L'Enfant turned next to former secretary of war Henry Knox, to see if he might be able to receive some pay for that abortive stint as supervisor of the fortification project at Mud Island in the Delaware below Philadelphia. One of the first obstacles that Knox might help him overcome, L'Enfant pointed out, was the loss of all record of his employment in an 1800 fire that destroyed the temporary quarters of the War Department in Washington.

Knox obligingly wrote to the current secretary, Henry Dearborn, pointing out that L'Enfant's inability to manage his financial affairs was as familiar to everyone who knew him as was the "excellency of his talents as an engineer." While Dearborn was apparently convinced that L'Enfant deserved some settlement, he did not get around to answering for more than three years.

In the meantime, L'Enfant's personal affairs spiraled steadily downward. In 1803, Samuel Davidson, one of the original Georgetown proprietors who had banked on the success of L'Enfant's plan in the early days, noted in his ledger book that he was forgiving the architect's long-standing debt of fifteen pounds, "knowing you now to be a pitiful dirty fellow and very poor."

In 1804, faced with a suit by his former partner Richard Soderstrom (who had kept careful records of every penny he had lent L'Enfant, and of who had paid for exactly what during their years of living together), L'Enfant signed over the lot he had purchased in Washington City back in 1791 and assigned to Soderstrom the rights to any future settlement he might receive for his work on the design for the Federal District. And though L'Enfant attempted to recoup the value of the bank stock he had lent to Robert Morris, that former tycoon went to his grave in 1806 virtually penniless.

Given the opportunity to add his name to the list of creditors pressing claims against Morris's estate, L'Enfant—in yet another of the many mystifying and contradictory actions he took relating to financial matters—refused to do so. Likewise, there is no record that he ever made any attempt to collect the military pension granted him by the French government, or to claim the small farm in Normandy that he had inherited upon the death of his father. Though his letters indicate that a sense of honor kept him from sullying the good name of others such as Washington and Morris with any legal filings, even when he faced the poorhouse, the question of why L'Enfant ignored his wartime pension and his inheritance remains unanswered.

In 1808, L'Enfant finally hit rock bottom. Facing eviction from Rhodes' Tavern, where he had been staying, just a stone's throw from the President's House on Pennsylvania Avenue, L'Enfant finally accepted a settlement from Congress and the Superintendent of Washington City. Though he had presented a claim for more than $95,000 back in 1801, L'Enfant was desperate enough to take what was offered: $4,600 and the lot that was originally offered him by the commissioners back in 1792.

Given the economics of the day, it might have constituted a windfall. But under the terms of his settlement with Soderstrom, about $4,150 went immediately to his former partner, who was now the

Swedish consul general. The building lot went to L'Enfant's attorney, as satisfaction for his fee. William Rhodes, who had been ready to turn L'Enfant out onto the street, picked up the $300 owed him. And that left L'Enfant with a little less than $150. Truly, it seemed that the architect was spectacularly inept when it came to managing his own finances.

Despite his willingness to accept the $4,600 payment in 1808, L'Enfant maintained that it was only a disbursement "on account," toward eventual satisfaction of that $95,000 claim. His continued appeals finally persuaded James Madison, who succeeded Jefferson in office, to sign a bill in May of 1810 awarding L'Enfant a supplemental payment of $666.66, plus interest dating from 1792. It all came to about $1,400, a sum that still fell far short of what he felt he was owed, but by that time a destitute L'Enfant was willing to accept anything.

Madison was far more sympathetic to L'Enfant than Jefferson had ever been. Seeking an appropriate way to improve the fortunes of the planner, less than a month after his declaration of war with Great Britain, the president directed then secretary of war William Eustis to offer L'Enfant an appointment as "professor of the art of military engineering in the Military Academy of the United States" in West Point, New York. Although he spent several days contemplating the offer, L'Enfant's reply of July 17, 1812, was another classic of its kind.

He began by begging Eustis to forgive the ten days it had taken him to formulate an answer. Truly, the "terrifying" state of his personal affairs had caused him to give serious consideration to the matter, he wanted Eustis to understand, and "indeed, the sudden unexpected mark of the President's esteem of my talents excited in my breast a conflict of sensations more felt than easy to describe." (Given that it had been twenty years since Washington had last applauded him publicly, there can be little doubt as to the sincerity of this statement.)

However, as L'Enfant explained, the various reversals he had been subject to seemed to dictate the need to remain in Washington, where he might more easily find redress for his various injuries. However pitiful his present circumstances, were he to remove himself to this proposed appointment, or as he put it, submit to a "confinement more dismal" out on the Hudson, he would be giving up any hope of a successful pursuit of his claims with Congress. Furthermore, he worried that any wages he might be paid would only cause him further grief: "The next consequence would be the exposure of my person to arrest and to persecution for debts in amounts far greater than possible to repay in *20* years time by the saving out of the salary of any office whatsoever."

Nor was L'Enfant "so well satisfied of my fitness to the office of Instructor of youths." He did not possess "the rigidity of manner, the tongue, nor the patience, nor indeed any inclination peculiar to instructors," he said, before adding what might have been—in anyone else's letter—the last word on the matter: "I am not fond of youth."

Lest these deficiencies be misconstrued as the perfect profile for a potential West Point professor, however, L'Enfant had more to offer: "Besides, I would have to encounter the difficulties of language and that of a memory not remarkable for retentiveness of technical terms." And then, as if he imagined fellow graybeards scanning his letter and murmuring, "Yes, yes, one of us, exactly what we're looking for," L'Enfant elevated his argument to even more dismissive heights. "I have no reverence for the name of modern academicians," he declared, "nor do I believe in the utility of this military academy as many people affect to believe."

It was his opinion that engineers were effectively trained in the field, and on the job, as he had been, and not by studying books in classrooms. If it was all the same to Eustis, L'Enfant suggested, he would prefer an appointment as a military and civil engineer, working on harbors, camps, and fortifications, where all the experience he had gained during the Revolutionary War and in his work on the Federal City (and for which he was still owed, Eustis was not to forget) might be put to good use and have some bearing on the current conflict.

Particularly worrisome was the prospect that no member of the Military Academy staff "shall be entitled to command in the army," and that his position as an instructor would reduce him "from the rank of principal engineer, an office to which I was appointed by President

Washington in 1793." At West Point, he might run the risk of becoming nothing more than "a subaltern to one of the academy professors whose functions are by no means of military nature." Hardly a welcome prospect for a man who treasured his rank as a colonel.

The appointment Eustis proposed was anathema to L'Enfant, who stated his determination to once and for all "secure myself against the possibility of new contradictions . . . base personal jealousy, cowards, rancor, the little malice of fools, and the speculation of avarice, excited against the best of my exertions in former employment." With a final exhortation that Eustis and the president keep in mind that satisfaction of the outstanding claims he had levied against Congress would be of as much value to the "reputation of the American name as it is of Importance to me," L'Enfant closed this remarkable letter with something of a mind-boggling postscript. All that Eustis had just read was to be understood thusly: "P. C. L'Enfant states his reasons for delaying answer to his letter of appointment—will want more time to answer it definitely."

Eustis may well have reread that last just to be sure he was seeing correctly. Perhaps he passed the letter along with a terse cover, something to the effect of "Fellow's intrigued—just wants to mull a few points." Or perhaps he simply bucked it up the line without saying a word.

In any case it was Secretary of State James Monroe who dashed off a reply to L'Enfant on the very same day. While he lacked the time to give L'Enfant a definitive answer on the several subjects he had raised, "my urgent advice to you is to accept the appointment," Monroe said. "It will deprive you of no claim . . . and provide you an honorable station and support. Your creditors have no prospect in your present situation. This appointment may afford some hope." Monroe suggested that L'Enfant could reiterate some of his concerns in a letter of acceptance—"all the considerations which you think proper." But there was one piece of advice to take above all: "Do not decline this appointment."

When L'Enfant still hesitated, Monroe wrote again, on July 28, begging that the planner not make a misstep. For the past two years,

Monroe said, he had fought Congress on behalf of L'Enfant's claims, and while he had not yet been successful, this appointment offered by the president would not only offer some income but bring L'Enfant back into the public service and pave the way for an eventual transfer to active duty if that was what he truly desired.

Meanwhile, duty at West Point, Monroe argued, was not only honorable, but guaranteed "a comfortable assylum and independence for life." This is the very best that could be managed for him, Monroe asserted. "Indeed you are the only foreigner in the country for whom as much could have been done. If you reject this appointment I have no hope of seeing you in any other," he said. "Accept the office. It is a beginning and may lead to something better."

He closed his letter by assuring L'Enfant that he would never advise "an old revolutionary friend" to do anything that was not "honorable and praiseworthy." Indeed, Monroe said finally, "I beg you to be assured of my best wishes for your welfare."

In the sanguine version of the life of Peter Charles L'Enfant, our petitioner, now entering the fifty-ninth year of his life, worn and edified by his many battles, rises from his desk after reading this missive from the president's adviser, and walks across a well-worn carpet to the window of his humble lodging. There he stares out at a dusty, wheel-rutted Pennsylvania Avenue where but a little traffic moves, and finally his chin begins to nod.

Surely, a glass partway full is far better than one three-quarters empty. And after all these years, is it not a blessing that at last the president and his men see fit to offer this sinecure, an undemanding post that will ease him into his final years with some comfort and security? If the partisan jackals roaming the halls of Congress have forgotten his name, at least the men who truly matter understand the value of his lifelong contributions.

And thus soothed by the balm of goodness bathing him like sunlight spilled from heaven, our honor-driven L'Enfant at last returns to his desk, where he sits to pen a reserved though grateful acceptance of this gift delivered, and our common sigh of relief sends the pages dancing.

BUT THAT HAPPY fiction is not the true account of L'Enfant's actual life. In truth, we will never know in what temper the architect read those plaintive words from James Monroe. He may well have been touched by the encouragement of "an old revolutionary friend." Or he may have found terrible insult in that patronizing assurance that no "foreigner" could have hoped for as much as he. All we can know for certain is that our L'Enfant—in his quintessential way—did not decline the president's offer. In making no further reply to Monroe, he simply did not accept.

31

Embers of Imagination

A REGULAR FEATURE OF L'ENFANT'S MANY PETITIONS concerning payment for his work on Washington was a reminder that had his advice been heeded from the outset, the development of the city would have progressed far more rapidly than it had in the first twenty years of its existence. The piecemeal sales of lots under agreements lacking any incentive for timely improvement would only encourage idle speculation, L'Enfant had warned back in 1792, and while the cash-strapped commissioners were in no mood to listen, time would prove the planner right in that respect as well as many others.

The British diplomat Augustus John Foster served two stints in Washington City between 1804 and the declaration of war in 1812, the first under Ambassador Anthony Merry. In November of 1804, following the usual route of foreign visitors to the American capital, Foster arrived in Norfolk, traveled by packet ship to Baltimore, then continued on to Washington by stagecoach. In a letter to his mother, Foster expressed dismay at what he found: "[T]his place looks like, what in fact it is, an infant colony. Every man has built his house . . . just where his fancy chose, so that there are hardly ten buildings together in the whole of this immense place." His boss Merry was even more blunt, referring to the city as "perfectly savage."

And as bad as the physical conditions were, Foster found the cultural deprivations even more distressing. "Imagination is dead in this country," he said. "Wit is neither to be found nor is it understood. . . . All the arts seem to shrink from it as you hear nothing but calculation and speculation in money or in politics." While traveling theater troupes such as Philadelphia's Chestnut Street Theatre Company made occasional stops in Washington during the city's first decade, horse racing, debates in Congress, and even appearances by "The Learned Pig" were just as popular. Visitors to the pig's five daily shows paid an admission fee of fifty cents to watch the animal (the sagacity of which was "equal if not superior, to any . . . ever exhibited") read, spell, tell the time of day "by any person's watch in the company," compute the number of persons in attendance, and add, subtract, multiply, and divide.

Foster, however, was apparently not among those who came to see the pig identify a card—any card—drawn from a pack, or proclaim the day of the week and month. Instead, as he wrote his mother, "I do nothing but read the Tempest and A Midsummer Night's Dream and Virgil to try and keep alive the embers of imagination."

Though most congressional wives were in Washington only during session, if they came at all, social entertaining was not unknown. The widowed Jefferson kept affairs at the White House to a minimum, often turning to Dolley Madison, the wife of his secretary of state, to oversee any events he felt it absolutely necessary to host. When Ambassador Merry paid his first visit to Jefferson in the White House, a determinedly unceremonious Jefferson (who wrote to Merry, "Nobody shall be above you, nor you above anybody; pele-mele is our law") met him in the hallway in his slippers. The incident quickly became legend in European ambassadorial circles, along with the president's penchant for inviting diplomats from warring countries—including France and England—to dine at the same table. Describing his encounter with the president, Foster said that he "thrust out his hand to me as he does to everybody and desired me to sit down. Luckily for me I have been in Turkey, and am quite at home in this primeval simplicity of manners."

Foster was dubious that things would ever get better, telling his mother, "I do not think that this ever will become a great city." And as for his estimation of the American Congress, he found that there might have been "about five persons who look like gentlemen. All the rest come in the filthiest dress and are well indeed if they look like farmers, but most seem apothecaries and attorneys. There is only one man who can speak well."

At the time, the entire diplomatic corps in Washington totaled three: the representatives of Great Britain and France, and the Spanish minister to Denmark. When the ranks were swelled by the arrival of the ambassador from Tunis, Foster passed along the news that while Sidi Suleyman Mala Manni "arrived here with the most splendid dress on I ever saw," the gesture was not reciprocated. "The President receives him in yarn stockings and torn slippers, as he does us all."

It was clearly a demoralizing posting for the young British diplomat, who was twenty-four when he arrived in Washington. "I do believe from my soul, that from the Province of Maine to the border of Florida, you will not find 30 men of truth, honor or integrity. Corruption, immorality, irreligion, and above all self-interest have corroded the very pillars on which their library rest," Foster lamented. "They have inherited all our faults without one of our virtues that I know of."

Little that happened during his initial posting changed Foster's dour opinion of the new country, and shortly after an 1808 incident in which four alleged British deserters were impressed from an American ship while still in U.S. territorial waters, the young diplomat was transferred to Sweden. Admittedly, Foster's assessment of the American character and the tenor of life in Washington were colored by the prism of his aristocratic background and the deteriorating relations between the United States and his home country. Still, he would return briefly as Britain's ambassador in 1812, and many years later he would somehow recall many of his experiences in Washington as favorable.

If there is any truth in Foster's observations of Congress, then L'Enfant's dogged effort to press a claim of nearly $100,000, based on appeals to honor and decency, with such a crass, self-serving body seems almost touching in its naïveté. And even if some members of the U.S. Congress were more honorable than Foster allowed, lack of cash in the national treasury was the chief obstacle not only to the satisfaction of such a claim but to the development of the city of Washington in its early days, and for that matter to the development of the nation as well. Money—or the lack of it—incited political passions at every level, from war-related issues regarding free trade with Europe to the question of where and in what manner the remains of the country's first president would be permanently interred.

Supporters of the late George Washington campaigned fervently for the erection of a suitable monument—equestrian or otherwise—in the city, and in January of 1801, Congress allotted $200,000 for such a purpose, though the vote, at 45–37, was close. In a prescient admonition, the pamphleteer (and notorious scandalmonger) James Thomson Callender wrote that even though the appropriation exceeded the $170,000 estimate for the planned mausoleum, "All such estimates fall greatly short of the ultimate expenditure." Callender advanced what would transform into a familiar trope for political rhetoricians—the guns-or-butter argument. In Callender's version, the funds voted for this heap of memorial stone would be far better spent on shirts and pants for the valiant survivors of the old Continental Army, he proclaimed.

Although the funding for a memorial to Washington was passed despite such protests, the rhetoric—indicative of the fundamental Federalist/Republican division over the legitimate scope and reach of a central government's authority—continued. For his part, President Jefferson walked a narrow line. The notion of the city as a repository of monuments to past grandeur was pure anathema to him, but he had come to understand the need for a centralized seat of government on the Potomac, if for no other reason than to prevent control of the affairs of the country from falling back into the hands of the moneyed interests of the Northeast.

Nor were such fears abstract. In the spring of 1804, for instance, Federalists, spurred by their enduring disdain for the Federal District and ever hopeful of moving the affairs of the government northward, introduced a bill on the Senate floor that called for the removal of the capital from Washington to Baltimore. In short order, rumors were flying about the Federal City that Philadelphia and New York were in covert support of the measure—"anything to dislodge the government from that wretched site on the Potomac" remained the mantra among die-hard Federalists. It took all of Jefferson's influence to see that the measure was defeated.

Jefferson was willing to complete the public buildings in Washington City, and particularly the Capitol, the seat and symbol of the democratic system. But his support for monuments was grudging, and given only to the degree that he believed they would secure the city's standing as the permanent seat of government. To ensure his control over the process, Jefferson successfully lobbied Congress to abolish the Board of Commissioners and replace that body with a single District Superintendent. On June 2, 1802, Jefferson appointed Thomas Munroe, former clerk for the commissioners, to fill the post; and the following spring, after he had signed a bill authorizing repairs to the chronically leaking roofs of the Capitol and the President's House, he appointed trained architect Benjamin Henry Latrobe as "surveyor of public buildings" for the city. If there had to be such structures—and monuments surrounding them—then at least they would be conceived of in harmony and built in good taste, Jefferson determined.

Jefferson met Latrobe in 1798 at a meeting of the American Philosophical Society, and in 1802 asked him to submit drawings for a set of dry docks Jefferson wanted to see built at the Navy Yard being developed on the western banks of the Anacostia River in Washington. Although Congress declined to fund the docks, Jefferson was greatly taken with Latrobe's apparent skills as an architect, so much so that he sweetened the job offer of 1803 with an additional commission, for the design of the as-yet-unbuilt South Wing of the U.S. Capitol.

THE OFFER TO complete the premier governmental structure in the new country was, as they say, one that Latrobe could not refuse, though his appointment dashed the hopes of a return to the project held by George Hadfield, the British architect who had spent the years from 1795 to 1798 as the building's supervising architect, warring with the District Commissioners to very nearly the same extent as his forebear L'Enfant. Like Hadfield, Latrobe was a trained architect. But just because Latrobe was highly qualified did not mean that he was any less subject to criticism and controversy.

Following an inspection of the shoddy workmanship of the roof and plastering in the completed North Wing and the foundations under way for the South (footings too narrow to bear the massive loads required, stones tossed one atop another, unsecured and without regard for fit), Latrobe issued a blistering report to the president that pointed up the shortcomings of the "stupid genius" William Thornton. Thornton responded in equally vituperative terms, declaring Latrobe's report insulting, uncivil, ungentlemanly, and false, beginning a round of mudslinging that would end in an epic court fight.

Meanwhile, Latrobe went forward with a revised plan for the South Wing, which, when finished, would constitute what is generally considered the finest example of architecture in the fledgling nation up to that time. First, he pleaded with the president to abandon the concept of a three-story-high House chamber. Moving the assembly hall to the second story would be far more practical, allowing for the installation of offices, fireproof records-storage rooms, and indoor privies on the ground floor. Once he had convinced Jefferson that those changes were indeed justified, he then undertook the demolition of the affectionately named "oven," the temporary House chamber that had been hastily thrown up atop the foundations of the South Wing in 1801. It would mean the return of the House to the space allocated to the Library of Congress in the North Wing of the Capitol building while the construction was under way, but it was the only way to proceed.

In order to secure sufficient appropriations from Congress, Latrobe promised that he would complete his work on the South Wing in approximately eighteen months, by December of 1805—a prospect that soon proved hopelessly optimistic. Shortages of labor and materials plagued construction, as did bad weather and Jefferson's insistence that Latrobe top the wing with a fabulous glass dome modeled after the Halle au blé in Paris, a feature that the president termed "the most superb thing on earth."

By December of 1806, the wing was still far from finished, and Latrobe was beseeching Congress for still more money in hopes that he might complete the job in 1807. Critics accused Latrobe of dragging his heels on the project in order to ensure his steady paycheck. On December 15, 1806, John Randolph of Virginia (the single member of Congress deemed an able orator by the British diplomat Augustus John Foster) became one of the first in a long line of elected officials to tackle waste in government spending, demanding a full accounting from Jefferson of monies spent to date on all public buildings: the President's House, the Capitol, the Navy Yard, the offices of the Cabinet, and a Marine Corps Barracks building nearing completion that Jefferson had ordered built in 1801 close by the Navy Yard.

Despite all the grumbling, Latrobe got another $25,000 from Congress to finish the South Wing, along with an additional $17,000 for furniture. The last great obstacle to be overcome was that infernally impractical roof that Jefferson was adamant about. Glass ordered from Germany as far back as 1805 had still not arrived by January of 1807, and when no domestic supplier could commit to the necessary quality and quantity he needed, Latrobe was forced to order it from England, with whom relations were spiraling rapidly downward.

The glass finally arrived from England in August of 1807, just weeks before Jefferson called a special session of Congress to consider various outrages perpetrated upon American merchant ships by

England's men-o'-war. In December 1807, sitting in their new chambers and in the glow of light diffused by British glass in the skylights high above, members of the House voted for an embargo closing all American ports to foreign trade. Had the legislation been proposed only a few months before, they might have had to count the votes by candlelight.

32

Stillness of the Grave

THE INITIAL RESPONSE TO LATROBE'S WORK ON THE South Wing was mixed. The editor of the *National Intelligencer* hailed the new House Chamber as "the handsomest room in the world occupied by a deliberative body." But others, including the silver-tongued Randolph of Virginia, noted that the acoustics of the room were less than ideal. Latrobe—who had worried from the beginning about the reverberation effects of the elliptical shape of the room forced on him by Thornton's design—dismissed some of the carping as slander typical of the Federalist press; but he nonetheless went to work hanging a series of heavy drapes that considerably muted the echoes.

Congress might have forgiven him for the acoustic problems, but there was another matter that the politicians had decided they simply could not overlook: cost overruns. When he had gone begging for a final appropriation to complete the building, Latrobe had stopped just short of swearing on his mother's soul that he needed not a penny more than $25,000. Yet in the end, he had spent more than $60,000. He came closer to keeping within the $17,000 furniture allowance, but he was still over budget at $21,000.

Representative Randolph led the charge against wasteful government spending, calling Latrobe's actions "illegal and unjustifiable." He admitted that the result was pleasing, but that was beside the point. In language that could have been found in the first outraged criticisms directed at L'Enfant's initial vision of a Grand Capital, Randolph noted that artists were "not very nice calculators in money matters."

Latrobe wrote a lengthy defense of his work and his management of the project's finances, pointing out that in the final analysis he had built the South Wing of the Capitol for $61,000 less than the North Wing. Finally, after more righteous thundering from Randolph and his sympathizers, the House voted 73–8 to cover the deficits.

It might have been a vote of confidence that would have had Latrobe congratulating himself, were it not for a scolding note that came from Jefferson on the very same day. The episode "has done you great injury & has been much felt by myself," the president said. He went to explain his concern in terms that would become the rallying cry for many an officeholder in years since: "It was so contrary to the principles of our Government, which makes the representatives of the people the sole arbiters of the public expense, and do not permit any work to be forced on them on a larger scale than their judgment deems adopted to the circumstances of the Nation."

Latrobe, stung by the president's words, wrote back in a way that L'Enfant would have applauded, reminding the president that it had been he who called for a rush to finish the building by the end of 1807, and insinuating that if his services were not appreciated, then perhaps he ought to resign. Jefferson, who had seen this card played before, dismissed Latrobe's complaints and ignored the talk of resignation altogether. Latrobe should simply take it as a lesson learned and get back to the business of building, advice that *this* architect heeded.

Suitably chastened, Latrobe was soon back at work on the rebuilding of the ill-designed and hastily thrown-up North Wing. There he found virtually all of the floor and ceiling joists and supports weakened by rot, a situation that forced him essentially to rebuild the entire structure within the skin, or outer walls, of the original.

During the course of this work, he was publicly assailed on a regular basis by Dr. Thornton. The first salvo was a letter from Thornton published in the *National Intelligencer* claiming that Latrobe had not, in fact, been trained as an architect, but had come to the profession as an apprentice "carver of chimney pieces in London." In response, Latrobe described Thornton's various claims as "too ignorant, vain, and despicable for argumentative refutation."

When Thornton published an account in the *Washington Federalist* of May 7, 1808, claiming that Latrobe had challenged him to a duel but was too cowardly to show up, it was the last straw. Latrobe published a brief reply that no more public comment would be heard from *him* on the matter—he had retained counsel and filed a libel suit against Thornton. The courts would decide whether or not Thornton, who considered himself the true designer of the Capitol building, was "an original inventor, or only a second hand retailer of falsehood."

It was not the only calamity that Latrobe encountered during his work on the North Wing. On Friday, September 16, 1808, while overseeing the construction of vaulting that Latrobe had designed and which was intended to support the new Senate chambers being relocated to the second floor of the building, the architect's assistant John Lenthall heard a terrible cracking sound above him. He glanced up in time to see the ceiling buckling, then the entire mass come crashing down. All of the workmen made it out safely, but Lenthall was buried under tons of brick and mortar. It took hours for workmen to unearth his lifeless body.

In the aftermath of the accident, Latrobe was again assailed by his critics in Congress, who blamed him—however unjustly—for Lenthall's death; they also took advantage of the opportunity to condemn the architect's progress generally, decrying his plans for remodeling and reconfiguration of the Capitol building, including the quarters of the Supreme Court and the Library of Congress, as simply too ambitious in scope. Pressed by Congress to lay out just exactly what it was going to take to finish the North Wing *and* the central building that would connect the two, as well as the landscaping, the paving, and any ancillary work, Latrobe responded with a chart that was as chilling to Congress as it was clear. In the architect's estimation it would take another $412,000 to finish things down to the last pane of glass and potted plant.

The news could hardly have come at a less propitious time. Jefferson's embargo on foreign trade—meant as a retaliatory strike against Great Britain and France—had proved an economic catastrophe for the fledgling nation. With most export trade suspended and imports greatly restricted, customs duties—which would provide the bulk of federal income up through the Civil War—were down more than 50 percent. Jefferson, who was nearing the end of his second term, had received literally hundreds of petitions calling for an end to the embargo, leaving an unenviable situation for his successor, James Madison.

Still, Latrobe pushed for the funds to finish renovating the Senate chambers in the North Wing in time for the 1809 session, and, following a grudging appropriation, managed to reopen that part of the building on February 10, 1810. He had fought for monies to complete work in that wing, but given the economic crisis, there was little hope he would succeed. As one House committee reported on January 11, "It is not deemed prudent at this time, when a resort to loans may be necessary for the support of the Government, that any improvements whatever should be made."

Congress's tight-fistedness put Latrobe in such a financial bind that when he asked for $77,500 for the 1810 building season and was granted about a third of that amount, he was forced to cut his staff of laborers to half a dozen men and sell off salvaged timbers and discarded furniture to try to raise money. It is difficult to imagine Pierre L'Enfant holding rummage sales in order to keep his work moving forward, but such efforts are telling proof of the dire financial straits of the nation.

Jefferson's Embargo Act had proven to be a gross miscalculation. Great Britain was scarcely inconvenienced—it simply turned to Spain for goods it had been importing from the former colonies (chiefly tobacco and other agricultural products). France, delighted to see any pressure applied to its enemy across the channel, happily turned elsewhere for its U.S. imports as well. Canada delighted in its status as a moneymaking conduit for smuggled goods both to and from the United States. In the end, the only country hurt by the Embargo Act was the one that brought it into being. U.S. exports, valued at $108 million in 1807, sank to $22 million in 1808. Imports fell from $60 million to less than a quarter of that during the same period. Ships were said to be rotting away at dockside in American ports, and virtually every merchant sailor was thrown out of work. "Our wharves have now the stillness of the grave," wrote the Newburyport, Massachusetts, *Herald*. "Nothing flourishes on them but vegetation."

In desperation, Congress repealed the fifteen-month-old act in March of 1809, substituting a measure that maintained prohibition of imports from England and France, but permitted American ships free trade with the rest of the world. In May of 1810, the so-called Non-Intercourse Act of 1809 was repealed and a new measure (Macon's Bill Number 2) passed, which reopened trade with England and France, providing, that is, that both nations would agree to rescind their restrictions on trade with nations neutral to their conflict.

In August, Napoleon responded with a decree known as the Cadore Letter, in which he promised to respect the rights of American vessels whether or not they might be bound for British ports (or were suspected of funneling goods bound for England through neutral ports). Madison was delighted with the letter, which he hoped to use to pressure the British to suspend its Orders in Council, the pretext for their seizure of American ships suspected of trading with France. But the British pointed out that Napoleon's letter was a farce—the French continued to seize American ships and had instituted a new series of tariffs that made U.S. trade on the Continent practically impossible. As a result, Madison reinstituted a ban on the importation of British goods as of February 1811, and recalled the American ambassador from London.

Shortly thereafter, Augustus John Foster, the British subminister who had found his earlier posting to Washington so dismal, returned for a second engagement, this time as British ambassador, and bearing a troubling set of demands for the new nation. So long as France continued to interfere with trade bound for Britain, Foster proclaimed, the Orders in Council would remain in effect—and it was no good waving about that sham of a letter from Napoleon. Furthermore, if the non-importation restrictions were not lifted immediately, Foster warned of grave consequences for the United States.

At the same time that the American economy remained strangled in the East, settlers hoping for a better life on the western frontiers also found themselves stymied by the British, albeit in far different form. In the Indiana Territory, the problem took the shape of regular depredations on settlements by the British-allied Shawnee tribes, reaching a crisis at the Battle of Tippecanoe in November 1811, when two hundred American regulars and militiamen under the command of William Henry Harrison were killed by the followers of Tecumseh. The British funneled support to the tribes through Canada, and the raids were seen by settlers as proxy attacks by the Crown. Tribesmen were referred to as "British savages" in the American press, and the conflict in the territories was often termed the "Anglo-Indian War."

By late 1811, Federalist-leaning merchants of the Northeast and Anglophobic Republicans of the South and West were rapidly approaching a consensus on what was needed for the new nation. By giving the British a good drubbing on the fields of war, the United States would not only solve its economic woes but also put an end to its second-class status on the international stage, once and for all.

The many slights and outrages perpetrated by Britain over the years were all part of a strategy to hold the nation down, Republicans believed; in their eyes, the Federalists, so eager to profit by trading with the former enemy, had allowed the country to remain, shamefully, a tacit colonial dependency. The *National Intelligencer* proclaimed on November 7, 1811, "Not only the rights of the nation, but the character of the government are involved," and even Federalists, who had opposed the many restrictive trade measures over the years and who now constituted only about 25 percent of the Congress, were ready to join the chorus. "By war," wrote Massachusetts's Elbridge Gerry to Madison, "we should be purified as if by fire."

While the so-called War Congress that convened in November of 1811 was full of rabid proponents of immediate engagement with

Great Britain, their enthusiasm was dampened by Treasury Secretary Albert Gallatin's estimate that it would cost about $10 million to increase the number of troops in the ground army and build sufficient warships to counter the powerful British navy on the seas. While there was enough, barely, in the treasury to meet the regular expenses of nationhood, Gallatin counseled that the only way to fund the war was through loans, the repayment of which would likely have to come from a series of internal taxes.

To Republicans, talk of taxes beyond import duties was as distasteful as was discussion of broad avenues and grand buildings in a national capital, but without money, how else were troops to be mustered and frigates built? While the matter of internal taxes was sidestepped for the time being, Congress voted approval of an $11 million loan to support the war. It would be two more years and several escalations of debt before a series of duties on imported salt, stills, retail and auction sales, sugar, carriages, and commercial documents was approved in 1813.

Though debate over actually engaging in combat continued through the spring, the issue had been essentially decided. In early June of 1812, the House voted 79–49 to send its forces, ill-prepared though they were, to war with the former master of the colonies, and on June 17 the Senate added its approval by a 19–13 margin. On June 18, Madison signed the measure into law, and the "Second War of Revolution" officially began.

33

The More Things Change . . .

I F, BY THIS TIME, MUCH OF THE COUNTRY'S POLITICAL
landscape—the internal schism between agrarian Republicans
and industrial, urban Federalists, and the external tensions between the United States and Great Britain—was little changed in
more than twenty years, the geography of the place was profoundly
transformed over the same period.

The original thirteen states had become eighteen by 1812, with
Ohio joining the Union in 1803 and Louisiana in April of 1812. The
population of the nation had grown from 3.9 million in 1792 to
7.2 million in the 1810 census, and, with the addition of the Louisiana
Purchase in 1803, the territorial size of the country had nearly dou-
bled as well.

For $15 million, or about three cents an acre, Jefferson brokered the
purchase of a little more than 820,000 square miles of mostly unex-
plored and sparsely populated land west of the Mississippi. Ultimately,
following negotiations with France and Spain, the deal included most
of present-day Arkansas, Missouri, Iowa, Kansas, Nebraska, Okla-
homa, and Louisiana. The acquisition of New Orleans and its port
was especially vital. Also included were parts of Manitoba, Saskatch-
ewan, and Alberta in the north, and parts of Montana, Wyoming,
Colorado, Texas, and New Mexico in the west.

The transaction drew the wrath of Federalists, who saw it as constituting not only a debt of monumental proportions, but as implicit financing and support of the French offensive against Great Britain. The deal also set the United States up for a later war with Spain, which claimed Texas and New Mexico as its own colonies. But for Republicans, and for expansionists in general, the purchase seemed to open glorious possibilities for the nation. Ultimately the bill sailed through Congress and, with a few pen strokes applied to treaty documents, an already vast country expanded by an area very close to the size of all Europe.

East of the Mississippi, where nearly all the populace resided, about half were British immigrants or their descendants, with the rest a roughly equal mixture: one-sixth were African-American (most were slaves, even though their importation was abolished in 1808); one-sixth were Scotch and Scotch-Irish; and the other sixth were of German and Dutch extraction. There were others, of course: most of the 76,000 or so inhabitants of the newly purchased Louisiana Territory were of French descent, and there were a few Swedes as well, though the great influx of Scandinavian immigration to the upper Midwest would not take place until the last half of the nineteenth century. Perhaps of most political and military significance were the 100,000 or so Native Americans who for the most part had been pushed to the edge of the country's northern and western territories.

About four in every five Americans were farmers at the time, and most lived in relative isolation, visiting towns and cities only when necessary. The largest population center—New York City—had yet to reach the 100,000 mark, and the five largest cities combined (New York, Philadelphia, Boston, Charleston, and New Orleans) had fewer than 300,000 residents among them. The citizenry of the City of Washington, despite all those glowing predictions made by its namesake, its eager proprietors, and its genius French planner, had grown to just 8,208, though that number did put it at number fourteen on the list of the nation's most populous cities.

On all those farms, work was powered by muscle, of man and beast. Sure-footed oxen were used primarily in the steep and rocky North, horses were employed upon the flatter terrain of the West, and mules did best in the hot and humid South. "Machinery" consisted primarily of plows, axes, hoes, shovels, scythes, and rakes. (More than a few of those wielding those tools in the early Republic came from the 20 percent of the population who were African-American: according to the 1810 census there were 1.4 million listed as black, 1.2 million of whom were slaves.)

There was one notable advancement in agricultural science, however. Eli Whitney's cotton gin, brought into common use in 1793, had revolutionized farming in the South, making that crop "King" in the region, though tobacco, rice, and cane were still important crops. One of Whitney's gins could clean the seeds from a hundred or more pounds of cotton in a day, whereas a skilled worker might be hard put to manage a single pound.

But those wondrous machines would be sitting idle unless more hands were found to pick and tote the raw bolls to their waiting maws. Thus, plantation owners were soon crying for more slaves, instead of fewer, and with the importation—if not the ownership—of slaves now banned, large growers became as interested in enhancing the reproduction rate among their human properties as they were in their livestock.

With textile mills and other forms of factory mass production still to come, there was little organized manufacture in the United States, though an enterprising fur merchant from New York City named John Jacob Astor realized that opportunities in the newly acquired Louisiana Territories could make a man with organizational capabilities rich. Astor set up trading centers as far away as the mouth of the Columbia River in Oregon, and though the War of 1812 would prove a temporary impediment, his American Fur Company would come to constitute the first industrial monopoly in the United States and make him one of its first self-made millionaires as well.

But for all the talk of a "civilized" part of the country (as opposed to near-barbaric Washington), there were relatively few luxuries for the likes of Astor to indulge themselves in. While farmers and their necessarily large families would have slept three to a bed on straw ticks, a prosperous city dweller would likely have retired for the night on a feather bed, probably extinguishing a whale-oil lamp (each of which emitted the light of ten candles) before doing so. Only the truly well-to-do would have enjoyed upholstered furniture or carpeted floors, and those would have been made by hand, as mass production of such items was still decades away.

Most food, with the exception of what might be dried or smoked or pickled, was fresh, as the technology of food processing was in its infancy. A rudimentary form of canning had originated in the 1790s in France, and while the process had migrated to Great Britain, one major difficulty facing its wider adoption was the fact that although the inventor had figured out how to sterilize and weld his sturdy containers securely shut, he had yet to devise a convenient means for getting them open. Until the invention of the can opener in the middle of the nineteenth century, hungry people were opening the tins with knives, chisels, and even rocks.

Pork and beef were the meat staples on tables in the North, while Western and Southern families relied far more on fresh-killed game including rabbit, squirrel, venison, and possum. To wash the food down, hard cider and beer were commonplace drinks at many family dinners, with whiskey finding its way more often to Southern than to Northern tables. The mint julep is said to have originated in Virginia during the first decade of the nineteenth century, as a highly touted morning "tonic," though it was probably made with brandy in its earliest form.

Transportation still took place largely in carriages, on the backs of horses, or by sail or raft or paddleboat, a particular challenge for a country with such vast distances to be bridged. There were a few steamships operating on American waters, but those were rudimentary in nature. Ambitious plans for a system of canals linking the Atlantic to the Mississippi remained just talk, and the beginnings of the fabled American rail boom were still twenty years away. On a good day, a stagecoach or freight wagon might cover twenty-five or thirty miles, depending on when the sun went down. Traveling the nation's rocky, deeply rutted roadways at night was literally suicidal, and for much of the still-forming country, a navigable stream or a roadway of any kind was nothing more than a fancy.

As a whole, the United States of 1812 was very much a rawboned adolescent of a nation, poised between a hardscrabble upbringing and a promising future, and this new war was a major test for the gangly upstart. If the first revolution had been prompted by reaction against subjugation, this attempt at finishing the fight was more about the determination to evolve than to escape. There were still factions in the Congress calling for a fracture of the tender Union into North and South—and even a few voices calling for a peaceful reconciliation with the King. But the great sense of possibility exuded by a landscape now twice the size of Europe had captured the imaginations of most of its citizens.

There might have been significant differences of opinion about what would make the new empire great, but there was no debate as to the possibility of greatness. It was this sense of promise that ultimately allowed for a consensus on the declaration of war in 1812—once rid of meddling foreign interests, once all barriers to trade on the seas and expansion on the western frontiers had been removed, the United States would achieve a status comparable to that of other sovereign nations on the world political and economic stage. And what dreams might take shape in the aftermath were beyond any man's attempt to say.

The British and their Indian allies, however, proved to be more formidable opponents than expected. By late 1814, that annexation of Canada, which was to be "a mere matter of marching," was a long-forgotten flight of fancy. While the alliance between the British and the native population had weakened following the death of Tecumseh at the Battle of the Thames in October of 1813, the many thrusts and counterthrusts along the northern borders had resolved into a stalemate, with neither British nor American forces able to prevail.

And the same was true on the seas as well. American naval forces had won impressive victories on Lake Erie and Lake Champlain, but were no match for the formidable British array enforcing their blockade of shipping along the Atlantic Coast. With Napoleon defeated at last, and the British free to devote all their military energies to this problem with the former colonies, some feared that the tide was about to turn.

Key to the renewed British offensive was the push to bring "hard war" to the American cities that were vulnerable to a naval assault. In their thinking, a swift decimation of prominent American targets would demoralize a war-weary nation and force the ambitious but ill-provisioned opponent into surrender. Ironically enough, Americans saw Washington City's lack of strategic value as its chief defense against an invasion. Given the new British strategy, however, its vulnerability made it the perfect place to begin what was essentially a terrorist campaign.

Such thinking had sent Cockburn and Ross marching down that blistering road toward Washington to begin with in August of 1814, and it is what moved them to go forward despite the timid second-guessing of their commander, Cochrane. Hard war had been called for, and hard war was what these upstart Americans were going to get.

34

Under a Different Belief

A S IT TURNED OUT, SECRETARY OF STATE—TURNED—army scout James Monroe had been having a difficult time of it in his new profession. His foray down the Patuxent to check on the British led him thirty-five miles southeast of Washington City to a fine vantage point atop a hill, about three miles to the northwest of Benedict. There he found Admiral Cochrane's fleet anchored. Unfortunately, Monroe discovered that in his haste he had left his spyglass behind in Washington and was unable to count the number of ships, or determine whether men were being landed onto shore.

Still, he was taking no chances. He dispatched a courier with an urgent message for Madison: "The general idea is that they are still debarking their troops. . . . The general idea also is that Washington is their object."

Unaware that Ross and his men were already ashore and marching toward the village of Nottingham, just north of Benedict, Monroe carefully worked his way closer to the British anchorage at Benedict. By the next morning he was close enough to count the ships and realize that the troops had debarked. He sent another message back to the president confirming that a force had landed and that he was on his way to catch up with them and fix their position. With his courier on his way, Monroe and his men galloped twelve miles up the main road from Benedict toward Washington, but found no sign of any advancing force.

Puzzled, he cut back across country toward the Patuxent and Nottingham. He found the town deserted, but no sign of any British troops there, either. Then, out on the water, he caught sight of Cockburn's flotilla, headed upriver toward where Joshua Barney's little fleet of raiders had fled for shelter.

At first Monroe entertained the notion of holding his position and calling in an additional force that would cut off Cockburn's retreat, but then he got a better look at the size of Cockburn's numbers. Moments after that, a scout rushed forward to report that the head of Ross's ground troops had been sighted. They were advancing from the southeast, toward the village on the road that ran along the river up from Benedict. He'd circled entirely around the British Army, Monroe realized. He and his two dozen men had stumbled directly into the path of four or five thousand infantrymen, with perhaps a thousand more marines on Cockburn's barges a few hundred feet offshore.

Monroe heard firing behind him, and turned in astonishment to see some of his men taking potshots at Cockburn's distant barges, unaware of the massive ground force that was advancing just minutes away. Monroe made a dash to stop the firing, then led his party on a frantic retreat from the village, just ahead of Ross's troops.

Monroe had managed to save himself and his men for the time being. Still, as they galloped toward General Winder's command post at Wood Yard, just east of Washington City, he could not have felt much confidence in their prospects. Winder had perhaps 2,000 men at his disposal, most of them volunteers, many of them raw and untrained. The British troops on his heels were battle-hardened veterans under the command of able and fearsome leaders. Worse yet, there was more than one approach to the city. Without a clearer sense of the plans of the British, they'd have to spread their paltry troops along a series of ultimately untenable positions.

It was hardly welcome news for Winder once Monroe galloped into his camp at about eight o'clock to explain what they had seen. But at least he knew the truth. Washington was a target after all. And he and his men were all that stood in the way.

AT TWO O'CLOCK on the morning of Monday, August 22, after considerable debate and soul-searching, Winder roused the several hundred men camped with him there at Wood Yard, about halfway between Washington and Nottingham, the small town where Monroe had nearly stumbled upon the invading troops. Winder had decided to advance toward Nottingham and engage the British there; if he waited at Wood Yard, the enemy might take a path that would skirt his position altogether, and march on Washington unopposed.

With that decided, Winder and Monroe rode back toward Nottingham with a small advance party ahead of the main force, reaching a strategic fork in the road just before dawn, where the general reckoned that the British would have to make their intentions clear. If the enemy tried to advance along the west fork, toward Wood Yard, it meant a certain assault on Washington. If they took the north fork toward Upper Marlboro, however, they might be bound for Baltimore after all. If so, he'd let them pass without engagement. He would send word ahead by rider for the forces at Baltimore to prepare, and then use his own forces to cut off any British retreat.

By the time Winder and Monroe reached the fork, however, they could already hear the rumble of the main British force bearing down. The main body of Winder's own forces would never arrive in time to engage at the crossroads. Whatever the British had in mind, he'd be helpless to do anything about it.

The general was mulling his options when he heard shouts from somewhere in the forest ahead. British scouts had spotted American soldiers among the trees, and the forward column of redcoats was swinging down the Wood Yard road, firing as they came. It was enough for Winder and Monroe, who turned their mounts and galloped quickly away, sure now that the British were on their way to Wood Yard and Washington City.

Meanwhile, on the upper reaches of the Patuxent, Cockburn had finally cornered Joshua Barney's fleet in the shallows. As Cockburn anticipated the slaughter that was about to ensue, a series of explosions shattered the air. Knowing he was facing certain annihilation, Barney had already ordered his men ashore and rigged his sloop, the *Scorpion*, and his gunboats with explosives, rather than have them fall into Cockburn's hands. Cockburn had to dive for cover as shards of the boats he had meant to sink or commandeer ricocheted across the bow of his craft.

Just a few miles inland, General Ross stopped his troops' pursuit of Winder's advance party. He had no intention of bothering with a party of scouts, and the outpost of Wood Yard was the farthest thing from his mind. The brief skirmish at the crossroads was nothing more than an unplanned diversion. He reassembled his forces and soon had them marching north toward Upper Marlboro, where he had been bound all along. His intention was to make camp there for the night, then cover the last sixteen miles to Washington the following day.

In Washington City, meanwhile, news of an impending British advance had spread, and the city was in a panic, with everyone who had a horse and cart or carriage in full flight for the Virginia and Maryland countrysides. As clerks at the State Department scrambled to pack documents into the bags that had been readied for just such an emergency—the secret journals of Congress, the Declaration of Independence, Washington's resignation of his commission—Secretary of War Armstrong stuck his head out of his office long enough to observe that all this commotion seemed terribly unnecessary. The British would never bother with Washington, Armstrong called out to senior clerk Stephen Pleasonton. "I replied that we were under a different belief," recalled Pleasonton, and kept on with his packing.

At the Navy Yard, Chief Clerk Mordecai Booth was in frantic search of wagons to move the stores of powder out of the reach of the invaders. He was offering as much as six dollars—a week's wage for a working man—for the rental of a horse and carriage, but even at that exorbitant price he was having a difficult time of it. Clerks at the House and Senate were just as hard put to find a conveyance of any kind for their priceless records. In the end, they had to scour the countryside to come up with a single cart and four oxen.

At the President's House, Madison made a momentous decision. He approached his wife Dolley and explained that he had decided to join General Winder and his troops in the field. Once he had determined the true intentions of the British, he would return. If she had the courage, she could wait for him in the President's House, he told her. If not, he could arrange for her to be taken away to safety. Doubtless Madison knew what she would tell him before the words left his mouth.

She would stay and wait for him, she said without hesitation. In the meantime, she would see to the packing of the Cabinet papers and whatever else she found it possible to carry away. They embraced, and Madison departed for Winder's new position at Long Old Fields, about eight miles east of the city. He left behind a detachment of a hundred guards under the command of Colonel Charles Carroll of Bellvue.

What the president found at Long Old Fields could not have been comforting. Though Winder's forces had been bolstered to more than 3,000 by the addition of Barney's retreating flotilla fighters and other volunteers, the general seemed distracted by the various possible avenues that the British might pursue.

Once his troops left Upper Marlboro, eight miles farther east, where they were camped for the night, Ross might decide to march southwestward to Fort Washington and join up with forces reported to be sailing up the Potomac, Winder worried. Or they might intend to march directly through Long Old Fields and enter Washington City from the south, using the bridge over the Anacostia River, where proprietors Young and Stuart had once prayed for any kind of traffic. And then there was Bladensburg, a village just a few miles to the north of Winder's present position, where another bridge offered Ross and Cockburn's armies immediate access to the capital. Fortunately a detachment of some 1,400 troops was in place there, under the command of General Stansbury, Winder noted. If Bladensburg was the target, perhaps Stansbury's men could hold out until he got there.

Despite Winder's indecision, the morning of August 23 came and went without any movement of the British troops massed in Upper Marlboro. An alarm was raised that the British had broken camp and were advancing on Annapolis, but it proved to be false. Then two British deserters were captured and brought into the camp, but the pair claimed to have no clue where their commanders might be headed, or when.

As the day wore on without incident, Madison decided to return to Washington, taking Ross and Cockburn's pause as a sign that they might well be gathering their forces for an advance toward Baltimore. No artillery or cavalry had been spotted among the British forces—this led him to assume that whatever the British had in mind would not take place until their ranks had been bolstered by such detachments. Given the limited size of the British force in Upper Marlboro, it was entirely possible that they were simply foraging and resting prior to a return to Benedict.

That morning, Madison had taken the time to pencil a note to Dolley, assuring her that he had found the British forces far less formidable than had been rumored and "not in a condition to strike at Washington." Unless there were new developments, he said, he fully expected to see her "later in the evening." By 2:00 p.m., he decided that in fact nothing new would develop, and he and Secretary of War Armstrong, who had come down grudgingly to survey the situation, mounted their horses to return to the city.

It was a significant miscalculation on the president's part. Hardly had he and Armstrong and their party ridden away from Long Old Fields than reports came of some movement among the forces at Upper Marlboro. Winder dispatched a small patrol along the road to Bladensburg to double-check, and soon afterward he heard gunfire erupting from that direction.

Perhaps it was just the patrol exchanging fire with some sentries, Winder thought, but soon his scouts were back with unsettling news. No, not a few sentries, they told him. They had stumbled onto the entire British force, now fully mustered and marching out of Upper Marlboro and advancing toward Bladensburg. The scouts were lucky to have escaped with their lives.

Though it seemed that the only sensible course open to Winder was to move his men immediately to Bladensburg to back up Stansbury's troops, still he hesitated. What if his intelligence was faulty? What if he vacated his present position and the British instead advanced along Long Old Fields Road to the two bridges over the Eastern Branch? That would give the enemy unfettered access to the Federal City.

In the end he decided to pull his men all the way back into the city, leading a hasty and dispirited march across the bridges over the Eastern Branch to an overnight camp at the Navy Yard. Once the British made their intentions clear, Winder declared, he would lead his men out to oppose them.

There might have been some logic in Winder's plan, but to his men the orders to repair to Washington City seemed to constitute nothing less than a retreat. Nor did it hearten the remaining citizens of Washington to witness the tired and confused troops pouring back into the city and collapsing in their makeshift camps.

James Monroe, who had witnessed the brief engagement between Winder's patrol and the British just west of Upper Marlboro, sent a rider to intercept Madison's return to the city, alerting the president that it seemed that their worst fears had materialized: "The enemy are in full march for Washington," he reported. "Have the materials prepared to destroy the bridges," he advised, then added, "You had better remove the records."

Madison stopped long enough to dash off another penciled note to Dolley, retracting his earlier optimism. He would not be returning home, after all. It appeared that the enemy was stronger than it first appeared, he told her. A significant British force was now marching on the Federal City with the intent to destroy it. She should ready a carriage and be prepared to flee at a moment's notice.

Instead of joining the exodus out of the capital, the First Lady continued her methodical packing away of Cabinet papers into trunks. Her servant Jean-Pierre Sioussat approached her with a suggestion. He could spike the barrels of the two twelve-pound cannons placed at the gates of the White House, he told her, and run a line of powder from them as a fuse. If the British stormed the residence, he would light the powder trail and the plugged cannons would explode, blowing the redcoats to kingdom come.

His mistress heard him out, then shook her head. She was a Quaker, and opposed war on principle. But if a war had to be fought, it would be fought fairly, she told Sioussat. She thanked him for his offer and congratulated him on his loyalty, but then went back to boxing up the records. There would be no booby-traps laid at the gates of the White House.

As Dolley Madison continued her packing and the citizens of Washington streamed from the city, Ross and Cockburn were camped for the night at Upper Marlboro, about twenty miles away, readying their final plans. They were in direct defiance of the orders of their commander, but they were seasoned warriors and the prize they sought lay only a few hours' march away. At daybreak they would move, and the city of Washington would be theirs.

35

Debacle at Bladensburg

THE VILLAGE OF BLADENSBURG SITS ON THE ANACOS-
tia, or Eastern Branch, north of the Federal City and some ten
miles upstream from where that river joins the Potomac. The
settlement was founded in 1742, when sixty acres of building sites
were carved from the surrounding forests, and by 1814 it had developed into a prosperous port town of about 1,500, situated on the main
post road from Georgia to Maine, enjoying plenty of trade and a number of taverns that enticed residents of nearby Georgetown and Washington City for regular outings.

Because it lay just over the northern border of the newly formed
District of Columbia and featured a flat field hidden by a hedgerow
just off the main road, Bladensburg also gained notoriety as a dueling
site for quarreling politicians. During a six-year period, beginning in
1808 with the shooting of Representative Barrent Gardiner of New
York by Representative George Washington Campbell of Tennessee
(over the "falsehood, meanness and baseness" that had arisen from
their differences on Jefferson's Non-Intercourse Act), more than fifty
duels had been fought in the village.

On the morning of August 24, 1814, however, there would be more
than a pistol shot or two ringing out over the low-slung hills in the area.
Cockburn and Ross chose to approach Washington from the northeast, through Bladensburg, in part because the more obvious route *was*

from the southeast, crossing into the city over the bridges near the juncture of the Anacostia and the Potomac. And in fact, after a feint in that direction by the British that morning, the American defenders destroyed those two bridges, as Monroe had advised.

Soon enough, Cockburn and Ross had their men back on the road toward Bladensburg, marching at a clip that quickly took its toll in the one-hundred-degree heat. "A greater number of soldiers dropped out of the ranks, and fell behind from fatigue, than I recollect to have seen in any march," wrote British ensign G. R. Gleig of his companions, who were still getting their legs under them after so many weeks at sea.

At last there remained no doubt of where the British troops were headed. James Monroe rode out ahead of General Winder's troops still encamped in Washington, hell-bent for Bladensburg. By the time Winder, now accompanied by Secretary of War Armstrong and President Madison, arrived on the scene, Monroe had begun shifting forces about, his enthusiasm unencumbered by much in the way of tactical acumen.

Madison, unaware of how quickly the attackers were advancing, had actually started across the Bladensburg bridge when he heard the rumble of British forces in the forest just ahead. The only American chief executive ever to set foot on the field of battle beat a wild retreat as a 1,100-man regiment of Ross's foot soldiers led by Colonel William Thornton stormed across the bridge behind him.

If anything, Thornton had proved himself even more impetuous than Cockburn and Ross. When the senior commanders spotted the array of forces that Monroe and Winder had managed to deploy about the hills of Bladensburg, they hesitated. Perhaps Admiral Cochrane had been right to order a retreat after all. They had next to no artillery support, and it looked as if there were actually a fair number of American soldiers amassed on the other side of the Anacostia.

Thornton, however, dismissed their fears. In his eyes, his men were crack soldiers, highly disciplined and trained. The American forces were a motley conglomeration of raw recruits and unorganized militiamen. Once the fighting began, experience and method would win out.

As it turned out, Thornton's first wave—his men restricted to moving three abreast over the narrow bridge—was turned back by a withering barrage of musket fire from American troops hidden in the trees on the Bladensburg side of the crossing. It was an auspicious beginning for the defenders, but then Thornton gave the order to fire the rockets.

Invented in India and developed for use by the British military by William Congreve in the early 1800s, these new devices consisted of heavy iron tubes weighing about thirty pounds and carrying incendiary or explosive warheads of various sizes. The rockets had a range of two miles and, while notoriously inaccurate, were quite effective in terrorizing an inexperienced enemy force as they flew erratically about, shrieking, showering sparks, and ending in daunting explosions.

If seasoned British troops in India had been unnerved by such devices, the callow Americans gathered at Bladensburg were sure to be undone. Colonel Thornton came galloping across the narrow bridge, saber raised, unmindful of a volley of musket fire and a swarm of deadly rockets buzzing wildly overhead. Suddenly the forward line of American forces had seen enough. They turned and began a mad dash toward Washington.

At that moment, Madison turned to Monroe and Armstrong, watching the action from a nearby hillside, and ventured the opinion that it might "be now proper for us to retire to the rear, leaving the military movement to military men." There is no record that either Armstrong or Monroe quarreled with the president's assessment.

As the president, the secretary of state, and the secretary of war galloped away from the contest, American artillery forces found that they had a more practical problem on their hands. As the British passed through the first lines of defense, the artillerymen, who had taken up positions on the hillsides, found themselves unable to lower the barrels of their cannon sufficiently to aim at the enemy.

And as their supporting batteries fled behind them, the riflemen who tried to maintain their positions were further unnerved by the steady advance of the British in the face of the most withering fire. Even when the front rows of the redcoats toppled over after a burst of musket fire, their places were taken by a fresh wave of forces from the rear, in fearless and methodical fashion.

General Winder saw that a tactical fallback and re-emplacement of his artillery forces was called for, but he hesitated, fearing that the frightened, inexperienced troops would mistake such a maneuver for an authorization of a full-out retreat. As he wavered, a contingent of the Baltimore militia that Monroe had placed as support for the gunners began to falter. As one commander would later put it, "There is a distinction between madness and bravery." In moments, the militiamen were in full flight.

Winder had no choice. He gave the defenseless artillerymen the order to retreat. The rout was on, and the Battle of Bladensburg was effectively over.

One observer would later characterize the ignominious, unformed retreat toward Washington as the "Bladensburg Races," and the battle, which lasted less than three hours, would go down as one of the most pitiful American military efforts in history. As to Madison's brief role as an actual battlefield commander-in-chief, one popular poem put these words in the president's mouth: "Nor, Winder, do not fire your guns / Nor let your trumpets play, / Till we are out of sight—forsooth, / My horse will run away."

The one stirring moment in the engagement took place when the advancing British forces stumbled into the path of Commodore Joshua Barney. Barney, who had only hours before destroyed his flotilla to keep Cockburn from getting his hands on the ships, was engaged in dragging his cannon through the woods back to Washington, where he figured they might be needed. As retreating American infantrymen fled past him and his men, Barney called a halt to his procession and ordered the cannons wheeled about and fired upon the advancing British troops. "I could not but admire the handsome manner in which the British officers led on their fatigued and worn-out soldiers," wrote one of Barney's men in describing the futility of their actions.

Finally, his cannons silenced for want of ammunition and facing overwhelming odds, Barney ordered his men to spike the artillery pieces and retreat. He would have joined them, but he had taken a round to the thigh, and every horse had been taken. Grimly, Barney sank to the ground and waited to be taken prisoner.

When a British infantryman approached cautiously, Barney snapped an order—he would surrender, but only to an officer. The British soldier went obediently away and returned with a young naval captain who served under Cockburn on the *Tonnant*. When Barney explained who he was, the young officer hurried back toward the British lines. Soon enough, he returned, accompanied by none other than General Ross and Admiral Cockburn.

When the young officer introduced his superior, using the British pronunciation of *Co*-burn, Barney affected surprise: "Cock-burn is what you are called hereabouts." Barney suggested that his adversary must be feeling some satisfaction, having got hold of his quarry at last, but even the overbearing Cockburn observed standards of professional courtesy. There was no need to speak of such things, Cockburn told Barney. "I regret to see you in this state." General Ross paroled Barney on the spot and asked where he would like to be taken for rest. After Barney identified a popular Bladensburg tavern, Ross ordered a surgeon forward to dress Barney's wounds and detailed several other men to stay behind as stretcher bearers and escorts for the commodore. Then Ross and Cockburn returned to an assessment of their own position.

Estimates of the number of casualties resulting from the brief battle varied widely on both sides, but no one disputes that the British lost many more men than did the Americans (Donald Hickey puts the figures at seventy-five U.S. troops lost, and 250 British). Ross believed there was a simple explanation: his opponents had fled so rapidly they had no chance to be killed.

Certainly, the ease with which the U.S. forces had been routed dictated what would happen next. Ross and Cockburn assembled a fresh brigade of men who had not seen action that afternoon, and by six o'clock they began the seven-mile march on toward Washington City.

36

Barbarians Through the Gates

THROUGHOUT THE DAY, AS THE SOUND OF CANNON FIRE from Bladensburg echoed along the streets of a virtually deserted Washington City, forty-six-year-old Dolley Madison strode through the corridors of the President's House, overseeing the final collection of papers and what few personal items she could not bear to leave behind. Though the one wagon she had managed to secure was packed nearly full with documents, she added a few items of silver, some books, a small clock, and—in perhaps her one moment of excess—the set of velvet drapes that she had chosen for the oval drawing room. Thomas Jefferson might not have cared a whit about the appearance of his residence, but to Mrs. Madison it was important to make a home—especially that of the First Family—*look* like a home.

Despite the obvious gravity of the situation, she clung to hopes that all her efforts would prove to be mere precaution. Anticipating the best, she ordered the servants to prepare for what had become the normal dinner party in recent weeks. At three o'clock or so, a group of forty or so men would convene, including her husband, his cabinet, military officers, and advisers. Accordingly, Paul Jennings, her fifteen-year-old personal servant, was bustling between the cellar and the dining room, placing flagons of ale, cider, and wine for the expected guests, when a rider was spotted approaching the house at a gallop.

"Clear out!" came the cry of Jim Smith, the president's freedman servant. "Clear out! General Armstrong has ordered a retreat!"

As she stared in apprehension, Smith dismounted and thrust another penciled note from her husband into her hand. What she read confirmed Smith's report. The battle at Bladensburg had proved a disastrous loss, Madison told her. She was to fly from Washington at once.

"If I could have had a cannon through every window," Dolley later wrote of the anguish she felt at finally abandoning the city and the President's House. "But alas! Those who should have placed them there, fled before me, and my whole heart mourned for my country."

Retreating troops were already pouring along Pennsylvania Avenue, sending up great clouds of dust as they rushed toward Georgetown and the forested haven of Virginia beyond. Although the detachment of guards under his command had long since fled as well, Charles Carroll of Bellvue had steadfastly maintained his post at the President's House. Hardly had Smith sounded the alarm than Carroll prepared a carriage for the First Lady; they should leave at once, he implored her.

But Mrs. Madison was not quite ready. She ordered the wagon bearing their few belongings and the state papers to be driven off in the direction of the fleeing crowds, then turned back into the house, beckoning for gardener Tom Magraw and the doorkeeper, Jean-Pierre Sioussat, to follow her. There was just one more matter that had to be taken care of.

As Carroll hurried along, beseeching her to heed the president's warning, Dolley led the group into the dining room, where the table lay set with food and drink. Could she be intending to have lunch before they fled for safety?

Food, however, was the last thing on the First Lady's mind. She pointed to Gilbert Stuart's full-length portrait of George Washington and told Magraw and Sioussat to pull it from the wall. The grandest work of art in the President's House—perhaps in all the city—would not be left behind for redcoats to disgrace.

The task was not as simple as it might have seemed. The painting had not been simply hung—its frame was screwed tightly to the wall.

Carroll tried to help them pry the piece away from its mountings, but had no better luck.

Carroll turned to Mrs. Madison. Forget the painting, he urged. There were six thousand troops out there pouring past the White House, and who knew how many bloodthirsty British on their heels. They had to get away. But the First Lady was resolute. "Save that picture," she told her men. "If it is not possible, then destroy it. Under no circumstances allow it to fall into the hands of the British."

Young Paul Jennings went to fetch an ax and delivered a blow to the wooden frame before Sioussat stopped him. They were sure to ruin the portrait that way. Instead, Sioussat withdrew a penknife from his pocket and sawed the portrait out of the frame. Sioussat might have next rolled up the eight-foot-by-five-foot canvas were it not for the appearance and intervention of New York merchants Jacob Barker and Robert DePeyseter, businessmen friends of the Madisons who had hurried to the residence to offer their help. Fearing that the paint would be cracked unless the portrait stayed flat, Barker and DePeyster agreed to take it away in a wagon of their own. They'd be responsible for its safety, the two assured the First Lady.

Only then did Mrs. Madison agree to leave. She hesitated for one moment to dash off a final note to her sister Anna Cutts. "And now, dear sister, I must leave this house, or the retreating army will make me a prisoner in it, by filling up the road I am directed to take," she said, showing that not even the threat of an invading army could rob her of her wry outlook. "When I shall again write you, or where I shall be tomorrow, I cannot tell." Finally, she and her personal servant girl, Sukey, climbed into the waiting carriage and Carroll snapped the reins, carrying them to the safety of his Bellvue estate. The White House was on its own.

MEANWHILE, AT THE Capitol, a few of General Winder's more dedicated troops had peeled away from the general rout toward Georgetown and were gathered to make a last-ditch stand in Washington

City if that was what their commander asked of them. Winder considered it. The two still-unconnected wings of the Capitol made formidable fortresses, and he had always thought that Jenkins Hill would offer an unassailable vantage point, if it came to battle on the streets.

But one look at the fatigued few men before him was enough to wipe thoughts of suicidal resistance from his mind. The hill could easily be surrounded by a superior force—they'd be out of ammunition, food, and water within hours. Better to run and fight another day, as Armstrong and Monroe were quick to agree, and besides, the heights of Georgetown were even more favorably situated for a confrontation.

Though a few of Commodore Barney's stout-hearted men stayed behind on the grounds, Winder ordered his forces to join the ragtag march to Georgetown. Now the Capitol too lay abandoned.

The work of all those years, so many political battles fought, so many careers and reputations made and lost. And now it seemed as if the words of every opponent who had ever spent breath decrying the Federal City finally had been made profoundly manifest. An invading army was on its way to accomplish the very thing that the city's critics could not.

37

A Disaster Striking and Sublime

AT TWILIGHT, ROSS AND COCKBURN LED THEIR forces into the city. Most of Washington City lay quiet and deserted, with those who had not been able to find a way out of the city apparently cowering in terror. The two commanders left their main force of about 1,400 men at the turnpike gates of the city and rode with a small advance party down Maryland Avenue toward the Capitol in the growing darkness. Although bucolic Washington scarcely resembled the urban landscape implied by the term "Federal City," the invading troops would still have found it an eerie experience, clopping unchallenged down a silent lane past one unlighted structure after another, not a soul stirring to shout an insult or a plea. What gutless foes the Americans had proved this time around; what craven cowards they were to desert their capital city, or hide beneath their bedskirts—or so the conquerors might have been thinking as they crossed Second Street Northeast on their way into the Capitol square.

But it soon became clear that not every citizen had fled Washington, nor were all those who remained pusillanimous victims. The silence was abruptly broken by a barrage of musket fire. Four of the British troops toppled, one of them killed instantly. General Ross too went down, his horse shot dead beneath him. Ross's stirrup had been blown from under his boot by an American sniper at Bladensburg earlier that day, and the aide who had come to repair it had in the next instant taken a mortal round to the forehead. Hard to say, then, if this latest near miss unsettled him or made him feel all the more invulnerable.

A call for reinforcements went out to the troops left behind, and soon a British company advanced to fire a volley of blazing Congreve rockets into the house from whence the shots—probably fired by Barney's men—had issued. In seconds the place was awash in flames.

Moments later a series of far more ominous explosions shook the ground around them, and in moments the surprised British troops saw that the whole of the southern sky was lit by a much bigger fire growing in the distance. Thomas Tingey, the chief of the Navy Yard, had seen the American defenders flee before the oncoming British assault and put the torch to his own command post on the Potomac. Half a million dollars' worth of ships—some finished and some nearly so—along with shops, mills, wharves, and warehouses packed with powder, rigging, cordage, sails, and lumber, went up in the inferno.

While Tingey's actions prevented the British from commandeering the stores, the glow from the fires at the Yard made their work at the Capitol square all the easier. Whether they kept the loss of the Parliament buildings at York in mind or not, Ross and Cockburn ordered that all public buildings in Washington City must burn. Private property alone would be spared, unless resistance was encountered or weapons found.

At the Capitol, the order proved unexpectedly difficult to carry out. Congreve rockets were fired onto the roof of the House wing, but nothing happened. Puzzled bombardiers finally discovered why: the roof was largely ironclad, a result of Thomas Jefferson's insistence on a skylighted chamber.

After firing a few rounds through the windows of the buildings, soldiers kicked down the doors and moved inside, piling up furniture, paneling, and curtains—anything that might burn. They laced their pyres with gunpowder, then used more rockets to set things going.

This time their efforts were rewarded. Soon both wings of Congress were ablaze—fed by the drapes and desks and leather chairs used by senators and representatives, the books of the Library of Congress and the records of the House and Senate, the library and documents of the Supreme Court. The sap-heavy pine floors steamed, hissed, then exploded into flame, the thigh-thick joists of floor and ceiling burning, then snapping like giant matchsticks. Though the thick limestone walls stood firm, the roofs of both House and Senate imploded, sending a wave of embers gushing up and outward in an airborne lava flow that ignited every nearby home of wood—including two that George Washington himself had built on North Capitol Street. British Ensign Gleig ghoulishly described the spectacle of utter destruction: "I do not recollect to have witnessed, at any period of my life," he said, "a scene more striking or more sublime."

At ten thirty, with the Navy Yard still burning and their business at the Capitol concluded, Ross and Cockburn gathered a force of about 150 men and made their way down Pennsylvania Avenue toward the President's House, where, as they told the one brave citizen who dared to ask, they intended to "pay a visit." Cockburn paused at Suter's Tavern long enough to send a message ahead to the President's House, offering Mrs. Madison an escort to any place she might choose. When the messenger returned with word that the house had been deserted, the commanders' party moved on.

Though Sioussat had locked the doors of the house before he left, Cockburn and Ross and their contingent had no trouble forcing their way inside. They strode about the empty hallways by torchlight and were no doubt attracted to the dining room by unexpected and mouth-watering odors. They had, after all, been on the move for more than twelve hours, with little time to eat or drink. What they discovered amazed and delighted the weary but exhilarated invaders. "So unexpected was our entry and capture of Washington," wrote Ross, "when our advance party entered the President's house, they found a table laid with forty covers." Lieutenant James Scott, one of Cockburn's subordinates, reported that "never was nectar more grateful to the palates of the gods than the crystal goblet of Madeira and water I quaffed off at Mr. Madison's expense."

The feasting and toasts quickly turned to plundering. Admiral Cockburn helped himself to one of the president's old hats. Lieutenant Scott slipped upstairs to Madison's bedroom, where he stripped off his filthy blouse and donned one of the president's own. Someone snatched a portrait of Mrs. Madison from her drawing room, and another soldier swept an armload of silver and plates into a tablecloth and slung it over his shoulder.

Finally, the souvenir-hunting at an end, Cockburn and Ross issued the inevitable order. Having learned a few things from their experience with the Capitol, the men built heaping piles of furniture in each of the main rooms of the President's House, then put the torch to those heaps. Up in flames went three dozen hand-carved, gilt and red-cushioned chairs in the oval drawing room. A massive sideboard in the dining room made fine kindling, as did the chairs and tables the invaders had sat upon. All the draperies and carpets and furnishings that Benjamin Latrobe and Mrs. Madison had painstakingly selected also became fuel for the fire. Soon the imported glass panes whose arrival Hoban had fretted over were popping away like spun sugar, and flames were pouring out of every casement. Once the walls and roof of the house were spouting flame, the band led by Ross and Cockburn traveled a brightly lit path to the Treasury Building, just across the street.

If the troops expected to decimate the national reserves and line their own pockets by hauling away greenbacks and gold by the wagonload, however, they had not been keeping track of the raging debate among the former colonists over the financing of the war. They found the Treasury's vaults as bare as any hag's cupboard, and even though their hopes lifted briefly when a hidden safe was discovered on the ground floor, they fell just as quickly when only musty documents were found inside. Still, those records helped to get a roaring fire going, and soon the flames rising from a ruined Treasury joined the many other pyres lighting the Washington sky.

A good night's work, all in all. The American Capitol building reduced to ashes. The President's House as well. The Navy Yard, torched by the hand of its own commander. The Treasury lay in ruins, and gone with the Capitol were the Library of Congress and the chambers of the Supreme Court, as well. The American president, his cabinet, the very government itself driven into ignominious hiding.

There was more work to be done, of course: the State Department building and that of the Department of War would have to be destroyed, as would the Office of Patents. Admiral Cockburn also had a score to settle with Joseph Gales, publisher of the *National Intelligencer* and a man given to the blithe besmirching of the admiral's reputation. Cockburn would find the presses of the *Intelligencer*, he vowed, and make sure that all the *C*s in the typesetting kit were destroyed, "so that the rascals cannot any longer abuse my name." But all that could wait until they were fresh, could wait for another day.

Cockburn and Ross and their men had destroyed just about all that the nation had managed to construct in its capital over the course of twenty-two years, and had taken just a few hours to do it. If such devastation had not taught these upstarts a lesson in "hard war," what could?

38

Thieves in the Night

THE BUILDINGS JUST WEST OF THE GUTTED WHITE House that housed the Departments of War and State went up in flames the following morning, though Cockburn spared the Patent Office following a desperate plea by William Thornton, the original architect of the Capitol. Thornton had raced a column of troops to the spot, to stand on the steps and block their path. Burning the building would destroy hundreds of priceless models and documents, all private property and the product of America's best minds; it would be an act of barbarism comparable to the Turks' immolation of the Library of Alexandria, Thornton argued as he held them off. If it must be done, why not carry out to the street anything thought to be public property and destroy it there?

While Thornton's Solomonic suggestion saved the Patent Office, it may also have given Cockburn food for thought when he led his troops to the offices of the *National Intelligencer*. Confronted by a pair of Washington matrons unable to find passage out of the city who begged him not to burn the newspaper offices for fear the fire would spread to their own homes next door, Cockburn responded courteously. The ladies would be just as safe with him as they would with President Madison, he assured them, then ordered everything inside Gales's offices brought into the street and set aflame.

While the troops torched files, shattered presses, and scattered type, one onlooker called out to Cockburn, "If General Washington had been alive, you would not have gotten into this city so easily." The words must have struck a chord in the normally abrasive admiral. "No," he responded thoughtfully. "If George Washington had been president we should never have thought of coming here."

It would be particularly poetic if, along with Dr. Thornton and the spirit of George Washington, a threadbare Major Pierre Charles L'Enfant and his faithful hound had confronted Cockburn and Ross with a passionate defense of his city and of *liberté*, but there is no record of any such event. Though it is easy enough to imagine him shaking his head over a pint in some safe retreat, or muttering to himself as he gazed out over the smoldering ruins of the city he championed, his location and emotions on that day are simply not known.

The day's high point for bravado actually came when John Lewis, a somewhat addled grandnephew of George Washington, mounted a steed and made a singlehanded charge on a group of British soldiers not far from the charred remains of the President's House. Lewis, who had run off to sea as a youngster only to suffer impressment at the hands of the British Navy, apparently found the possibility of carrying out his long-promised revenge upon the Crown too tempting to pass up. He managed one shot from his pistol in the general direction of the startled British troops before they sent a far better-aimed volley in return. Lewis, mortally wounded, toppled from the saddle as his terrified horse galloped on across F Street—no one dared venture out to pull his body from the gutter until the following day.

The British took some of their worst casualties of the entire attack later that afternoon when a detachment entered the American arsenal at Greenleaf's Point, the southernmost corner of the city, where the Eastern Branch emptied into the Potomac. Though the retreating American troops had burned the fort itself, more than a hundred barrels of powder still remained in the magazine there, and the British intended to destroy them before the Americans could make any use of them. As British troops tossed barrels into a deep well, a spark sent the entire mass of powder up in a thunderous explosion. Thirty men died instantly and nearly fifty more went down with bones broken or limbs blown away.

Soon after the echoes of that horrific explosion died away, the skies turned dark and huge peals of thunder were heard as a storm of epic proportions rolled in. The force of the winds was great enough to flatten several poorly built wooden homes and rip the roof off the Patent Office that Thornton had prevailed upon Cockburn to spare only hours before.

"Great God, Madam!" a disbelieving Admiral Cockburn is reported to have asked one local woman. "Is this the kind of storm to which you are accustomed in this infernal country?"

"No, sir," she replied. "This is a special interposition of Providence to drive our enemies from our city."

Reports of several such encounters survive. For all the devastation wreaked upon official Washington, the British maintained a respect for any stranded inhabitants and their property that seems almost quaint from a modern perspective. On several occasions, General Ross acquiesced to the appeals of citizens when they argued that the destruction of certain buildings—the Marine Barracks among them—would endanger nearby private property. When Cockburn was informed by Doctor James Ewell (in whose home Cockburn and Ross had bivouacked) that the Bank of America was housed in a private building, it too was spared.

One British soldier was flogged for having stolen a goose, and another was summarily executed for a series of thefts. When a prostitute showed up in tears at Dr. Ewell's house, bruised and bloodied, and accused a sailor of rape, Cockburn ordered all his men mustered for a lineup. The assailant was to be shot on the spot. In the end, the woman was too distraught to proceed, and—at Dr. Ewell's urging—the matter was dismissed.

Shortly thereafter, a group of bedraggled citizens of Alexandria arrived at Ewell's doorstep, soaked from a trip through the rainstorm and bearing a dripping white flag. They wanted to surrender their city, they told Cockburn, who suspected that the sight of a supporting fleet under the command of Captain James Gordon advancing up the Potomac had put the fear of further destruction into them. Not so, they assured him, they had seen no advancing fleet. They simply wanted to surrender.

To Cockburn, the idea seemed preposterous. One surrendered when one was staring down the barrel of an enemy's gun. But still, he was agreeable. If the good men of Alexandria promised not to engage in any covert hostile actions, he pledged to respect their property and even pay for any supplies that he might have to take. With that, the grateful citizens made their exit, and the city of Alexandria was officially in British hands. On their heels, a group of Georgetown citizens led by Mayor John Peter approached General Ross offering to surrender their city, too, if he would spare their homes. Ross assured the men of Georgetown that they could rest easy; he had no designs on their property.

In truth, Ross was anxious to decamp from Washington as soon as possible, before General Winder and other American troops in the vicinity regrouped and mounted a counterattack. He had heard rumors of American forces massing in the western hills abutting Washington, and he did not want to wait. The mission he and Cockburn had chosen for themselves had been successful beyond the most sanguine expectations, but the troops were exhausted, and—with no supply lines, no cavalry, and no artillery—they were in no shape to hold a position.

In the end, the British occupation of Washington lasted scarcely twenty-four hours. Shortly after nightfall on August 25, Ross and Cockburn ordered a series of bonfires built, to give the appearance that camps had been established for yet another night. Then, with the hooves of their few horses muffled, driving what cattle they could quickly rustle, and all the supplies they could muster loaded onto wagons, the British simply vanished from the devastated city into the night.

39

Scorn and Execration

THE NEWS OF THE ATTACK ON WASHINGTON WAS RE-
ported in terms that would have warmed the hearts of Ross
and Cockburn, and might also have tempered the anger of
Admiral Cochrane, who had seen his two subordinates ignore clear
orders to abort the assault and return to his ships at once. "When
General Ross's official account of the battle and the capture and destruction of our capitol is published in England, it will hardly be credited by Englishmen," wrote the *New York Evening Post*. "Even here it
is still considered as a dream."

"In what words shall we break the tidings to the ear?" was the plea
of the *Richmond Enquirer* on August 27. "The blush of shame, and of
rage, ringes the cheek while we say that Washington has been in the
hands of the enemy."

Outraged Washingtonians voiced their dismay with messages
scrawled on the walls of the still-smoldering Capitol Building: "George
Washington founded this city after a seven years' war with England,"
one read. "James Madison lost it after a two years' war." "James Madison is a rascal, a coward, and a fool," proclaimed another graffitist,
who completed his message with a sketch of the president fleeing in
terror, minus his hat and wig. "Armstrong sold the city . . . The Capital of the Union lost by cowardice."

Following a scathing editorial in Philadelphia's *United States Gazette* demanding that the country's leaders be "constitutionally impeached and driven with scorn and execration from the seats which they have dishonored and polluted," Secretary of War Armstrong—in an action as bizarre as his conduct in office—issued his resignation via a letter published in the *Baltimore Patriot* on September 3 and reprinted in the *National Intelligencer* on September 8. Defiant and oblivious to the end, Armstrong wrote that he would rather step down than allow his actions to be dictated by the whims of a mob "stimulated by faction and led by folly." He depicted himself as a scapegoat for the failures of others: "It became a system to load me with all the faults and misfortunes which occurred," he said, and, in the end, he blamed the debacle on the cowardice of American troops. Had the men at Bladensburg "been faithful to themselves and to their country," Armstrong asserted, "the enemy would have been beaten and the capital saved."

As for Madison, who was described by an acquaintance as appearing "shaken and woe-begone . . . as if his heart was broken" upon his return to the ruined city, he had no intention of capitulating to editorial writers, public opinion, or the British forces still in the area, including the fleet of Captain Gordon sailing up the Potomac toward Alexandria. He appointed James Monroe as acting secretary of war and issued a warning that anyone found trying to contact the British with appeasement or surrender in mind would find himself facing a bayonet.

To counter any impression that the capital was still in the control of the British, Madison issued a proclamation published in the *National Intelligencer* of September 3, stating that the city was back in the hands of the elected government and calling on all Americans for a "manly and universal determination to chastise and expel the invader." A previous generation had made great sacrifice to secure liberty, Madison reminded his audience—now an equal resolve would be necessary to maintain the nation's independence. The president's message succeeded in shifting the prevailing mood from dismay and finger-pointing toward outrage and determination. "The spirit of the nation is roused," proclaimed the *Niles Weekly Register*. "War is a new business to us, but we must 'teach our fingers to fight' . . . Wellington's *invincibles* shall be beaten by the sons of those who fought at *Saratoga* and *Yorktown*."

"Believe us, fellow citizens," the *Albany Register* admonished. "This is no moment for crimination and recrimination. . . . Let one voice and one spirit animate us all—the voice of our bleeding country and the spirit of our immortal ancestors." Even Alexander Hanson, a vitriolic opponent of Madison and publisher of the *Federal Republican*, called for unity: "The fight will now be for our country," he proclaimed, "not for a party."

Leading Federalists in government followed suit. New York senator Rufus King called for an immediate, all-out attack on the British, announcing, in a break with his party's fiscal conservatism, his support for loans to finance the operation and making the rather startling pledge of his personal fortune toward the effort as well. Vermont governor Martin Chittenden, who had earlier refused to allow his militiamen to fight outside the borders of his state, made a turnabout of his own. The situation had changed, he declared, and he urged that "all degrading party distinctions and animosities . . . ought to be laid aside; that every heart may be stimulated and every arm nerved for the protection of our common country, our liberty, our altars, and our firesides." Lamentable, perhaps, that it had taken the destruction of the Federal City to achieve such unity of purpose, but then again, of what matter were the petty distinctions of political preference when the very survival of the nation was at stake?

Many Britons were jubilant, of course. The prince regent called the campaign "brilliant and successful" in a commendation of Ross, and Sir George Prevost, governor-general of Canada, crowed that "the proud capital at Washington has experienced a similar fate to that inflicted by an American force" at his own capital of York. Still, there were those on the opposing side who, if they failed to fully calculate the impact of the attack in uniting Americans, still felt that Ross and

Cockburn might have gone too far. The *Annual Register* for 1814, a chronicle of British and world history, noted that the actions of the commanders had resulted in "a heavy censure on the British character," and the *London Statesman* added, "The Cossacks spared Paris, but we spared not the capitol of America."

In the end, the righteous charge levied by James Monroe in a letter to Admiral Cochrane on September 6, 1814, seems to have carried the day. "In the course of ten years past, the capitals of the principal powers of the continent of Europe have been conquered," Monroe scolded the British commander, "and no instance of such wanton and unjustifiable destruction has been seen."

Cochrane welcomed Ross and Cockburn back to his command with open arms and pronounced himself well satisfied with how things had turned out, apparently having decided to ignore their blatant insubordination. In fact, Cochrane was so buoyed by their success—terming it "as fine a thing as any done during this war, and a rub to the Americans that can never be forgotten," according to Colonel Arthur Brooke, one of Ross's subordinates—that he agreed to Cockburn's suggestion that they carry out an operation against Baltimore next.

Despite General Ross's fears that, following the assault on Washington, the Americans could not possibly be caught unawares at Baltimore, the attack went forward. At 7:00 a.m. on September 12, Ross landed a force of 4,500 men at North Point, about fifteen miles southeast of the city. While Cochrane began a bombardment of Fort McHenry at the mouth of Baltimore Harbor, Ross began his march overland. He and his troops made it less than halfway toward their target when they spotted American forces arrayed to stop them; in the next moment, a shot rang out from an American rifleman, and Ross toppled from his horse, dead on the spot. Though the ground troops would push the Americans all the way back to the limits of the city, the naval bombardment—kept at long range by the accurate fire of American gunships and the fort's batteries—was proving less effective. Given the loss of their commander and the steadfast resistance of the Americans, Colonel Brooke decided not to press the ground engagement further. By three o'clock the next morning, he and his men were in ignominious retreat toward their ships.

Meanwhile, witnessing the assault on Fort McHenry from the deck of a ship—where he had been taken by the British after having helped negotiate the release of an American prisoner taken during the assault on Washington—was Francis Scott Key, an attorney, staunch Federalist, and member of a volunteer artillery company from Georgetown. It was there and then that the frustration, the outrage, the pride, and the passion that had been stirred by the British attack on Washington finally took its most lasting form.

As he and companion John Skinner witnessed the seemingly endless shower of screaming Congreve rockets and the thunderous barrage of British mortars descending upon the fort, Key could not help but despair. And yet, when the bombardment had finally ceased and the first light of dawn fell upon the scene, he was astonished to see that it was not a British flag that flew above the battered fort, but the Stars and Stripes. The assault on Baltimore was over, and the British had turned tail. Compelled, as he put it, by an irresistible force, Key snatched an envelope from his pocket and began to scribble notes as fast as his pen would fly, striving to catch everything before memory and inspiration might fail: Congreve rockets with their ruddy red glare, those many mortar bombs bursting in air . . . and the flag, star-spangled, still waving there.

Key called the resulting four verses "The Defence of Fort M'Henry" and suggested it be sung to the tune of a British musical society's anthem with which he was familiar: "To Anacreon in Heaven." The tune, if not the title, stuck, and although it took some time, in 1931 "The Star Spangled Banner" officially became the U.S. national anthem.

40

Dishonest, Avaricious Men

THE WAR WOULD LIMP ALONG INCONCLUSIVELY FOR A few more months, but the British withdrawal at Fort McHenry was to set the course for its final resolution. Cochrane, still hoping to win a clear-cut victory through an assault on the American West via the Mississippi River, prepared a doomed offensive against the forces of General Andrew Jackson outside New Orleans. Britons, weary from their continuing involvement in the Napoleonic Wars, began to reconsider the wisdom of continuing a costly and increasingly unpopular war with their former dependency that seemed to have no end in sight.

The forces that had clashed on the battlefield shifted their focus toward a conference table in Ghent, Belgium, where high-ranking American officials met with delegates of the Crown to negotiate the end of fighting. Meanwhile, the debate, seemingly long settled, over the federal government's permanent home was resurrected in Washington by the actions of the British invaders. Congress reconvened on September 19, less than a month after the city had burned, using as their cramped chambers the Patent Office Building that William Thornton had managed to save.

The first item on the House of Representatives' agenda was a proposal to move the capital to a temporary base in Philadelphia, but

debate on the matter had to wait when a fistfight prompted by its introduction broke out between the abrasive Alexander Hanson, publisher of the *Federal Republican*, and Representative Willis Alston of
North Carolina. When order was restored and a preliminary vote
taken, the results evoked uneasy reminiscences of the deep divisions
that had plagued the nascent republic: Connecticut, New Hampshire,
Rhode Island, and New Jersey voted for immediate removal of the
government to Philadelphia. Fiercely opposed were the delegations
from North Carolina, Georgia, Maryland, Tennessee, and Virginia. The
swing states were New York, Pennsylvania, and Kentucky, with their
delegations split on the matter.

While local businessmen wrung their hands in fear that Washington City, already suffering from the massive destruction of the invasion, was about to become a ghost town, the debate in Congress raged
on into October, when a sharply divided House finally resolved the
matter with a vote of 83–74 against removal, following a third—and
final—reading. Washington would remain the seat of government,
and rebuilding the devastated city became a federal priority.

IT WOULD BE many years before the scars of war were removed from
the landscape of the Federal City, but every journey begins with first—
sometimes uncertain—steps. And one of those, as fate would have it,
was undertaken by a figure familiar in the saga of the capital on the
Potomac.

In September of 1814, shortly after the defeat of the British at Baltimore and during congressional debate over the future of the capital,
the acting secretary of war, James Monroe, determined that the devastated Fort Washington, which had been abandoned to England's
Captain Gordon by a cowering Captain Samuel Dyson, would have
to be rebuilt, at once. The capitulation of the fort, about twelve miles
south of the Federal City—and the resultant ease with which Gordon's fleet commandeered Alexandria shortly after Ross and Cockburn
had departed Washington—convinced Monroe that if Washington

was to stand in perpetuity, the Potomac approach must be effectively protected against future incursions at all costs.

There were many men the secretary might have deputized for the task, of course, but it is poetically just that the one he actually picked was one Pierre Charles L'Enfant. Once more, the architect would be given an opportunity for public service, and who could fail to wonder whether this might be the occasion with which L'Enfant might finally redeem himself and his fortunes?

It all began on July 25, when Monroe's predecessor, Robert Armstrong, received a complaint from the fort's commander, Captain Dyson, bemoaning the abilities of his ill-prepared eighty-man force as well as the general disrepair of the facility and its armaments. In response, Armstrong dispatched none other than Major L'Enfant to inspect the installation and report his findings—this was an engineer who had worked (however maddeningly) at bolstering Fort Mifflin near Philadelphia in the aftermath of the Revolution, after all. L'Enfant, who had long been a champion of an enhanced network of defenses for the nation's seaports, went eagerly to Fort Washington and was soon back to confirm the opinions of its commander:

"The whole original design is bad," L'Enfant assured Armstrong, "and it is therefore impossible to make a perfect work of it by alterations." The installation would require a substantial appropriation for its redesign and for the addition of a number of heavy guns. Furthermore, L'Enfant said, what was really needed was the construction of another fort somewhere nearby.

If he had been hoping for a few suggestions for a quick and inexpensive fix, Armstrong had clearly sent the wrong man. Whatever he thought of L'Enfant's ideas, there were no funds available for such an ambitious overhaul, and besides, with the British operations heating up elsewhere, Armstrong had a thousand other things to do nothing about. Whether or not Armstrong's foot-dragging was responsible, in late August, following the devastation of Washington, when Captain Gordon and His Majesty's ships approached the installation perched on a hill nearly two hundred feet above the Potomac, Captain Dyson wasted no time in blowing up his own magazine and leading his forces in a hasty retreat, leaving the rest for the British to burn. These ignominious actions led to a court-martial for Dyson and his eventual dishonorable discharge from the armed services.

Given this background and L'Enfant's previous involvement with Fort Washington, as well as Monroe's enduring sense of obligation to "an old revolutionary fellow soldier and friend," it must have seemed a golden opportunity for the new secretary. He had, after all, been behind the idea to offer L'Enfant a teaching position at West Point to compensate him for his many claims against the government, and he no doubt still considered the man an able architect and designer. Furthermore, L'Enfant was a close friend of a prominent Washington figure by the name of Thomas Digges, whose British-born father had founded a plantation named Warburton Manor across the Potomac from Mount Vernon, scarcely a quarter-mile from Fort Washington (its proximity led the installation to be referred to often as Fort Warburton, in fact).

Digges, making use of his family connections, had spent a good deal of time abroad during the Revolution, serving as an agent (detractors claimed he was actually a double agent) attempting to barter a secret peace agreement between the upstart colonies and the Crown. Benjamin Franklin, in particular, was suspicious of Digges's loyalties, and the resulting controversy led some Maryland detractors of Digges to attempt to have his estate confiscated on the grounds that he had been a traitor to the cause of independence. But Digges managed to retain his holdings, and since 1798, following a twenty-year career as a government agent, had been living at Warburton, a great favorite of George Washington and a frequent dinner guest at Mount Vernon during the last years of the president's life.

Digges may have first met L'Enfant during a period of their mutual involvement with Alexander Hamilton's Society of Useful Manufactures in Paterson, or they may have struck up a friendship later, in the first decade of the century, when both spent some time in residence at Rhodes' Tavern in Washington. In any case, they remained close, and Digges was happy to extend his hospitality at Warburton to L'Enfant as he carried out his duties at the nearby fort.

As L'Enfant's biographer Kenneth Bowling puts it, "It was a match made in heaven—two old worldly Catholic bachelors [L'Enfant was by then sixty] who shared a house and meals in harmony, each pursuing his own claim against the federal government." Digges, it seems, had filed a number of petitions regarding alleged damage to his property caused during the construction of the adjacent fort just prior to the war in 1812, and he was entirely sympathetic to the litany of similar complaints L'Enfant had filed with an uncaring bureaucracy.

In letters to friends, Digges described the arrangement as "better than a hotel with me as the bar keeper of a tavern—all however pro bono," praising L'Enfant as an able engineer as well as "a faithful agent to his employers and an inflexibly honest upright man." Though his relationship with Digges could not have proceeded more favorably, the ties between L'Enfant and his employers quickly soured.

When, during a tour of the grounds of the fort with L'Enfant and Digges, Monroe made a few suggestions concerning the work to be undertaken, L'Enfant dashed off a haughty letter to the secretary making it quite clear who was the expert in building and design. And though the architect talked of ambitious plans and ordered 1,000 pieces of stone and 200,000 of brick, by the middle of 1815 he had failed—despite several requests from the clerk of the War Department—to deliver any formal plan of his intentions.

Once again, the status of his employment reached a crisis. The continual calls for plans and progress reports had reduced him to such a state as to make him "pray for death," L'Enfant wrote back to Monroe. He described himself as a "naked cast away" struggling for survival "on a strange shore without home without friend without resources," and he reiterated the irony that he had to suffer so in a country "for whose service I bled and spent a good fortune."

On June 23, 1815, L'Enfant sent off a lengthy explanation of the

difficulties he was facing at Fort Washington to A. J. Dallas, who succeeded Monroe as acting secretary of war. He had not submitted a
formal plan for the work, L'Enfant explained, because he had been
ordered to work on temporary artillery emplacements in case of a
British return to the area. His progress had been further handicapped,
he pointed out, "without the aid of clerk and of copyist draftsman
whom I had not."

Furthermore, he had been assured when he was hired that he
would have plenty of time to crystallize a formal plan: "I simply asked
and I was readily granted the permission of the reserve of those ideas
in order for the better perfection of them." Further distractions to that
"perfection of ideas" had come in the form of contractors who "would
never bring any thing in time, neither in quantity nor quality suitable"; a "treacherous" master mason; and the failure of the department
to supply him with a sufficient number of laborers, carts, or oxen.

And as for another asinine suggestion that had passed to him down
the chain of command, L'Enfant was resolute: "[W]ith respect to the
idea of carrying on work with the assistance of men from the army to
the exclusion of other—I must be explicit: *that cannot be done*." Soldiers might be employed from time to time at common labor, he
pointed out, but what he needed to complete this job was a dedicated
corps of masons, stonecutters, carpenters, blacksmiths, "and all the
hord of those mechanic journeymen as will soon be wanted."

He closed his letter to Dallas with a lament on the chicanery of the
contractors and suppliers drawn to a noble project meant to bolster
the defense of the nation. He could have made himself a rich man by
accepting a mere fraction of the bribes offered him, L'Enfant assured
the secretary, but he stopped himself short of a full exegesis on that
matter, for, "indeed it would here carry me too far to describe the va-
rieties of winding ways which avaricious, *dishonest avaricious* men, can
safely pursue in effecting their own aims of plunder."

Whether this early observation on the corruption of defense contractors caught the secretary's attention is doubtful. This much, though,

is certain: according to Department of the Interior archives, "operations were suspended on July 8, 1815, and on September 6, Lieutenant Colonel Walker K. Armistead succeeded Major L'Enfant at Fort Washington." The formal service to his adopted country by P. Charles L'Enfant, architect and engineer, was finally at an end.

41

Phoenix Rising

WHILE L'ENFANT'S LAST PUBLIC DRAMA PLAYED OUT, momentous developments in the final course of the war were taking place as well. On Christmas Eve, 1814, British and U.S. negotiating teams meeting in the Belgian town of Ghent agreed to end all hostilities in what had turned out to be an inconclusive and unpopular conflict, and to revert to *status quo ante bellum* (as things were before the war). Other than formally proclaiming "a firm and universal Peace," the treaty changed very little between the two countries, declaring simply that all land and property would be returned to prewar owners or paid for, including Canadian lands and American slaves.

Nothing in it addressed an end to the impressments of American seamen, but the practice had been discontinued anyway—with the Napoleonic Wars at an end, there was no need for the British Navy to bolster its forces in such a way. Similarly, the end of hostilities with France and her allies made retributive trade restrictions a meaningless issue as well. And finally, with an understanding that the border between the United States and Canada should remain exactly where it had been before the war began, the British had no reason to continue to incite Indian depredations on that frontier.

Though neither side achieved a clear military victory, in the aftermath of the war it became clear that the United States had finally won coequal status with its former master, ending a period of discontent that had endured since the Revolutionary War. Contemporary observers believe the end of the War of 1812 marks a gradual reversal of roles between the two powers, as Britain's empire waned and the United States grew stronger.

News of the treaty's signing only reached the United States by packet ship the second week of February. In the meantime, Cochrane's flotilla reached the Louisiana coast below New Orleans, and ground troops began an assault on the city defended by troops under the command of General Andrew Jackson. Jackson had been spoiling for the contest for several months, ever since word of the debacle at Washington had reached him. On September 26, he wrote to a colleague, "was it not for the national disgrace I am glad of it—It will unite America and learn the rulers of our nation, to prepare for defence before it is too late." Had he and his "Tennesseens" been there, Jackson declared, "the capital would have been defended—and saved."

What happened at New Orleans suggested the truth of those bold words. In an epic battle that took place on January 8, Andrew Jackson's forces soundly defeated the British, killing, wounding, or capturing about 2,500 of the enemy, and losing just thirteen of their own. Although the battle was inconsequential in practical terms, the overwhelming victory swelled American pride and made such a hero of Jackson that he would eventually ride the triumph into the presidency fourteen years later.

Following the ratification of the peace treaty in February, and with the issue of the permanence of Washington City settled at last, the restoration of its public buildings could begin in earnest. Former chief architect George Hadfield estimated that it would take $692,000 to restore what the British had destroyed, and an unusually generous Congress appropriated $500,000 toward the task. As usual, preliminary estimates and appropriations would prove only a fraction of the eventual total, but it was a mark of the Federalists' diminished influence that the bill went forward with little debate.

Dolley and James Madison, who had returned to view the ruins of the President's House on August 27, two days after the British decamped, moved into Octagon House, the former home of the French ambassador, just west of the White House at 18th Street and New York Avenue NW. While the First Lady reportedly burst into sobs at any mention of the British for months afterward, she soon resumed a series of entertainments in her new quarters and vowed a meticulous reconstruction of her old ones.

President Madison resurrected the District Board of Commissioners, which had been abolished by Jefferson, and they in turn hired James Hoban to rebuild the President's House, which he had originally seen to completion, along with the Cabinet buildings, which had been torched on the second day of the occupation. At the opposite end of Pennsylvania Avenue, Benjamin Latrobe, who had gotten crosswise with Congress over ever-increasing cost overruns before the war, was put back at work on the Capitol.

Hoban soon discovered that while the exterior walls of the White House remained standing, the heat had weakened them terribly. In the end, though most of the foundation supports were salvaged, the exterior shell of the President's House had to be torn down and rebuilt.

Though the pace of work proceeded rapidly—it would take only three years to rebuild most of what had taken ten years originally— James and Dolley Madison would never again reside in the President's House. In fact, it was not until New Year's Day of 1818, almost a year after James Monroe succeeded Madison in office, that the White House was officially reopened. Even then, much of the interior detail work and furnishing awaited completion. And though he is credited with the completion of the project, in his haste Hoban had taken certain shortcuts (such as replacing ruined inner partitions of brick with wood, and using soft pine for flooring) that would require a virtual second rebuilding of the White House in 1948.

Meanwhile, and while Latrobe was at work on the Capitol, Congress at first continued to use the Patent Office for its sessions, later relocating to a tavern that Latrobe hastily enlarged just east of the Capitol at the southeast corner of First and A Streets NE. Though he had agreed to the same $1,600-a-year salary as Hoban, Latrobe was far more the artiste (or the careful craftsman) than his counterpart at the White House, and simply could not confine himself to mere reconstruction. He was intent on correcting what he had always viewed as flaws in the original design of the building.

The situation was exacerbated when, in the spring of 1816, Madison decided to abolish both the recently reconstituted Board of Commissioners and the office of the City Superintendent and replace them both with a one-man post he called the Commissioner of Public Buildings. To this position Madison appointed a detail-oriented if pedestrian-minded former military officer named Samuel Lane.

Lane was the sort who demanded regular reports and strict attention to details, such as showing up for work regularly and on time. Given that Latrobe had proclaimed his workday to begin at 10:00 a.m. and to end at 3:00 p.m., Lane did not think it too much to ask that these hours be faithfully observed. Latrobe, however, was cut from the same bolt of cloth as L'Enfant when it came to answering to authority, and soon contentious memos were flying back and forth between the commissioner and the architect. "The enclosed has been sent by mistake to my address," ran one rejoinder from Latrobe to Lane, when the latter had requested that the architect try to be more punctual and reliable in maintaining his hours. "It was apparently intended for somebody who was supposed to have neither the habits, the education, nor the *spirit* of a Gentleman."

Latrobe's standing among the members of Congress was also suffering. While work progressed fairly smoothly on the North Wing, where the Senate would reside, a delay in the delivery of the marble columns necessary to support the roof of the South Wing meant that virtually no work was going on there. In addition, Latrobe's habit of sending Congress requests for additional funds without any supporting detail had begun to make some lawmakers share Lane's concerns about the architect.

Matters worsened early in 1817, when the newly elected Monroe, anxious to move the pace of work forward, declared that Latrobe should drop his plans for extremely heavy brick domes above the two wings and install less durable but more easily built wood frames instead. An incensed Latrobe protested, and even suggested to Lane that it might be time for him to resign.

Meanwhile, on March 28, 1817, Monroe himself traveled to the quarry where the marble for the South Wing columns was being excavated, to try to speed along that process. After a look at the high-quality stone convinced him that it was worth the trouble to stick with marble for the supports, the president reassigned Robert Leckie, director of the U.S. Arsenals and a former quarry master, to the project. Leckie would be in charge of having the stone cut from the earth and John Hartnet, the present master, would turn his efforts solely to the final shaping of it. Monroe also installed a clerk at the quarry site who would keep the books, pay the workers, and oversee the flow of necessary supplies. He was to receive progress reports every Monday morning, Monroe declared. All fooling around in this matter was going to end.

Having taken these steps, Monroe embarked on a three-month tour of the New England states that would take up the entire summer. Before his departure, he made it clear that he expected the White House and the Capitol to be completed upon his return. Latrobe and Lane were to bury their differences and concentrate on the task at hand, he added, or someone's head was going to roll.

When Monroe returned from his travels in September, he found far less than what he had demanded. The prospect of finishing work on the buildings in such a short time had been far-fetched to begin with, and the unforeseen delays common to any complex building project, including in this case the collapse of the canal used to transport the marble columns from the quarry, meant that little had been accomplished over the summer.

An irate Monroe had, shortly after his inaugural, named a pair of army engineers to an informal panel meant to advise the president on expediting the construction of public buildings, but that only added another layer of bureaucracy in the way of progress. Latrobe was assailed by constant requests from Monroe, Superintendent Lane, and panel members that he explain this or that aspect of a complex undertaking, the very oversight of which might have required the totality of a supervisor's attention.

The orchestration of any major building project involving the efforts of hundreds of specialized workers is a trying task under the best of circumstances. Compounding the difficulties at the Capitol was the fact that Latrobe was doing his best to carry out his work within the confines of an existing, though seriously damaged, footprint. Every day's work revealed an unforeseen issue that would have to be corrected before the new work could proceed. As many a builder has had to explain patiently to a homeowner hoping to save a few dollars by remodeling an existing structure, it is a far simpler, quicker, and cheaper process to build from scratch than to add on or re-create.

Under such circumstances, it is a teeth-grinding experience for a project manager to be called away from an attempt to simply keep things rolling to sit down with a client—or, worse yet, the emissary of a client, a person who almost assuredly has never held a hammer or driven a peg—and explain, for instance, why the wet plaster seems to look a lot darker than what was expected, or just why all those men are needed on a job when some of them seem to be simply standing around and watching.

Such constant heel-nipping finally did Latrobe in. Saddled with debt accrued in the years following his first dismissal from work at the Capitol, and greatly saddened by the recent death of his son from yellow fever, he was nearing emotional collapse when, on November 20, the president called him to a summit conference with Superintendent Lane after Lane had dismissed Latrobe's chief carpenter and replaced him with a favorite of his own.

The meeting had not proceeded far when Latrobe snapped. As Latrobe's wife describes the scene, her husband suddenly jumped from his chair and fell upon Lane (who had lost the use of one arm and walked with a limp as a result of injuries sustained in the recent war), seizing him by the collar. "Were you not a cripple I would shake you to atoms, you poor contemptible wretch," Mary Elizabeth Latrobe reports her husband as saying. "Am I to be dictated to by you?"

An astonished Monroe tried to intervene, asking the distraught Latrobe, "Do you know who I am, sir?"

Latrobe released Lane and tried to gather himself. "Yes, I do," he told the president, "and ask your pardon, but when I consider my birth, my family, my education, my talents, I am excusable for any outrage after the provocation I have received from that contemptible character."

With a last angry glance at Lane, Latrobe left the president's chamber and returned home, where he quickly dashed off his letter of resignation. In a fashion of which fellow architect L'Enfant surely would have approved, Latrobe chose to pretend as though no "superintendent" existed; he extended his thanks and his most sincere apologies for leaving solely and directly to President Monroe.

GIVEN THE FATE of L'Enfant, Hallet, Thornton, Hadfield, and Latrobe, it might have seemed a tall order to entice any capable practitioner to a project that had proven itself to be a veritable graveyard for architects. But a request to spearhead the construction of the foremost governmental structure in the nation was a lure that transcended ordinary cautions. Scarcely had Latrobe left Washington City for a fresh start in Baltimore than Charles Bullfinch, a Harvard graduate from Boston and, though self-trained, considered the best architect in New England, agreed to take the job for $2,500 a year, less than the $3,500 he asked for, but still enough to entice him to the Potomac.

Following his appointment on December 12, 1817, Bullfinch went quickly to work on the completion of renovations to the damaged North and South wings. He also designed the central building and oversaw its completion, capping it with a low stone-and-wood dome over the rotunda below (a dome that would be replaced with the taller cast-iron dome we know today in 1856–64 renovations). He completed the eastern portico with its striking sculpted tympanum (*Genius of America*), and effected a major change to the western façade facing the Mall, creating an impressive projecting portico where Latrobe had envisioned a recess, thereby creating additional space for much-needed meeting rooms. The earth and masonry terraces that he added there not only framed the building appropriately but provided camouflage for the necessary privies and other service structures. He also was responsible for landscaping the Capitol grounds and adding a fence that kept tree- and shrub-hungry cattle from their regular incursions there.

Aided by a willingness to suffer both fools and apt criticism, and able to justify his decisions and expenditures in a way that left Congress with little to do but shrug at the ever-rising costs of doing business, Bullfinch left the office of Architect of the Capitol in 1829, shortly after the inauguration of Andrew Jackson, having accomplished what so many before him had only dreamed of. Thirty-six years after it was begun, the U.S. Capitol had been made whole.

42

Ad Astra

"REBUILDING" WASHINGTON WAS SOMETHING OF AN OPEN-ended process, making it difficult to say just when all that the British had destroyed was finally put right again. What new structure, for instance, will take the place of what existed on the footprint of the Twin Towers—or wipe away the memories of what took place there? Just when and how are such losses repaired?

For one thing, work on the Capitol did not stop when the Senate and House wings were made serviceable again. It could be argued that once the President's House was restored and Bullfinch had finished with the Capitol—the two buildings that Washington, L'Enfant, and others saw as the necessary poles—then the enterprise of the city was at last established. But even that is debatable. Cities change organically and, except for those that have died altogether, they are always in flux—growing here, shrinking there, ever changing in their character.

The Treasury Building was rebuilt quickly following the departure of the British troops, but it was again destroyed by fire in 1833. The story is told that Andrew Jackson, weary of delay and debate over the site for its replacement, walked out from the President's House one day, jammed his cane into the earth at the corner of 15th Street and Pennsylvania Avenue and said, "Here, right here, I want the cornerstone laid." Accordingly it was, and the building was completed in 1842. It lasted only until 1866, however, when it was torn down and replaced again. The 1842 replacement had cost about $600,000. The next, completed in 1869, took $6 million. But then in 1907 the sandstone facing of the building's east wing was removed to match the granite of the west, and so the process would continue. All of the buildings that make up the governmental core of the federal city similarly would be in a constant state of renovation, reconstruction, and repurposing.

A new Patent Office building went up in 1836, and a General Post Office in 1839, though the latter would become the General Land Office when the "new" Post Office (now a shopping mall) was completed in 1899. A Pension Office that commentators found "impressive" was dedicated in 1885, and a "remarkable" building for the Departments of State, War, and Navy in 1888. There was to be the Customs House (1857), the Bureau of Engraving and Printing I (1878) and II (1914), the Department of Agriculture (1903), and on and on.

By the time Bullfinch completed his work, the cost of building the Capitol alone had reached nearly $2.5 million, a significant outlay given that the original estimate for constructing *all* the public buildings in the city was about $1 million. But these figures pale in comparison to what it took to add the massive dome that was added in the 1850s, its crowning Statue of Freedom, and the new Senate and House wings in the mid-nineteenth century. By 1870, the tally for the building was at $12,256,150, and it has been rising ever since.

The Library of Congress resided in rooms at the Capitol until 1814, when the British-set fire consumed its 3,000 volumes. Bullfinch dedicated a space for the Library in the reconstructed building, and there it stayed until its own home was built across the street in 1897 for about $6.5 million. The Supreme Court, which had also met in the Capitol before the British invasion, was relocated to a private home until its reinstallment at the Capitol in 1819. The justices would convene there, in one room and another, until the present Supreme Court Building was completed in 1935.

The Navy Yard, also reduced to ashes, was quickly rebuilt and put back into service, and famously Robert Fulton would turn from development of steamboats to experiments on torpedoes there. In 1855 the Smithsonian Institution was founded and housed, the gift of a British scientist; there would also be a War College (1907), office buildings for House and Senate members (1907 and 1909), and much more.

What L'Enfant had envisioned as the third focal point around which all the other public buildings in Washington would be located did not come into being until 1884, when the long-debated monument to the city's namesake was finally completed, nearly forty years after it was begun. Though everyone in Washington had always agreed that a proper memorial to the first president was not only appropriate but necessary, the nature and placement of the thing itself had been the subject of nearly as much debate as had the location of the capital itself. Jefferson had been indifferent to the matter of a monument, and his administration was followed closely by the devastation of the British invasion. So no action was taken for the first third of the new century, until 1833, when a group of citizens took the matter into their own hands, raised the necessary funds to sponsor a design competition, and, after approving his concept for a six-hundred-foot-tall obelisk, finally hired architect Robert Mills to carry it to fruition.

Congress donated thirty-seven acres of land just slightly south and east of the site that L'Enfant had chosen, reasoning that such a colossus needed to be built on stable, solid ground rather than in the marshy spot L'Enfant had picked out for purposes of symmetry and the sight lines to the Capitol and the President's House (though it might be remembered that L'Enfant had only an equestrian statue in mind). While donations were far short of the $1 million price tag on Mills's design, supporters began construction anyway, figuring that a respectful populace would find some way to finish what had been started. They were right, as it turned out, but delays in funding and occasional distractions such as the Civil War stalled construction near the two-hundred-foot level for nearly twenty years. By that time the original source of stone had been depleted, and the resultant band where the addition of new material ensued is still clearly visible.

THE ORIGINAL ARCHITECT never reemerged in the public affairs of his city. Following the debacle at Fort Washington, L'Enfant spent the remainder of his earthly years under the protection and patronage of Thomas Atwood Digges.

The first portion of that time was spent at Warburton Manor, and though the colorful Digges sometimes acknowledged a wish to visit his former cronies in Washington City, he wrote in 1815 to his friend Archbishop John Carroll that he did not see how he could possibly simply decamp from Warburton and leave the poor old major (not to mention his valued property) alone. "For although himself temperate, quiet, worthy and ever orderly, my doors open to Him would become the Conductor to dinners, lounging night visitants, &ca., &ca. And You as a family man can guess the result."

In 1816, Digges penned a similar note to James Monroe explaining that he would love to spend more time in the Federal City, but that the presence of "my old Chum Major, the want of a housekeeper &ca. yet prevents me." Digges went on to paint a portrait of his aging ward, lamenting not only the state of L'Enfant's wardrobe, "broken shoes, rent pantaloons, out at the elbows, etc. etc. etc. etc.," but his mental condition as well: "manifestly disturbed at his getting the go by, never facing towards the Fort, tho' frequently dipping into the eastern ravines and hills of the plantation—picking up fossils & periwinkles."

It seemed that L'Enfant had not abandoned industry altogether, for Digges described him as "early to bed & rising—working hard with his instruments on paper 8 or ten hours every day as if to give full & complete surveys of his works &ca." But as to exactly what those surveys and works might have consisted of, Digges admitted, "I neither ever see or know."

Ultimately, Digges was unable to resist the lure of nearby Washington, and he spent most of the winter months of 1817 in the city. Following a hailstorm that seriously damaged the manor house in May of 1818, Digges determined never again to return to Warburton, though he insisted that L'Enfant stay on. In the summer of that year, Digges wrote James Madison that he would have closed down the house and used the grounds solely for a tobacco plantation, were it not for the presence of "the old major (a harmless honorable minded man & though a Great Oddity I believe as good an Engineer as any one we have.)"

L'Enfant, meantime, continued to make his own forays into the Federal City, stoically pressing his case, and noting to his most recent attorney that he reckoned the district commissioners had by that time realized nearly $100,000 from sales of copies of his city plan in Holland. In his *Reminiscences*, newspaperman Benjamin Perley Poore describes L'Enfant's ceaseless quest. "He was to be seen almost every day slowly pacing the rotunda of the Capitol," Poore wrote, describing a tall, thin man in a close-fitting blue military coat flapping at his heels and buttoned to his throat, with no sign of a shirt underneath. "His hair was plastered with pomatum close to his head, and he wore a napless high beaver bell-crowned hat." In one hand, L'Enfant swung an imposing silver-headed hickory cane, and in the other—just as formidable, it must have been his hope—he clutched a thick sheaf of papers that would surely someday prove his claim.

For all his disappointments in the halls of government, however, L'Enfant would never jettison his steadfast loyalty to his adopted land. When a census taker visited Warburton Manor in 1820, the acting master of the house identified himself as P. Charles L'Enfant, a white male "over the age of 40" (he was by this time nearly sixty-six years old). In what might be seen as his most significant statement, L'Enfant informed the census taker that he was a citizen of the United States. There is no record to be found that L'Enfant ever formally applied for citizenship, but in his own mind he was a citizen. What else could possibly matter?

L'Enfant's tenure at Warburton might have continued indefinitely were it not for the death of Thomas Digges in 1821. Digges's nephew William Dudley Digges wrote at once to L'Enfant to say that he was entitled to the property and that L'Enfant should of course stay on.

But Thomas Digges's younger sister, Elizabeth—daughter-in-law of Daniel Carroll of Rock Creek, one of the original commissioners so at odds with L'Enfant—sued to take possession of the estate. In 1824 she prevailed, and the seventy-year-old L'Enfant was about to find himself out on the street.

That, however, was not a prospect that Digges's nephew could countenance. On March 15 he sent a driver to Warburton with a message: L'Enfant's belongings were to be loaded up and carried back to Green Hill, William Digges's plantation in northern Prince Georges County, Maryland, where the planner would be his guest. "I think you had better come up and take your quarters with me," William Digges wrote. "Here you are welcome and your coming will give me great pleasure."

While Digges clearly revered the major's contributions and felt it his duty to honor his uncle's commitment to care for the elderly gentleman, it is unclear whether his wife felt the same way. She, it turns out, had been born Eleanora Carroll, daughter of Daniel Carroll of Duddington, whose road-blocking house L'Enfant had destroyed some thirty-two years before.

Still, L'Enfant's stay with William Digges was by all accounts pleasant, if brief. On June 14, 1825, the weary old major died, less than two months shy of his seventy-first birthday and not many days after having presented yet another petition seeking payment for services rendered to his government. An inventory of his personal goods showed that he had accumulated three watches (one silver, two gold, valued at thirty dollars), three compasses (twelve dollars), and a few books, maps, and surveying instruments. Perhaps others had profited to the tune of hundreds of thousands of dollars from his work, but the author of the "Grand Plan" was worth exactly forty-five dollars when he died.

Digges, who preserved L'Enfant's papers—assigned no value by appraisers—discovered while combing through them a copy of the lien that Robert Morris had so long ago assigned to L'Enfant in partial payment of the bank stock loan. The enterprising Digges pressed for payment and was awarded $1,839.76—an award that may have done L'Enfant no good, but it provided something of a return to the Digges family for its eleven years of generosity.

An obituary in the *National Intelligencer* of June 25, 1825, credited "this interesting but eccentric gentleman" with the original conception of the plan of the City of Washington, "and with which his name ought to be gratefully associated." The writer summarized L'Enfant's many disappointments in receiving his just due, and characterized his later years as a "life sequestered from society, and austere privation."

"Notwithstanding his apparent infatuation," the writer continued, "he was a man of great scientific attainments, of profound research, and close and intelligent observation." The writer acknowledged the many contributions of the Digges family to L'Enfant's welfare, and closed with this: "The grateful task of smoothing the downhill path of the veteran L'Enfant has been cheerfully and most kindly performed by the liberal gentleman at whose house he breathed his last."

L'Enfant was buried at Green Hill in a "fine and private place" located amid a copse of cedar trees not far from the Digges manor home. And there he might have remained if not for the obstinacy of good work and loyal friends.

43

Honor and Reward

B Y THE END OF THE NINETEENTH CENTURY, SOME SEV-
enty years after the planner's death, James Dudley Morgan,
physician and grandson of William Dudley Digges, was still
carrying on the efforts of his forebears to have L'Enfant's work on the
City of Washington given the credit they believed was due. Morgan
titled an address before the city's historical society on February 18,
1895, "Major Pierre Charles L'Enfant, the Unhonored and Unrewarded Engineer," and began with the observation that "it is a lasting
disgrace upon the American Congress and people that one like Pierre
Charles L'Enfant, in whom we find so much to admire and to reward,
who has done so much for America, its Capital and the American
people, should have in the early summer and autumn of his life . . .
depended upon charity for the most ordinary necessities to sustain
life."

Even Morgan's efforts to resurrect L'Enfant's reputation might
have ended up in history's dustbin of noble intentions, however, if it
hadn't been for the convergence of a number of forces at about that
time. There had been periodic gestures toward rectifying the matter,
including a bill introduced in Congress in 1884 seeking an appropriation for a monument to L'Enfant. And in 1895 another measure was
introduced, this time seeking $50,000 for that same purpose. No
action was taken in either case.

However, in 1900, the centennial of the permanent relocation of the federal government to Washington City excited considerable interest, not only in what had been accomplished over the previous one hundred years, but in what might be undertaken in the ensuing century. While the Washington of 1900, with almost 300,000 citizens, was no longer the "sheep walk" that Secretary of War Armstrong could not believe to be worthy of enemy attack in 1814, much of the recent development seemed at odds with the concept of a grand and coherent "City Beautiful." It was the concept of orderly planning that had been enthusiastically received in the form of the "White City" at the World's Columbian Exposition in Chicago in 1893, and one that the Federal City seemed desperately in need of.

For all the economic growth and the mighty buildings that sprouted here and there, there were also signs of disarray. Railroad tracks ran across L'Enfant's Mall at Sixth Street, and grade crossings snarled traffic elsewhere in the city. The Smithsonian Building projected onto the Mall's borders as well, and the Botanical Gardens that had been planted in front of the west entrance to the Capitol obscured its connection with Washington's monument and the rest of the city. Many of the small triangles formed at the intersections of streets and the diagonal "avenues of convenience," intended by L'Enfant to be reserved for green spaces and monuments, had become repositories for trash. City offices were scattered, parks were practically nonexistent, and slums had sprung up within a stone's throw of the nation's most esteemed edifices.

On March 8, 1901, Senator James McMillan of Michigan, head of a joint congressional task force, named a blue-ribbon commission that was to formulate a definitive plan for the orderly future development of Washington. Those named to the commission constituted the brain trust behind the Columbian Exposition and a who's-who of American design: Daniel Burnham, chief of construction and visionary of the "White City;" noted landscape architect Frederick Law Olmsted Jr.; sculptor Augustus Saint-Gaudens; and architect Charles F. McKim.

After the august committee had completed a thorough study of the future needs of the capital, revisited a number of the foremost cities of Europe, and engaged in considerable debate as to how best to proceed, they reached unanimous agreement: the perfect plan was already in place.

And it had been since 1791, when an untrained architect named L'Enfant had drawn it up in the space of a few weeks and handed it over to the president. The "Grand Plan" of P. Charles L'Enfant would not only serve as the template for a modern center of government, Burnham and his associates declared, but it should direct the development of the entire District of Columbia as well.

No more need be said. Railroad tracks were buried; gardens moved; trash heaps carted off and replaced with parks and fountains. The L'Enfant Plan would govern the Federal City forever more.

THOSE CHAMPIONS WHO had argued loud and long for a reassessment of the planner's value had found their leverage at last. In 1908, with the enthusiastic support of President Theodore Roosevelt, Congress passed the Sundry Civil Bill, which provided among other things that "one thousand dollars is made available for the Commissioners of the District of Columbia to remove and render accessible to the public the grave of Major Pierre Charles L'Enfant."

Accordingly, on April 22, 1909, a party that included Dr. Morgan, city clerk and historian William Tindall, and City Commissioner Henry MacFarland traveled to Green Hill, Maryland, where the unmarked remains of L'Enfant were disinterred and transferred to a casket. On April 28, the coffin was carried to the rotunda of the U.S. Capitol, where thousands, including then president William Howard Taft, came to honor the planner of the city at last. Only seven others— among them Abraham Lincoln, James Garfield, and William McKinley—had ever lain in state beneath that dome. Later in the afternoon, the casket was transferred to Arlington by military caisson at the head of a procession said to stretch a mile long. A place had been chosen for L'Enfant on a hillside, with a sweeping panorama of the city below.

At the interment ceremony, French ambassador Jules Jusserand summed up the career of L'Enfant: "To plan this city, [President] Washington selected a French Officer, whose qualities of character and faults of temper, he had for thirteen years many occasions to appreciate; gifted, plucky, energetic, but difficult to handle." And in closing, Reverend William Russell of St. Patrick's Church assured those who had gathered, "L'Enfant needs no monument of marble or of bronze. The City Beautiful at his feet is the proudest and most endearing monument we can erect to his memory."

Despite Reverend Russell's sentiments, a competition for the design of a monument did ensue, won by the well-known sculptor William Welles Bosworth (who, fittingly enough, went on to oversee a restoration of the Palace of Versailles in the 1920s). Bosworth, interviewed late in life by L'Enfant biographer Hans Paul Caemmerer, recalled that the design of the tomb was complicated by military regulations governing the size of monuments at Arlington: "L'Enfant, being only a major, could not have a monument exceeding a fixed height of seven feet," Bosworth explained.

And while the correctly proportioned design that Bosworth submitted was the one chosen by the judges, the army regulations had started them thinking. The panel approached the sculptor with an unusual idea: Might Bosworth be willing to abandon his winning proposal and design something like the sort of marker prevalent at the time of L'Enfant's death? He might indeed, Bosworth replied, and thus the final result: a simple but elegant table tomb supported by graceful columns, with the Plan of Washington engraved on top of the slab and the remains in the ground below.

"The President made a fine address, also Monsieur Jusserand and several others whose names I've forgotten," Bosworth said of the dedication, which took place on May 22, 1911. "It was a fine, clear summer afternoon, not hot; a large audience; color, music; and all honors were paid to L'Enfant and Washington, and to Franco-American friendship and collaboration."

Elihu Root, secretary of state at the time, commented, "Few men can afford to wait a hundred years to be remembered. It is not a change in L'Enfant that brings us here. It is we who have changed, who have just become able to appreciate his work. And our tribute to him should be to continue his work."

In the end, then, the vindication that a dramatist might have granted to L'Enfant in his lifetime was left for others to carry out, long after his demise. But that does not alter the fact that his city and his nation finally recognized his efforts, nor does it decrease the incalculable value of the design that he created, or diminish the remarkable strength embodied in the streets and buildings and monuments arrayed in the distance before his tomb.

It is by and large a quiet vigil beneath the sheltering maples there in Arlington, looking out across the sheen of the Potomac at what Washington has become. From time to time, the subdued voices of passersby seeking out the resting place of a family member or a famous person can be heard, and sometimes there is the excited chatter of schoolchildren set free from a stifling bus and fairly indifferent to the stones surrounding them.

And occasionally the quiet is broken by the roar of jet engines from planes descending toward nearby Reagan National Airport. It is difficult to hear that sound without thinking of other jets descending toward Washington, and of the awful destruction at the Pentagon . . . and with that, also the thought that it was not fighter planes, not anti-aircraft fire, not any military marvel that brought that fourth plane down on September 11, 2001—simply a band of ordinary citizens who were willing to lay down their own lives before they'd see other lives taken and a part of their nation destroyed.

Impossible, really, to avoid thoughts of foreign zealots and citizen defenders as we stare out across the Potomac at the city that has served as a symbol of our nation, and therefore both a target and a place to be defended. While the most able and revered of statesmen established the philosophical underpinnings and devised the laws that guide the United States, it was a self-trained architect and lover of liberty named L'Enfant who created the vessel that carries them down through time. If the Declaration of Independence and the Constitution and the Bill of Rights constitute the covenant of a government with its people, then the City of Washington—"a pedestal waiting for a monument"—is its ark.

Acknowledgments

I AM GREATLY INDEBTED to many fine scholars and writers who have covered portions of this ground before me, but foremost among them is Kenneth R. Bowling of George Washington University, whose expertise concerning the founding of Washington, D.C., and treatise on the life and work of P. C. L'Enfant stand as models. Also of particular note is the work of the architectural historian Pamela Scott, whose insights and knowledge concerning Washington, D.C., architecture were invaluable to me.

I would also like to thank a number of those who have been of great assistance as I read and researched the matters taken up in this book: Rusty Roberts, Chief of Staff for Congressman John L. Mica; former Florida congressman Dan Miller; Melissa C. Naulin, Assistant Curator, Executive Residence at the White House; Barbara A. Wolanin, Curator for the Architect of the Capitol; David M. Songer, Director of the Kiplinger Research Library housing the records of the Historical Society of Washington, D.C.; Tom Sherlock, Historian at Arlington National Cemetery; and Adis Beesting, Reference Education Librarian at Florida International University.

I also owe a great debt to Rachel Klayman and Lucinda Bartley at Crown Publishers and to Kim Witherspoon at Inkwell Management. Without the support, advice, and aid of these three remarkable individuals, this book could have not become a reality.

Finally, I want to extend many thanks to my colleague James W. Hall, for his close eye and his unfailing encouragement, and to my family, for helping me make the time and for making this work seem important. They, however, are most important: my wife, Kimberly, and my children, Jeremy, Hannah, and Zander.

Selected Bibliography

A full study of the themes in this volume, including the transition of the British colonies from a state of disarray into a single united nation, the struggle to place and build the u.s. capital, the causes, conduct, and culmination of the War of 1812, along with the monumental personalities involved, might take up the better part of a lifetime. For those interested in delving more deeply into any aspect of this narrative, however, I append a list of publications that were of particular interest and great value to me.

Two of the most important manuscript sources are the letters of Pierre Charles L'Enfant, found in the Digges-L'Enfant-Morgan papers at the Library of Congress, and the George Washington papers, also in the Library of Congress. Many of L'Enfant's writings, as well as the letters of Washington relating to the founding of the "National Capital," are transcribed in the records of the Columbia Historical Society, now known as the Washington Historical Society and housed in the Kiplinger Research Library, the city's original Carnegie library.

Any serious student of the materials pertaining to L'Enfant will note discrepancies between the original documents written in the architect's own hand and the various transcriptions, including those produced by the society, as well as those by L'Enfant's biographers. It can be a trial of patience to follow the circumlocutions, oddities of phrasing, and other peculiarities through the crabbed hand of a man whose exuberance often outdistanced his mastery of his second tongue; I have varied in my presentation of L'Enfant's words, sometimes hewing to the original for the sake of authenticity, at other times using a transcribed version for the sake of clarity. For those inclined, there is, of course, nothing like sitting with a sheaf of the letters of a man as passionate as L'Enfant in hand, and for that we have the foresight and care of the Digges and Morgan families of Maryland to thank.

Adams, Henry. *History of the United States During the Administration of Jefferson and Madison*. New York: Scribner, 1891.

Allen, William C. *History of the United States Capitol*. Washington, DC: U.S. Government Printing Office, 2001.

Allgor, Catherine. *A Perfect Union: Dolley Madison and the Creation of the American Nation*. New York: Henry Holt, 2006.

Arnebeck, Bob. *Through a Fiery Trial: Building Washington 1790–1800*. Lanham, MD: Madison Books, 1991.

Boller, Paul F., Jr. *Presidential Wives: An Anecdotal History*, New York: Oxford University Press, 1988.

Borneman, Walter R. *1812: The War That Forged a Nation*. New York: Harper-Collins, 2004.

Bowling, Kenneth R. *The Creation of Washington, D.C.: The Idea and Location of the American Capital*. Fairfax, VA: George Mason University Press, 1991.

———. *Peter Charles L'Enfant: Vision, Honor, and Male Friendship in the Early American Republic*. Washington, DC: Friends of the George Washington University Libraries, 2002.

Bowling, Kenneth R., ed. *Coming into the City: Essays on Early Washington, D.C.* Washington: Historical Society of Washington, D.C., 2000.

Boyd, Julian, ed. *The Papers of Thomas Jefferson*, 27 volumes, Princeton, NJ: Princeton University Press, 1950–.

Brant, Irving. *James Madison, Commander in Chief, 1812–1836*. New York: Bobbs-Merrill, 1961.

Caemmerer, H. Paul. *The Life of Pierre Charles L'Enfant*. (Washington: National Republic, 1950). Reprint, New York: Da Capo, 1970.

Caffrey, Kate. *The Twilight's Last Gleaming: Britain vs. America, 1812–1815*. New York: Stein & Day, 1977.

"Capture of the City of Washington," *American State Papers*, Military Affairs, v. 1, 524–599.

Carter, Edward C. *The Journals of Benjamin Henry Latrobe, 1799–1820*. New Haven: Yale University Press, 1977–1980.

Clark, Allen C. *Life and Letters of Dolley Madison*. Washington: W. F. Roberts, 1914.

Coles, Harry L. *The War of 1812*. Chicago: University of Chicago Press, 1965.

Elias, Robert H., and Finch, Eugene D., eds. *Letters of Thomas Attwood Digges*. Columbia, SC: University of South Carolina Press, 1982.

Ewell, James. *Planter's and Mariner's Medical Companion*, 3rd ed. Philadelphia: Anderson & Meecham, 1816.

Ford, Paul Leicester, ed. *The Works of Thomas Jefferson*. Federal Edition. 12 vols. New York & London: G.P. Putnam's Sons, 1904–5.

Freneau, Philip M. "Federal Hall," *New York Daily Advertiser*, March 12, 1790: 1.

Greenblatt, Miriam. *The War of 1812*. New York: Facts on File, 1994.

Hamlin, Talbot. *Benjamin Henry Latrobe*. New York/Oxford: Oxford University Press, 1955.

Harris, C. M. "Washington's Gamble, L'Enfant's Dream: Politics, Design, and the Founding of the National Capital." *The William and Mary Quarterly*, 3rd Series, v. 56, no. 3 (July 1999): 527–64.

Hazelton, George C. *The National Capitol: Its Architecture, Art, and History*. New York: Taylor, 1902.

Hickey, Donald R. *The War of 1812: A Forgotten Conflict*. Urbana: University of Illinois, 1989.

Hitsman, J. Mackay. *The Incredible War of 1812: A Military History*. Toronto: University of Toronto, 1965.

Ingersoll, Charles J. *Historical Sketch of the Second War Between the United States of America and Great Britain*, Philadelphia: Lea & Blanchard, 1849.

Jennings, J. L. Sibley. "Artistry as Design: L'Enfant's Extraordinary City." *Library of Congress Quarterly Journal*, Summer 1979.

Jennings, Paul. *A Colored Man's Reminiscences of James Madison*. Brooklyn, NY: G. C. Beadle, 1865.

Jensen, Amy La Follette. *The White House and Its Thirty-three Families*. New York: McGraw-Hill, 1962.

Jusserand, Jules. "Major L'Enfant and the Federal City." In *L'Enfant and Washington 1791–1792* (Elizabeth Kite, 1929). Reprint, New York: New York Times, 1970.

Kimball, Fiske. "Origin of the Plan of Washington, D.C." *Architectural Review* 7 (September 1918: 41–45).

———. "Pierre Charles L'Enfant." *Dictionary of American Biography* (1932). Reprint, Farmington Hills, MI: Thomson Gale, 2006.

Kite, Elizabeth. *L'Enfant and Washington 1791–1792*. (Baltimore: Arno, 1929). Reprint, New York: New York Times, 1970.

Lambert, Tallmadge A. "Observations on the Development of the Nation's Capital." *Records of the Columbia Historical Society*, 2, 1899, 272–92.

Lear, Tobias. *Letters and Recollections of George Washington*. New York: Doubleday, 1906.

"L'Enfant, Pierre Charles." *Encyclopedia of World Biography*, 2nd ed. Detroit: Gale Research, 1998.

"L'Enfant's Memorials." *Records of the Columbia Historical Society*, v. 2, 1899, 72–110.

"L'Enfant's Reports to President Washington, March 26, June 22, and August 19, 1791." *Records of the Columbia Historical Society*, v. 2, 1899, 26–47.

Lord, Walter. *The Dawn's Early Light*. New York: W.W. Norton, 1972.

Mahon, John K. *The War of 1812*. Gainesville: University of Florida, 1972.

McClure, Stanley W. "Memorandum on the Strategic Location of Fort Washington." *National Park Service Archives*, May 26, 1941.

McCullough, David. *John Adams*. New York: Simon & Schuster, 2001.

———. "Washington on the Potomac." In *Brave Companions: Portraits in History*. New York: Prentice Hall, 1992.

Mitchell, Stewart, ed. *New Letters of Abigail Adams 1788–1801* (1947). Westport, CT: Greenwood, 1973.

Morgan, James Dudley. "Maj. Pierre Charles L'Enfant, The Unhonored and Unrewarded Engineer." *Records of the Columbia Historical Society*, v. 2, 1899, 118–157.

Moser, Harold D., et al., eds. *The Papers of Andrew Jackson, v. III, 1814–1815*. Knoxville: University of Tennessee Press, 1991.

Muller, Charles G. *The Darkest Day: The Washington-Baltimore Campaign During the War of 1812*. New York: Lippincott, 1963.

Olszewski, G. J. *A History of the Washington Monument 1844–1968*. Washington, DC: National Park Service, 1971.

Osborne, John Ball. "The Removal of the Government to Washington." *Records of the Columbia Historical Society*, v. 3, 1900, 136–60.

Ovason, David. *The Secret Architecture of Our Nation's Capital: The Masons and the Building of Washington, D.C.* New York: HarperCollins, 2000.

Pack, James. *The Man Who Burned the White House: Admiral Sir George Cockburn 1772–1853*. Annapolis: Naval Institute, 1987.

Partridge, William. "L'Enfant's Vision: A Discussion of Development from a City on Paper to a City in Actuality." *Federal Architect* 7 (1937): 103–7.

Peets, Elbert. "Washington as L'Enfant Intended It." In *On the Art of Designing Cities: Selected Essays of Elbert Peets*, edited by Paul Spreirgen. Cambridge, MA: MIT Press, 1968.

Pitch, Anthony S. *The Burning of Washington: The British Invasion of 1814*. Annapolis: Naval Institute, 1998.

Poore, Benjamin Perley. *Perley's Reminiscences of Sixty Years in the National Metropolis*. 2 vols. Philadelphia: Hubbard Brothers, 1886.

Rakove, Jack N. *James Madison and the Creation of the American Republic*. 2nd ed. New York: Longman, 2002.

Reiff, Daniel D. *Washington Architecture, 1791–1861: Problems in Development*. Washington, DC: U.S. Commission of Fine Arts, 1971.

Remini, Robert V. "Becoming a National Symbol: The White House in the Early Nineteenth Century." In *The White House: The First Two Hundred Years*, edited by Frank Freidel and William Penack. Boston: Northeastern University Press, 1994, 16–30.

Reps, John W. *Monumental Washington: The Planning and Development of the Capital Center*. Princeton, NJ: Princeton University Press, 1967.

"Ross, Robert." *Dictionary of National Biography*. Oxford: Oxford University Press, 1967–68, v. 17, 274–77.

Scott, Captain James. *Recollections of a Naval Life*. London: Bentley, 1834.

Scott, Pamela. "Pierre Charles L'Enfant." *American National Biography*. v. 13. New York: Oxford University Press, 1999.

———. *Temple of Liberty: Building the Capitol for a New Nation*. Oxford/New York: Oxford University Press, 1995.

Seale, William. *The President's House: A History*. 2 vols. Washington, DC: White House Historical Association, 1986.

Seale, William, ed. *The White House: Actors and Observers*. Boston: Northeastern University Press, 2002.

Simpson, Sarah H. J. "The Federal Procession in the City of New York." *New-York Historical Society Quarterly* 9 (1925), 39–57.

Skeen, C. Edward. *Citizen Soldiers in the War of 1812*. Lexington: University Press of Kentucky, 1999.

Tindall, William. *Standard History of the City of Washington: From a Study of the Original Sources*. Knoxville, TN: H. W. Crew, 1914.

Torres, Louis. "Federal Hall Revisited." *Journal of the Society of Architectural Historians* 29, no. 4 (1970): 327–38.

Tucker, Glenn. *Poltroons and Patriots: A Popular Account of the War of 1812*. 2 vols. Indianapolis: Bobbs-Merrill, 1954.

Tully, Andrew. *When They Burned the White House*. New York: Simon & Schuster, 1961.

Washington, H. A., ed. *The Writings of Thomas Jefferson*. 9 vols. New York: John C. Riker, 1853–54.

Wharton, Anne Hollingsworth. *Social Life in the Early Republic* (1902). Reprint, New York: Bloom, 1969.

Wiencek, Henry. "Slaves and Slavery in George Washington's World." *Common-Place*, v. 6, no. 4 (July 2006).

Williams, John S. *History of the Invasion and Capture of Washington and All the Events Which Preceded and Followed*. New York: Harper & Brothers, 1857.

"Writings of George Washington Relating to the National Capital." *Records of the Columbia Historical Society*, v. 17, 1914, 3–49.

Notes

Many of the particulars referred to in this book have been widely written about and are part of the public record. Where I have relied on information or analysis unique to a particular author, I have done my best to attribute it as such, either in the text or the notes below. Quotations or observations drawn from contemporary press accounts are identified in the text, and in most cases can be found in microform in the Library of Congress and other comprehensive libraries. I have attempted in these notes to go beyond simple identification of sources and to introduce readers to some of the most intriguing books I encountered during my research. Anyone interested in delving further into the life of L'Enfant and the founding of Washington will find many avenues of exploration in the notes that follow.

AUTHOR'S NOTE

The reference to W. H. Auden is from "In Memory of W. B. Yeats," where the pronouncement is amplified. The version is from *The Norton Anthology of English Literature, Volume 2*, 1974 (2350).

NOTES TO ILLUSTRATIONS

L'Enfant silhouette: Profile portraiture, or silhouette artistry, was something of a cottage industry in the United States prior to the development of daguerreotype photography in the 1840s. Ms. DeHart's rendering of L'Enfant is one of some 250,000 of the profiles estimated to have been executed by professional and amateur practitioners of the art during the first years of the republic. The profile was also a favorite of Madame Pompadour, mistress of Louis XV, whose finance minister Etienne de Silhouette encouraged the use of the inexpensive profile as a cost-cutting form of portraiture—thus, the common name of the form and the likelihood that L'Enfant was familiar with its practice. (D. Brenton Simons, "New England Silhouettes: Profile Portraits ca. 1790–1850," *New England Historical and Genealogical Register*.)

Stuart painting of Washington: The provenance of the so-called fourth of the "Lansdowne" renderings of Washington has been murky from the beginning. An October 2004 issue of *ARTnews* summarizes the controversy surrounding the painting, which was commissioned originally in 1797 by Charles Pinckney, the newly appointed American minister to France, following Stuart's execution of similar works for Lord Lansdowne of England, Pennsylvania senator William Bingham, and New York merchant William Constable. Pinckney never received the painting, but a fourth version of the work surfaced in a private museum in New York in 1798 and was later sold to the White House in 1800. In 1802, Stuart was reported as saying of the White House version, "I did not paint it, but I bargained for it." Some say that Stuart meant to disown what is generally considered the weakest of the four efforts, and others feel that he was trying to skirt the issue of having resold a painting for which he had already collected a commission from Pinckney. More recently, a former director of the National Portrait Gallery, Marvin Sadik, declared the painting a forgery, a charge adamantly disputed by current White House curators.

Stuart painting of Jefferson: Stuart was no stranger to controversy—chronically short of cash, he often accepted advances for more work than he could deliver on time. Even the so-called "Edgehill" portrait of Jefferson is tinged with suspicion. In 1800 Stuart accepted a commission for a portrait from Jefferson, just prior to his election to the presidency. Five years later, Stuart had still not delivered the painting, telling Jefferson that he was simply not satisfied and was still tinkering with the image. Then, in 1805, came James Bowdoin III, newly appointed ambassador to Spain, with a request that Stuart paint portraits of both Jefferson and secretary of state Madison to be taken abroad—Stuart convinced the then president to sit for the new commission, pointing out that it would allow him to finally finish the painting he owed his subject. It took Stuart two years to deliver Bowdoin his portrait, but he continued to stall Jefferson—the artist did not present the "Edgehill" to Jefferson until 1821, and experts today believe it may have actually been executed shortly before its delivery. (Ellen G. Miles, "Presidential Portraits," *Colonial Williamsburg Journal,* Spring 2007.)

1. SENTINEL

The geographical boundaries and physical makeup of Washington, D.C., are the source of no little confusion. The bounds of the triangular walk described in the text lie within what was originally referred to as the "Federal City" or "Washington City," and the three main points referred to—the White House, the Capitol, and the monument to Washington—were considered the anchors for an efficiently operating center of government by L'Enfant. However, what a layman or a tourist might refer to as downtown Washington, D.C., takes up a relatively small part of the 68-plus square miles presently contained within the entire Federal District, or District of Columbia. The Residence Act of 1790 resulted in the creation of a diamond-shaped district of 100 square miles with its southernmost point in Alexandria, Virginia; its westernmost near Arlington; its northernmost near Silver Spring, Maryland; and its easternmost in Prince Georges Country, Maryland, across the Anacostia River (the "Eastern Branch" of the Potomac) and several miles from Capitol Hill. In 1847, the nearly 32 square miles of Virginia lands within the original bounds of the District were returned to that state (where Arlington National Cemetery and the Pentagon are located). Today, the southwestern boundary leg of the District runs along the southern bank of the Potomac River. Georgetown, originally a city in Maryland, maintained its identity as a separate entity within the District of Columbia until the early 1870s, when all internal city boundaries within the District were dispensed with. Today, Georgetown is one of the more than one hundred D.C. neighborhoods, which include Dupont Circle, Capitol Hill, Downtown, Foggy Bottom, Navy Yard, and many more. The mayor of Washington, D.C., is in fact the mayor of the entire District.

Kenneth Bowling titles his monograph *Peter Charles L'Enfant* (2002) and begins in a lively fashion by sharing his puzzlement as to why the architect anglicized his name when he purchased a lot in as-yet-unbuilt Washington, D.C., in 1791. Bowling's succinct analysis of L'Enfant's life and career occasioned a *Washington Post* review calling for a full-blown modern biography of the architect, whose life had been chronicled previously through a series of public documents printed by Elizabeth Kite in *L'Enfant and Washington 1791–1792* and in a 1950 biography by Washington historian Hans Paul Caemmerer, *The Life of Pierre Charles L'Enfant* (Washington: National Republic), which is thorough, if perhaps overly reverential toward its subject. These, along with the original manuscripts and materials already mentioned, provide the basis for the portrait in this book. The *Post*'s call for a comprehensive biography of L'Enfant was finally answered in 2007 by Scott W. Berg in *Grand Avenues: The Story of the French Visionary Who Designed Washington, D.C.* (Pantheon), a well-received volume published after the completion of this manuscript.

The sentiments of Abigail Adams upon being displaced from her New England home to the wilds of Washington have been widely explored. My primary source is Stewart Mitchell's *New Letters of Abigail Adams 1788–1801* (1947), reprinted by Greenwood in 1973.

In an interview at the American Film Institute in 1984, Robert Wise mentioned to me that he had enjoyed his work directing *The Day the Earth Stood Still* as much as anything he had done up to that point. (He had already edited *Citizen Kane* and *The Magnificent Ambersons* for Orson Welles, and he went on to direct *West Side Story* and *The Sound of Music*.) Of the scene during which young Billy Gray discusses the nature of freedom with as-alien Michael Rennie, Wise said, "Pure hokum . . . but it was *good* hokum."

Arlington National Cemetery historian Tom Sherlock went to some lengths to determine that the lofty point from which L'Enfant maintained his vigil was 571 feet above sea level.

For those eager to experience the Washington, D.C., of yore as a living, breathing entity rather than a symbol, there is no better place to start than with David McCullough's touching "I Love Washington," originally published in *American Heritage* in 1956 and updated for its inclusion in a collection of essays entitled *Brave Companions* (1992).

2. If You Build It, They Will Come

My first exposure to the particulars of the British invasion of Washington came via a guided tour of the White House I took as an eighth-grader, and White House Assistant Curator Melissa Naulin graciously conducted a more recent tour. I gained a much deeper appreciation of those events by reading Andrew Tully's *When They Burned the White House* (1961), Charles G. Muller's *The Darkest Day* (1963), Walter Lord's *The Dawn's Early Light* (1972), and Anthony Pitch's assiduously researched *The Burning of Washington* (1998).

3. The Winds of a War

As I point out, Professor Hickey's is among the earliest comprehensive histories of the War of 1812 to call for a reevaluation of a conflict often given short shrift by those who came before him. Walter Borneman's *1812: The War That Forged a Nation* (2004) makes a similar case in a style that is perhaps geared more toward the general reader. But it is not as if historians were clueless all along as to the importance of the conflict. Even such general treatments as a Facts on File volume published in 1944 notes the impact of the war on a nascent country and offers a quote from a Vermont newspaper of 1815 that the United States had gained "the fear of our late enemy: / The respect of the world; and / The confidence we have acquired in ourselves" (119).

In his 1999 book *Citizen Soldiers in the War of 1812*, C. Edward Skeen, professor of history at the University of Memphis, provides valuable perspective on the often woeful performance of the state militias used to conduct the war and points out that these shortcomings led to the formation of a standing professional army.

4. First Orders of Business

In *Peter Charles L'Enfant*, Kenneth Bowling points out that L'Enfant's father signed his paintings without an apostrophe and further theorizes that the cane that the architect relied on after his injuries in the Revolutionary War might also have been part of a larger pattern of self-aggrandizement (5, 70).

L'Enfant's appearance is a matter of some conjecture. While it is vivid, Bowling notes (48) that William W. Corcoran's description of L'Enfant comes sec-ondhand, "as reported to" Washington historian Hugh T. Taggart in his manu-script "Old Georgetown," published by the Columbia Historical Society in 1908. Though it is far less detailed, Bowling places more faith in a letter in Corcoran's own hand that refers to his childhood memories of L'Enfant as "very poor and very proud" and "a great pedestrian" who often came to visit Corcoran's father, the mayor of Georgetown. See Taggart, v. XI, 216–17, *Records of the Columbia Historical Society;* Corcoran to Representative John Kasson, April 17, 1884, Hugh Taggart Papers, Library of Congress.

The only known contemporary likeness of L'Enfant is a silhouette executed by Sara DeHart in 1785, hanging today in the Diplomatic Reception Room at the U.S. Department of State.

The cover of Bowling's biography of L'Enfant features a "conjectural por-trait" of L'Enfant executed in 1990 by Bryan Leister, which is based on a con-temporary portrait of L'Enfant's father, the DeHart silhouette, and the scraps of contemporary description that survive. The Leister portrait hangs today in the Washington Historical Society.

American Eagle as symbol: See Pamela Scott, *Temple of Liberty* (11–12).

References are to L'Enfant materials in Digges–L'Enfant—Morgan Papers, Library of Congress—*Records of the Columbia Historical Society,* by date.

5. COMING OF AGE

A visit to St. Paul's, where Washington regularly worshipped, and which miraculously escaped damage on September 11, 2001, will allow the curious to make up their own minds about the quality of L'Enfant's talents as a sculptor. *Glory* is a rendering of Mount Sinai beset by clouds and lightning, with the Ten Commandments, as delivered by "YHWH," featured at the base.

Many of the details of L'Enfant's life and career were first set down by Jules J. Jusserand (then the French ambassador to the United States) in his 1916 book, *With Americans of Past and Present Days,* which won the first Pulitzer Prize for history the following year. Jusserand's essay, based in large part on materials in the Digges/Morgan collection, the Papers of the Continental Congress, and other primary sources, was reprinted as the introduction to Elizabeth Kite's 1929 work on L'Enfant.

6. A NEW AMERICAN ORDER

Franeau's "Federal Hall": Franeau, 1750–1832, an intimate of James Madi-son's, is sometimes referred to as America's first poet. Though several collections of his work, including occasional poems written to commemorate various pub-lic events, are still to be found, his nine-stanza effort on behalf of "Federal Hall" comes from the archives of the newspaper that published it.

Mrs. Washington's tour of Federal Hall: The letter addressed to L'Enfant on the matter, dated June 11, 1789, was written by President Washington's secretary David Humphreys (DLM/LOC).

In her book on the building of the Capitol, Pamela Scott discusses L'Enfant's work on Federal Hall and laments the fact that no drawings or engravings of its interior remain. The 1970 article by the Department of the Army's Louis Torres includes a summary of contemporary descriptions and offers the closest approximation of a visual tour of the original.

7. QUID PRO QUO

Kenneth Bowling's *The Creation of Washington, D.C.*; Bob Arnebeck's *Through a Fiery Trial: Building Washington 1790–1800;* and George Brown Tindall's *Standard History of the City of Washington* are the essential guides to an understanding of the maneuvering and political forces involved in the selection of the site and the actual making of the capital.

In an address presented to the Columbia Historical Society on January 4, 1897, Washington historian Tallmadge A. Lambert argued that the idea of a united group of colonies required the symbolism of a national capital. *Records of the Columbia Historical Society*, v. 2, 277–278.

Pellatiah Webster's comments are cited by Bowling and find their full flowering in "Citizen of Philadelphia," *Essay on the Seat of the Federal Government and the Exclusive Jurisdiction of Congress Over a Ten Miles District*, Philadelphia: 1789, 15–29.

The writings of Jefferson I refer to in this chapter are in the Jefferson Papers in the Library of Congress. Primary sources include the nine-volume collection compiled by H. A. Washington (1853–54), as well as Paul Leicester Ford's twelve-volume *The Works of Thomas Jefferson (1904–05)*.

8. COURT OF PUBLIC OPINION

For a full record of the correspondence between Jefferson and Washington, see Julian Boyd's monumental and ongoing *The Papers of Thomas Jefferson*.

9. GREATNESS OF EMPIRE

Despite its grammatical shortcomings and the naïveté of its tone, L'Enfant's appeal to Congress for the establishment of an Army Corps of Engineers (DLM/LOC) is perhaps his most cogent and concise composition. As to his general failings in "orthography," countryman Jules Jusserand noted in his 1916 essay that L'Enfant was even more slipshod in his native tongue; though Jusserand theorized that this was probably owing to L'Enfant's "familiarity" with

French, one can only imagine how difficult it was for his countrymen to follow the architect's prose.

William Smith's letter to Otho Williams is quoted by Bowling in *The Creation of Washington, D.C.* (213).

10. HABITATION AND A NAME

"The Writings of George Washington Relating to the National Capital" are reproduced in Volume 17 of the *Records of the Columbia Historical Society* (1914), 3–49.

11. GRAND DESIGN

L'Enfant's early (1791) reports to Washington are reproduced in the *Records of the Columbia Historical Society*, vol. 2, 1899, 26–48.

Calculation of acreage/lots comes from Lambert (*Records of the Columbia Historical Society*, 2, 281).

The account of the laying of the cornerstone comes from Tindall (*Standard History of the City of Washington*, 93).

12. GLORY DAYS

"L'Enfant Proceeds." Carroll's letter to Madison, April 23, 1971, *Papers of James Madison*, Library of Congress.

The account of that first and fateful encounter between L'Enfant and Daniel Carroll comes from Arnebeck (*Through a Fiery Trial*, 53).

13. HEADWAY

Arnebeck deftly recounts the maneuvering between L'Enfant and the commissioners regarding the Carroll matter (*Through a Fiery Trial*, 56–57).

Kite (*L'Enfant and Washington*, 60) is apparently the first to note L'Enfant's outraged annotations on the August 18 letter from Jefferson mentioning Ellicott's name.

14. A PLAN WHOLLY NEW

Commissioner Stuart's letter to Washington reporting on the results of the sale is quoted by Arnebeck (*Through a Fiery Trial*, 70).

Among the many historical maps and charts made available in digital form by the National Oceanographic and Atmospheric Administration is a detail of old Washington City, including lot numbers, drawn from Ellicott's revision of the L'Enfant Plan.

The account of Washington's first public rebuke of L'Enfant comes from Caemmerer (*The Life of Pierre Charles L'Enfant*, 175).

Cf. Kite's defense of L'Enfant's dealings with Carroll of Duddington (*L'Enfant and Washington*, 80–82).

15. ALL THINGS REASONABLE AND PROPER

For Kite's comparison of Goethals and L'Enfant, see *L'Enfant and Washington*, 87–88.

The quote concerning the extent of Goethal's power comes from David McCullough's account of the building of the Panama Canal, *The Path Between the Seas* (New York: Simon & Schuster, 1977, 511).

Bowling (*Pierre Charles L'Enfant*, 14) points out that L'Enfant had served as a member of the panel overseeing work on Federal Hall.

16. ENDGAME

Carroll of Duddington to Madison, cited by Kite (*L'Enfant and Washington*, 91).

Manuscript sources for letters to and from the commissioners and matters attendant to their business are found in the Records of the Commissioners, housed in the National Archives. These letters have been widely reprinted in various accounts, including those of Tindall, Kite, Caemmerer, Bowling, Arnebeck, et al.

Perhaps the most thoroughgoing narrative of the intricate contest among L'Enfant, Washington, Jefferson, and the commissioners is found in Arnebeck's *Through a Fiery Trial*.

17. DITCHES IN THE MIDST OF WINTER

Roberdeau's letters to L'Enfant, as well as L'Enfant's lengthy letter and detailed report to Washington, are reproduced in Kite (*L'Enfant and Washington*, 105–132).

18. WRIT OF TRESPASS

Regarding matters surrounding the arrest of Roberdeau, see Tindall (*Standard History of the City of Washington*, 136–38).

19. PUREST PRINCIPLES

Jefferson's letter to L'Enfant terminating the latter's services is reproduced in Tindall (*Standard History of the City of Washington*, 139).

20. LEAST OBEDIENT SERVANT

The fulsome defense of L'Enfant by the proprietors is reproduced in Tindall (*Standard History of the City of Washington*, 140–41).

Kite (*L'Enfant and Washington*, 171) calls attention to a note in L'Enfant's hand scrawled on the reverse of a copy of the proprietors' letter to the president.

The note suggests that L'Enfant did not receive a copy of the missive and was not aware that the proprietors had attempted to intercede on his behalf for some time; L'Enfant suggests in his note that had he known of this letter, he might not have so quickly resigned his commission.

21. IN THIS GREAT CASTLE

The number of houses constructed at that time comes from Robert King Jr., "An Enumeration of the Houses in the City of Washington made November 1801," *Records of the Historical Society of Washington*. King was surveyor of the city at the time, and, according to John Stewart, it was the last map to be executed for more than thirty years. (*Records*, v. 2, 64–65.)

For the temporary location of the Department of War, see Elaine C. Everly, "The Local Impact of the War Office Fire of 1800," in *Washington History*, 8.

Hawkins's map and its method is found in "The City of Washington in 1800: A New Map," *Washington History*, 12 (1), Spring/Summer 2000, 74–77.

The description of Lancaster is based on a drawing titled *Lancaster, Pennsylvania*, by Benjamin H. Latrobe, ca. 1801, Maryland Historical Society.

Details of Adams's directive for the removal of public offices to Washington come from Amy LaFollette Jensen, *The White House and Its Thirty-three Families*, New York: McGraw-Hill, 1962, 10.

Details of the President's House as Adams found it come from William Seale, "Like No Other House," in *The White House: Actors and Observers*, Boston: Northeastern University Press, 2002, xvii.

In an essay included in *The White House: The First 200 Years*, Robert Remini points out that in addition to their other privations, the Adamses were forced to use an outdoor privy. Jefferson would have none of that, however; he had the privy removed and had two water closets installed on the building's second floor ("Becoming a National Symbol: The White House in the Early Nineteenth Century," 21–22).

22. REVOLVING DOOR

Arnebeck (152, *passim*) deftly summarizes the trials of the many who followed in L'Enfant's footsteps with the commissioners, and he is the source for the commissioners' decision not to face the interior walls of the President's House with brick (163).

Jusserand sketches L'Enfant's adventures in Paterson (in Kite, 24–25), and Caemmerer (248–256) elaborates, providing a map of the proposed S.U.M. site as well as reproductions of the L'Enfant letter and local news story.

Speculation on the significance of Hallet's design is drawn from Arnebeck (126) and from William C. Allen in his definitive *History of the United States Capitol* (14–17).

Washington's architectural advice comes in a letter to the commissioners dated July 23, 1792, and reproduced in the *Records of the Columbia Historical Society*.

Results of the commissioners' second public sale are summarized by Arnebeck (136).

Hallet's quote is reproduced by Pamela Scott in *Temple of Liberty* (38).

For illustrations that clarify the similarities in the Hallet and Thornton designs, see Scott, *Temple of Liberty* (118).

See C. M. Harris, "Washington's Gamble, L'Enfant's Dream: Politics, Design, and the Founding of the National Capital," *The William and Mary Quarterly*, 3rd series, v. 56, no. 3 (July 1999), 527–564.

23. PLAGUE

Caemmerer (252) provides the stirring description of L'Enfant's proposed aqueduct.

Peter Colt's remarks are cited by Bowling (*Pierre Charles L'Enfant*, 38). The relationship between Peter Colt and the grandson whose idea of a "useful manufacture" was the Colt .45 is laid out in a 1916 *New York Times* obituary for yet another member of that prominent family: "Col. Samuel P. Colt Dies of Paralysis," *New York Times*, August 14, 1921 (19).

Arnebeck (170) describes the efforts of the commissioners to portray Washington, D.C., as a disease-free oasis.

William Seale's two-volume set, *The President's House*, published in 1986, provides the definitive history of the building of the White House. Seale provides the description of Walker's recruitment of the original Scottish workforce (62–63).

For the influence of L'Enfant's design on Hallet and Thornton, see Scott, *Temple of Liberty* (54).

Caemmerer (259–262) details the work of L'Enfant on the home of Robert Morris, and Bowling (*Pierre Charles L'Enfant*, 40–42) elaborates.

24. NO MATCH FOR THE ROGUES

For details of the deemphasis of the presidency in the Capitol design, see C. M. Harris (556).

Thornton's note on Hallet's dismissal is quoted by Scott (*Temple of Liberty*, 55).

Latrobe's reflections on Hadfield come from Edward C. Carter's edition of Latrobe's *Journals* (3:72).

Isaac Weld's commentary on the Morris home comes from Allen C. Clark, *Greenleaf and Law in the Federal City*, 1901, 28–30.

For details on the Greenleaf scheme, see C. M. Harris (552, 557).

The call in Congress to pull down the unfinished President's House is cited by C. M. Harris (559).

25. RAISE HIGH THE ROOF BEAMS

The state of Washington development, the comments of Moodey, and the antibrick sentiments of mason Collen Williamson are cited by Arnebeck (290, 293, 299–300).

Blagden's method is detailed by White House historian Seale (*The President's House*, 68–69).

Washington's suggestion that the commissioners deemphasize decoration in the President's House is contained in a letter dated February 20, 1797.

Washington's edict that both the president's home and the Capitol be completed by the 1800 deadline is dated February 15, 1797.

26. RACE TO THE FINISH

Seale (*The President's House*, 74–75) details the pace of work at the President's House in 1797–98, as well as the commissioners' firing of the stonecutters working there.

Capitol historian Allen (*History of the United States Capitol*, 38) cites the commissioners on Hadfield's deficiencies as an architect.

Hoban's efforts as the newly appointed superintendent are described by Allen (40, *passim*).

The commissioners' bonus to Hoban is cited by Seale (75).

Adams's declaration that he would as soon rent private quarters as live in the President's House is cited by Seale in *The White House: Actors and Obervers*, xviii.

Seale (162, 654, 1088) and others point to instances where the term "White House" was used in print as early as 1812, thus debunking the myth that the building got its name when it was repainted to cover soot marks following the British attack. The President's Mansion formally became the White House at the order of President Theodore Roosevelt in 1901.

Details of the death of Washington come from Tobias Lear's diary entries for December 14, 1799, and are reproduced in Lear's *Letters and Recollections of George Washington*.

Adams's initial reaction to the President's House comes from Seale, *The White House* (xvii).

Letters between Commissioner Stoddert and William Thornton on readying the President's House for Adams are cited by Seale (*The President's House*, 78).

Pamela Scott's article "Temporary Inconveniences" is collected in Bowling's edition, *Coming Into the City: Essays on Early Washington, D.C.* (70–73).

The note on the Capitol privy comes from Allen (41).

27. A RESIDENCE NOT TO BE CHANGED

Mrs. Thornton's diary is quoted by Seale (*The President's House*, 81).

Seale (79–80) summarizes the reaction to the Stuart portrait of Washington.

Secretary Wolcott's remark on the dearth of lodging in Washington, D.C., is quoted by John Ball Osborne in "The Removal of the Government to Washington," *Records of the Columbia Historical Society*, vol. 3, 1900, 157.

The passages from Abigail Adams are taken from *New Letters of Abigail Adams* (256, 259–60).

The remarks of President Adams boosting Washington, D.C., are cited by Allen (42).

Seale (86–88) quotes Jefferson and others in characterizing the election of 1800 as a mudfest.

28. A CONCURRENCE OF DISASTROUS EVENTS

Caemmerer (266–67) documents L'Enfant's work at Fort Mifflin and reproduces letters to and from the architect pertaining to it (437–444).

Bowling (*Pierre Charles L'Enfant*, 42–44, *passim*) is the source for details on the relationship between L'Enfant and Soderstrom. In an aside, 50–52, Bowling points out that an individual's sexual preferences had not yet become the stuff of public discourse at the time, leaving historians with little but speculation to go on in such matters.

L'Enfant's memorials to Congress are reproduced in *Records of the Columbia Historical Society*, vol. 2, 1899, 72–110.

Given his chronic difficulties with money, it is entertaining to imagine L'Enfant's reaction to the news that on December 11, 2007 (the anniversary of Lafayette's birth), Sotheby's auctioned a copy of one of the medals he designed for the Society of Cincinnati. The medal, made especially for Lafayette by L'Enfant at George Washington's request, sold for $5.3 million.

L'Enfant's petition to Jefferson and Jefferson's reply are reproduced in Caemmerer (241–47).

29. DESTROY AND LAY WASTE

Cockburn's pledge to Ross is taken from Captain James Scott, *Recollections of a Naval Life*, vol. 3, London: Bentley, 1834, 283. The remark is quoted both by Anthony S. Pitch in *The Burning of Washington*, and Charles G. Muller in *The Darkest Day: The Washington–Baltimore Campaign During the War of 1812*.

The comments of Daniel D. Tompkins are found in Hugh Hastings, ed. *Public Papers of Daniel D. Tompkins, Governor of New York, 1807–1817* (3 vols., New York and Albany, 1898–1902) vol. 3., 26–27.

Jefferson's comment on the dispatch with which the war would be fought is found in a letter to William Duane, August 4, 1812, in the Jefferson Papers (Library of Congress).

Editor Gales's comments are cited by Muller (75).

Armstrong's assurances are contained in Van Ness, November 23, 1814, *American State Papers*, Military Affairs, 1:581.

Cochrane's blanket orders to Cockburn are quoted by Pitch (20).

30. THE LITTLE MALICE OF FOOLS

Latrobe's reference to L'Enfant and his dog is reported by both Arnebeck (626) and Bowling (*Pierre Charles L'Enfant*, 48) and is taken from John C. van Horne and Lee W. Formwalt, eds. *The Correspondence and Miscellaneous Papers of Benjamin Henry Latrobe* (3 vols., New Haven: Yale University Press 1984–88), Vol. 2., 230.

Samuel Davidson's patronizing message to L'Enfant is cited by Arnebeck (626).

Jusserand's commentary on the failure of L'Enfant to claim his pension from the French government is reproduced in Kite (26).

The letters exchanged between L'Enfant and Monroe on the subject of the architect's appointment to the faculty at West Point are reproduced in the appendix to Caemmerer (445–450). Melville enthusiasts may find certain parallels between L'Enfant's manner of refusing to refuse and that of Bartleby the Scrivener, the protagonist of Herman Melville's 1853 novella of the same name.

31. EMBERS OF IMAGINATION

Augustus John Foster's reflections on his experiences in Washington, D.C., are contained in "Chronicle of a British Diplomat: The First Year in the 'Washington Wilderness,'" by Marilyn K. Parr, in *Coming into the City*, 78–89.

A handbill describing the "sagacity" of the learned pig is reproduced in "Remembering the Ladies: Women, Etiquette, and Diversions in Washington City, 1800–1814," by Cynthia D. Earman, collected in *Coming into the City*, 102–117.

Callender's condemnation of the memorial to Washington as well as the opposition of Jefferson is described by Rubil Morales-Vazquez in "Imagining Washington: Monuments and Nation Building in the Early Capital," *Washington History*, vol. 12, no. 1, (24, 26).

Latrobe's insult directed at Thornton comes from Latrobe to John Lenthall, May 6, 1803, in Edward C. van Horne, ed., *The Correspondence and Miscellaneous Papers of Benjamin Henry Latrobe* (New Haven: Yale University Press, 1984), vol. 1, 290–292.

Allen summarizes the acrimony between Latrobe and Thornton (60) and quotes Jefferson on his enthusiasm for the *Halle au blé* (63).

32. STILLNESS OF THE GRAVE

In a chapter titled "Jefferson and Latrobe," Allen (49–91) uses the materials collected by van Horne to weave a deft narrative of Latrobe's work on the Capitol.

Hickey (*The War of 1812*, 21) provides the gloomy statistics on the economic impact of the war.

The quote from the Newburyport *Herald* is from Greenblatt (*The War of 1812*, 22).

Hickey (22–24) summarizes events leading to the recall of the American ambassador from London in February of 1811; he also cites the inflammatory rhetoric of the *National Intelligencer* and of Elbridge Gerry (27, 28).

33. THE MORE THINGS CHANGE . . .

Much of the information concerning the nature of American life at the time is drawn from records of the U.S. Census.

34. UNDER A DIFFERENT BELIEF

Monroe's urgent message is found in Monroe to Madison, August 20, 1814, *American State Papers*, Military Affairs, vol. 1, 537: "The best security against this attempt is an adequate preparation to repel it," Madison added. Monroe's missives to the president during the assault on Washington form a part of a congressional committee report on the "Capture of Washington," submitted to the House of Representatives on November 29, 1814. The report of the committee, chaired by R. M. Johnson of Kentucky, is essentially the first published narrative of the assault on Washington.

Pleasonton's reply to the blundering Armstrong comes from Pleasonton to Winder, August 7, 1848, in John C. Hildt, "Letters Relating to Capture," *South Atlantic Quarterly* 6 (1907): 58–66, and is quoted in Pitch, *The Burning of Washington* (48).

The detail of Clerk Booth's frantic search for transport out of the city comes from Lord (*The Dawn's Early Light*, 73–74).

Dolley Madison's refusal to quit Washington, D.C., in the face of the British invasion has become the stuff of legend, and is well summarized in the prologue to the 2006 biography *A Perfect Union: Dolley Madison and the Creation of the American Nation*, by Catherine Allgor (1–4). Both Lord (77–78) and Pitch (49–50) provide similarly stirring accounts of Mrs. Madison's actions.

Madison's reassuring note to Dolley is quoted by Lord (83).

Monroe's often-quoted note confirming the worst to Madison is found in Monroe to Madison, August 22, 1814, *American State Papers*, Military Affairs, vol. 1, 538.

35. DEBACLE AT BLADENSBURG

Pitch (*The Burning of Washington*, 72) delivers a lively summary of Bladensburg as a dueling center.

Gleig's description of the battle-worthiness of his associates comes from his own manuscript, *The Campaigns of the British Army at Washington and New Orleans*, originally published in London in 1827 and reprinted in the United States in 1972 (54). His observations on the assault on Washington are perhaps the most useful from the British perspective.

Hickey (*The War of 1812*, 78–79) points out that the standard firearm issued by the government to American troops was a .70 caliber smooth-bore musket that fired a one-ounce lead ball, with an effective range of about one hundred yards. The use of an unrifled weapon made hitting anything at that distance a matter of luck, however—and the flintlocks on the pieces were said to misfire at a rate of 15 percent. Far more fortunate were those who brought along their own personal rifles, .40 caliber weapons with a range of about three hundred yards.

Madison's suggestion that it might be time to retreat comes from Henry Adams, *History of the United States During the Administrations of James Madison* (1016).

"A distinction between madness and bravery" comes from Colonel Lavall (Colonel Lavall, October 31, 1814, *American State Papers*, mil. 16, vol. 1, 571) and is quoted by Pitch (77).

"The Bladensburg Races" was originally published in the *Georgetown Federal Republican*, January 7, 1815. As one might suppose, it enjoyed widespread reprinting and enduring popularity among opponents of Madison and his administration.

The quote lauding their British opponents comes from Charles Ball, *A Narrative of the Life and Adventures of Charles Ball, a Black Man* (New York: John S. Taylor, 1837, 468), and is cited in Borneman (*The War That Forged a Nation*, 228).

Lord (*The Dawn's Early Light*, 138–39) provides a detailed description of Barney's surrender to Cockburn.

Hickey's estimate of American and British casualties at Bladensburg is found on 198.

36. BARBARIANS THROUGH THE GATES

Mrs. Madison's cry for a cannon in every window of the White House comes from Allen C. Clark, *Life and Letters of Dolley Madison* (166).

Mrs. Madison's often-quoted assertion that the Stuart painting would not fall into British hands comes from her letter to Robert de Peyster, February 3, 1848, *Dolley Madison Papers* (Library of Congress).

Mrs. Madison's letter to Anna Cutts is dated August 24, 1814, and is found in the *Dolley Madison Papers* (Library of Congress).

37. A DISASTER STRIKING AND SUBLIME

If the lack of transport out of the besieged city was a problem in 1814, a recent Washington Post Service story ("Area Disaster Planning Gets More Muscle," September 7, 2007) suggests that things have not improved much. The paper reported that based on a 2006 study, the Department of Homeland Security had described the preparations of Washington, D.C., for a major disaster as "not sufficient." In a statement that eerily echoes the past, one member of the region's Emergency Preparedness Council (which includes representatives of thirteen state and local governments) lamented, "There's no one really in charge."

Gleig's memorable quote as to the beauty of the city burning before him comes from page 70 of his memoir.

General Ross's comment upon finding the president's dinner table laid comes from the *Dictionary of National Biography*, vol. 17, 276.

Scott's poetic description of the quality of Madison's wine is drawn from his *Recollections of a Naval Life*, published in London in 1834 and quoted by Pitch (*The Burning of Washington*, 117).

Cockburn's vow to destroy all the C's in Joseph Gales's typesetting kit is passed along by Adams in his *History of the United States*, p. 1015.

38. THIEVES IN THE NIGHT

Early reportage on Thornton's brave stand to save the Patent Office is found in Charles J. Ingersoll, *Historical Sketch of the Second War Between the United States of America and Great Britain*, vol. 2, p. 184.

Cockburn's aside on Washington was recorded in James Ewell, *Planter's and Mariner's Medical Companion*, 3rd ed. (Philadelphia: Anderson & Meecham, 1816, 655).

Detail of John Lewis's ill-advised charge on British emplacements is found in Ingersoll (188).

Both Lord (*The Dawn's Early Light*, 180–81) and Pitch (*The Burning of Washington*, 138–39) paint vivid pictures of the self-immolation of the British troops at the Navy Yard.

The exchange on the fury of the storm involving Cockburn comes from "Early Washington: An Old Resident's Recollections of the War of 1812," *Washington Evening Star*, March 31, 1888, and is quoted by Pitch (142).

39. SCORN AND EXECRATION

The *Evening Post*'s observation on the ease with which the British stormed Washington is reproduced in Tucker (*Poltroons & Patriots*, 584).

Several examples of scorn and outrage were reported by Henry Bradshaw Fearon in *Sketches of America* (London: Longman, Hurst, Rees, Orme, & Brown, 1818, 284–85), and are quoted by Pitch (*The Burning of Washington*, 163).

The description of a drawn Madison comes from a letter written by Washington attorney William Wirt to his wife and is quoted by Lord (*The Dawn's Early Light*, 216).

Monroe's threats to bayonet traitors come from "James Monroe's notes respecting the burning city in 1814," in the *Papers of James Monroe* (Library of Congress) and are reproduced in Pitch (164).

The appeals of King and Chittenden are cited by Lord (217–18).

Borneman (*The War That Forged a Nation*, 234–35) and Hickey (*The War of 1812*, 202) provide a summary of the British response to the assault of their troops on Washington.

Colonel Brooke's *Diary* is quoted by Pitch (147).

Key's vantage point during the assault on Fort McHenry: It is sometimes reported that Key watched the naval bombardment from the decks of a British ship, where he had gone to negotiate the release of the American prisoner. But Lord (256) and Pitch (191–93, *passim*) point to documents, including reminiscences of Key's companion John Skinner, published in the *National Intelligencer* on June 4, 1849, that bear out that the two were actually transferred back to their own vessel at least one day in advance of the bombardment (though they there remained under the watch of British guards until the attacker's fleet finally left the area on Friday September 16, long after the battle was over).

40. DISHONEST, AVARICIOUS MEN

Pitch (*The Burning of Washington*, 223–24) details the final attempt to remove the seat of government from Washington.

Caemmerer (*The Life of Pierre Charles L'Enfant*, 270) quotes L'Enfant's initial letter to Armstrong on the deficiencies at Fort Washington.

Bowling's characterization of the match between L'Enfant and Digges is found in *Pierre Charles L'Enfant* (61).

The record of correspondence to and from L'Enfant concerning his work on Fort Washington comes from the DLM papers (Library of Congress) and is reproduced in the appendix to Caemmerer (451–62).

The final word on L'Enfant's service to his adopted country comes from Stanley W. McClure, "Memorandum on the Strategic Location of Fort Washington," *National Park Service Archives*, May 26, 1941.

41. PHOENIX RISING

Jackson's letter to Andrew Hynes concerning the burning of Washington is found in *The Papers of Andrew Jackson, v. III, 1814–1815*, ed. Harold D. Moser, et al. Knoxville: University of Tennessee Press, 1991, (147).

Hadfield's estimate and the congressional appropriation are reported by Seale (*The President's House*, 139).

Seale (142–43) summarizes the haste to rebuild the President's House and the resultant shortcomings.

Tindall (*Standard History of the City of Washington*, 327–28) details the temporary quarters of Congress in the Patent Office and the tavern remodeled by Latrobe.

In a widely quoted letter to a mutual friend, Margaret Bayard Smith wrote that Mrs. Madison could barely speak of what had happened "without tears." (Margaret Bayard Smith Papers, Library of Congress, August 30, 1814.)

Latrobe's spiteful letter to supervisor Lane is quoted by Allen (*History of the United States Capitol*, 113).

Allen (117–19) details Monroe's direct intervention in the drive to complete the building of the Capitol.

Latrobe's confrontation with Lane was recorded by Latrobe's wife, and the architect's response to the president is cited by Talbot Hamlin in *Benjamin Henry Latrobe* (477).

Latrobe's resignation to Monroe is cited by Allen (121–22).

For a full description of the work of Thomas Bullfinch in completing the U.S. Capitol, see Scott (*Temple of Liberty*, 60–65) and Allen, "The Bullfinch Years," 125–166.

42. AD ASTRA

Tindall (*Standard History of the City of Washington*, 435, 437, *passim*) provides the definitive record of public building in early Washington.

All that one might wish to know about the tortured history of the monument to our first president is contained in G. J. Olszewski's *A History of the Washington Monument, 1844–1968*.

Digges's letter to Archbishop Carroll is dated August 18, 1815, and is reproduced in the *Letters of Thomas Attwood Digges*, edited by Robert H. Elias and Eugene D. Finch.

Digges's letter to Monroe on the work habits of the elderly L'Enfant is dated October 26, 1816 (Elias and Finch).

Digges's "Great Oddity" letter to Madison is dated July 17, 1818 (Elias and Finch).

L'Enfant's reckoning of the commissioners' windfall from sales of copies of his plan are contained in L'Enfant to William Bayley, November 18, 1823, DLM Papers, Library of Congress, cited in Bowling (*Pierre Charles L'Enfant*, 63).

The picture of a pomatum-plastered L'Enfant haunting the halls of Congress comes from Benjamin Perley Poore, *Perley's Reminiscences of Sixty Years in the National Metropolis*, vol. 1 (54).

Bowling (63) describes L'Enfant's encounter with the census taker during the architect's last years.

William Digges's letter of invitation to L'Enfant is reproduced in the *Records of the Columbia Historical Society*, vol. 2, 1899, 136.

L'Enfant's final days and the inventory of his personal effects comes from James Dudley Morgan, "Major Pierre Charles L'Enfant, the Unhonored and Unrewarded Engineer," *Records of the Columbia Historical Society*, vol. 2, 1899, 123.

The story of the pursuit of the claim against the estate of Morris by Digges is related by Bowling (64).

43. HONOR AND REWARD

Details of Digges's address are found in the *Records of the Columbia Historical Society*, 2, 1899 (118–57).

The work of the McMillan Commission in reviving an appreciation of the L'Enfant Plan is detailed in Caemmerer (*The Life of Pierre Charles L'Enfant*, 319–34).

Details of the struggle to honor L'Enfant at last are contained in James Dudley Morgan, "The Reinterment of Major Pierre Charles L'Enfant," *Records of the Columbia Historical Society*, vol. 13, 1910.

Caemmerer's interview with tomb sculptor Bosworth, as well as the quote from Elihu Root, is found in his *The Life of Pierre Charles L'Enfant*, 295–303.

Index

About the Author

LES STANDIFORD is the author of ten novels, as well as the critically acclaimed nonfiction works *Last Train to Paradise: Henry Flagler and the Spectacular Rise and Fall of the Railroad That Crossed an Ocean* and *Meet You in Hell: Andrew Carnegie, Henry Clay Frick, and the Bitter Partnership That Transformed America*. Recipient of the Frank O'Connor Award for Short Fiction, he is director of the Creative Writing Program at Florida International University in Miami. He lives in South Florida with his wife and three children. Visit his website at www.les-standiford.com.